1 MONTH OF
FREE
READING

at

www.ForgottenBooks.com

———◇———

By purchasing this book you are eligible for one month membership to ForgottenBooks.com, giving you unlimited access to our entire collection of over 700,000 titles via our web site and mobile apps.

To claim your free month visit:

www.forgottenbooks.com/free193450

ISBN 978-0-483-53681-4
PIBN 10193450

For support please visit www.forgottenbooks.com

HARD SAYINGS

A SELECTION OF MEDITATIONS AND STUDIES

BY

GEORGE TYRRELL, S.J.

AUTHOR OF " NOVA ET VETERA,"

" Durus est hic sermo, et quis potest eum audire?"—*Joan.* vi. 61.

LONGMANS, GREEN, AND CO.

39 PATERNOSTER ROW, LONDON

NEW YORK AND BOMBAY

1898

Nihil Obstat:

        GULIELMUS ROCHE, S.J.,

                Censor Deputatus.

Imprimatur:

        HERBERTUS CARD. VAUGHAN,

                Archiep. Westmonast.

THE Author wishes to thank those who have in various ways helped him in the task of producing the present volume; and more especially Mr. C. Kegan Paul, who kindly read through the proofs.

b

INTRODUCTION.

——

ALTHOUGH the following conferences and meditations were in no way originally designed to be parts of a whole, written, as they were, at sundry times and in divers manners, yet there has been some imperfect attempt at method in their selection and arrangement which, though not very apparent on the surface, may make itself felt in the unity of their effect upon the reader's mind. Their purport is to illustrate and, so to say, turn over in various ways a very few of the deepest and most wide-reaching principles of Catholic Christianity, by which they are pervaded and upon which they have been built up with a somewhat dialectical severity which can hardly escape unfavourable criticism, as seeming to encourage an excessive rationalizing in matters too delicate for the coarse hands of the logician. The writer has had this danger continually before his mind as something to guard against, but since his aim has been confessedly to simplify, explain, and co-ordinate, it would be too much to hope that he has avoided all the errors and extremes which usually beset such an undertaking.

For indeed there is a most unpardonable narrowness as well as impertinence in the desire to represent the intercourse between the created spirit and its indwelling Creator in terms as sharp and exact as those which describe the dealings of father and son, master and servant, ruler and subject, husband and spouse. These familiar relationships bear a distant analogy to those subsisting between God and the soul, but fall immeasurably short of the reality. They are as a few rough, suggestive strokes drawn by a skilful hand, which will serve to bring to our mind all the meaning and expression of a face if only it be already familiar to us by experience. But an inordinate love of clearness, an overpressing of analogies and similitudes is a form of rationalism very fruitful in fallacies, and not very uncommon in ascetical writings. If, however, we use these metaphors with a full reflex consciousness of their imperfection, then indeed we may do so fearlessly and abundantly, trusting that where one is weak another may be strong, and that from many faulty adumbrations some vague image of the whole truth may shape itself in the mind.

What we have to guard against is the narrow pride of that rationalism which inclines some to be impatient of all ideas that are in any way obscure and imperfectly defined; to cast out of the mind as worthless those that are not clear and distinct; to apply the methods and criteria of the "exact sciences" to matters of a wholly different order; to be abhorrent of all that savours of mysticism. For this is to forget that every new idea that enters our soul, so far as it is new and incomparable, and unlike what we have previously known, is fringed with mystery, and is only very gradually defined and analyzed as to its full contents; it is to ignore the simple fact that our mind comprehends fully only what it has itself created—forms and numbers, and figures and relations; and that of the least atom of God's creations it can at best grasp a side or a surface or a corner, but can penetrate nothing. Still more evident is it that most of the truths relating to the commerce of God with the soul are necessarily veiled, and obscure to us in our present embodied condition, since they can never be properly expressed in terms of anything that falls under our senses—in terms of the only language we are skilled in. Ultimate truths, those which are concerned with the Alpha and Omega of our existence, are from their very nature set at the extreme limit of our intellectual horizon, so that we never see all round them or beyond them. Our mind is made for what lies between: for movements and processes and the laws by which they are governed; but

before the " Ultimates," the unchanging realities of
the timeless, spaceless world, whose existence is
postulated in our every thought, our progress is
abruptly arrested as by a dead wall, behind which
all is impenetrable mystery: " Hitherto shalt thou
come and no further, and here shalt thou break thy
swelling waves."

Yet these are the truths most essential to our
spiritual life, and ignorance of which is chiefly to
be deplored.   They are, moreover, truths for which
man has by nature a most insatiable intellectual
curiosity that breaks out everywhere, even in the
most barbaric and uncultivated minds; and yet with
regard to which he is as helpless, as much in need
of God, as the babe is of its mother's breast; and
if his craving for the mysterious, the wonderful, the
supernatural, be not fed by true religion, it will feed
itself on the garbage of any superstition that is
offered to it.

Indeed, the soul will never be raised higher or
further strengthened by any truth which it has once
thoroughly penetrated or comprehended, and which
therefore retains for it no element of mystery or
wonder, for it is only by straining to comprehend
what exceeds its present grasp that it grows great.

Mysticism deals with such half-veiled, half-
revealed truths as we speak of. There is no doubt
a false mysticism which values obscurity for its

own sake, and wraps up the simplest truisms of morality in clouds of confusion till they loom great and mysterious; and which on this score lays claim to special gnosis and prophetic insight. But this child of affectation, or self-delusion, or ignorance, no more discredits the true mysticism of à Kempis or of St. Teresa, than spiritualism discredits spirits, or jugglery discredits the miracles of Christ.

Having thus insisted on the reasonableness and necessity of mysticism, as opposed to crude rationalism and to the non-sense of *soi-disant* " common sense " in spiritual things, we must equally insist on the importance of using all the light and help that reason rightly used affords us in these matters; of recognizing here, as elsewhere, progress and development in our understanding of Divine truth (itself unchanging)—a progress in distinctness and coherence of idea and statement; a continual and faithful retranslation of the words and forms of one age or country into those of another; an adaptation of immutable principles, to the ever mutable circumstances of human life. For where this work is neglected, the language and conceptions of a former generation become, first, tasteless and commonplace; and then distasteful and repugnant to the changing fashions of thought and speech in succeeding generations—except in the case of those rare works of genius and inspiration which, like the Scriptures or the *Imitation*, are catholic and eternal.

Thus much, then, in justification of what might seem to be a too dialectical treatment of subjects to a great extent beyond the reach of so rude a method.

Again, the writer may be reproached with a certain indecency and irreverence in attempting to make bare to the public gaze many of those deeper mysteries of our holy religion which the instinct of more delicate minds has ever hidden in a language "not understanded of the people." This *disciplina arcani* the Church has learnt from her Divine Master, whose parables were "words to the wise," mercifully veiling from the many the light which they could not bear, and which would have been only to their ruin and not to their resurrection. Also there is a sacred duty of guarding the higher truths of the Eternal Kingdom from the profanation of being discussed, perhaps ridiculed and blasphemed by those whose minds and hearts are void of the first principles whence a sympathetic understanding of them might be evolved. As it is, there is scarce a hireling journalist who is not as ready with his flippant criticisms on the mysteries of the Kingdom of God as he is with those on political or scientific or literary topics. Nothing is sacred from his omniscient pen. Is it then season-

able thus to cast pearls before those who will but
trample them under foot and turn again and
rend us?

If after some hesitation the writer has determined to face the possibility of such ill-conse-
quences, it has been from a conviction that it is
rather through an insight into the high and all-
satisfying ethical conceptions of the Catholic religion
that men are drawn to embrace it than through any
more speculative considerations. *Loquere ad cor
populi hujus*—Speak unto the heart of this people,
was the Prophet's commission; nor can it be denied
that it was because He knew what was in man that
Christ had such irresistible power over the hearts of
men; for here if anywhere knowledge is power. So
there is nothing that establishes and confirms our
implicit faith in the Catholic religion of Christ more
than the clear conviction that she alone knows what
is in man, and holds the secrets of life's problems;
that she alone has balm for the healing of the
nations; that she alone can answer firmly and
infallibly what all are asking, with an answer harsh
at first sounding, and austere, but on reflection kind
and consolatory, and, like the "hard sayings" of
her Master, "full of grace and truth."

It is not till men's hearts are deeply drawn
towards the Church for one reason or another,
that their minds are sufficiently freed from the

natural bias against a creed so exacting and imperious in many ways, to make them desirous or capable of listening to her claims.

For this reason, therefore, it is to the heart we must make our first appeal, by bringing together as far as we can those various truths which embody the Church's explanation of life as we find it; by showing their mutual bearings, their harmony with one another, and with the stern facts they deal with and explain. If the Church has an answer which will give a meaning to pain and temptation and sin and sorrow, which will point to law and order where otherwise there is nothing apparent but painful darkness and confusion, which will verify and connect what is to all seeming manifold and dis-connected, even though that answer be hard and repulsive in its very simplicity, surely it should make every honest truth-seeking mind pause to see if indeed these things be so, if indeed darkness can be so touched with light, and sorrow so turned into joy. If the solution fits the problem it may indeed be the result of chance, but it is a chance that becomes ever more incredible as the conditions of the problem are seen to be multiple and intricate: and the more we know of life's complications on the one hand and of the Church's simplification on the other, the less possible is it for us to doubt that she is from on high, the work of those hands which fashioned the human soul, and which provide for the needs of every creature they have fashioned.

We do not mean that our needs demand and explain every point of Catholic teaching, as though that religion were merely the complement of our nature's exigencies, and were not also supernatural, giving more than our heart as yet knows how to desire. But the whole idea of personal trust and faith is that those whom we have found loving and true to us in matters we can test, should ever be accredited with the same love and truth in matters beyond our criticism. So it is with faith in God, with faith in Christ, with faith in the Catholic Church; we understand enough to warrant full trust in what we cannot understand, or cannot even expect to understand.

It is, then, the belief that a deeper and more comprehensive view of the Church's ethical and spiritual ideals; of her conception as to the capacities, the dignity and destiny of the human soul, of the hope that she inspires in the midst of so much that is otherwise disheartening, of the light which she sheds over the dark abyss of sin and temptation and sorrow—it is the belief that such a comprehensive view may in some cases serve far more effectually than any direct apologetic to win, to establish, or to confirm an abiding faith in her divine origin and operation, that must partly excuse or justify an otherwise reprehensible popularizing of the " secrets of the King."

Not indeed that any one mind however broad and deep can ever hope to grasp the Catholic idea in its entirety, or can ever count itself to have comprehended perfectly what by reason of its magnitude must elude all but an infinite thought. If every advance in the knowledge of Nature advances us in knowledge of our ignorance of Nature, the same holds good of our study of the Christian revelation, of the idea of Christ and the Church. Man's brain grows-to and outgrows religions that are its own creation, the provisional expression and images of that Reality which touches him in conscience, and cries out to him in Nature. But it does not, and cannot, outgrow that revelation in which God has expressed for him, albeit in faltering human language, realities which are beyond all reason and experience. Our conception of one whom we meet and observe daily will grow in depth, in volume, in accuracy; but our conception of one whom we know only by hearsay cannot go beyond what is contained in that hearsay. Yet this content may be infinite in potentiality, like some mathematical expression from which a process of endless building-up can be started. And so it is with that conception of Himself and of His Christ and of His Church which God has given us in the Christian revelation.

It is an idea which admits of infinite evolution, which the Church keeps and broods over and ponders in her heart; in which the best thought of every age finds its highest ideals satisfied and surpassed. Superficial critics who shrink from the labour of a wide induction, are perpetually treating this idea as it is found in some particular mind or nationality or period, and by consequence confounding what is accidental with what is essential, and failing to distinguish its morbid from its legitimate developments.

And indeed it is to the Church, who watches over this process, that we must look for our guidance as to results already obtained. But starting where she leaves off and following in the direction of the lines she has laid down, the minds of her children will ever press on towards a fuller intelligence of the mysteries of faith, turning back at times to gain her approval or to receive her rebuke or to listen to her counsel; and thus, under her supervision, they will purify the Catholic idea more and more from all foreign admixture and build it up member by member, nearing, yet never reaching, a perfect disclosure of its organic unity, its simplicity in complexity, its transcendent beauty.

Finally, in choosing *Hard Sayings* for a title, allusion is made to the occasion when many of the disciples of Jesus turned back and walked with Him

no more, because of His doctrine concerning the
great Mystery of Divine Love, in which all the other
mysteries of the Catholic faith are gathered up.
That this Man should give us His Flesh to eat, that
bread should be His Body, is indeed a "hard
saying" for the many who are the slaves of their
imagination, and who fancy that they know something of the constitution of matter and the limits of
Divine omnipotence. But for the more thoughtful it
is a far harder saying that God should so care for
man's love as to come down from Heaven, and take
flesh that He might woo man in man's own
language—the language of suffering. And if these
things are hard to the understanding, it is still
harder for the weak will to hear that God must be
loved back as He has loved us, with a love that
yields pain for pain, sacrifice for sacrifice, death for
death.

Here the Church has ever been faithful to her
Master. Others have, with false kindness, mitigated
the "hard sayings," and prophesied smooth things,
and drawn away the weak from her side. But
with all her human frailty, ever shrinking from the
stern ideal of the Cross, from the bitterness of the
Chalice of her Passion, when asked she has but one
ruthless answer, namely, that it is only through
many tribulations that we can enter the Kingdom
of God; that Christ's yoke is easy, not because

it is painless, but because love makes the pain welcome.

To whom then shall we go but to her who has the words of eternal life, who for two thousand years has kept all these sayings and pondered them in her heart?

G. T.

Wimbledon.
SS. Peter and Paul, 1898.

CONTENTS.

THE SOUL AND HER SPOUSE.

Veni, Electa Mea, et ponam in Te thronum meum.
" Come, My Chosen One, and I will stablish My throne in thee."

THE end of man is, to save his soul—*Salus animæ.* But what this health and well-being consists in is specified when St. Ignatius[1] tells us that it is in praising, reverencing, and serving God, in these three manifestations of Divine love, that salvation is realized. Health lies in the right balance of nutrition, in regularity of function, in the orderliness of our bodily conditions; and our spiritual health, in like manner, means *ordination;* the due proportion and subjection of all our faculties to God their Creator and Lord; the submission of our mind to the rule of Divine truth; of our affections to the rule of Divine love. Hence the whole aim of the Spiritual Exercises is to secure *ordination;* to induce that all-mastering love of God in which the soul is saved, perfected, and brought to its highest state and noblest activity.

As the natural life of the soul depends on God's dwelling in its substance, so the supernatural life or Eternal Life of the soul is God, who dwells as light

[1] This discourse has reference to the opening words of the Spiritual Exercises of St. Ignatius Loyola.

B

in the mind and as love in the heart, and who is the object of that light and love.

Here and hereafter alike, the life and health of the soul lies in seeing God, though the mode of seeing is different; here, it is through a glass darkly, in a riddle, there, face to face; here, in part, there, wholly and perfectly; here, as a child, there, as one who has put away the things of a child. A little girl thinks herself absolutely happy when she nurses her first doll. As a woman, with a living babe at her breast, she looks back on that former bliss and laughs. In Heaven she greets her child once more; and once more she wonders that she could ever have rejoiced before.

Eternal life is God *in* the soul. God is the soul's soul. As the body corrupts when abandoned by the soul, so too, the soul corrupts, morally and intellectually, it becomes fœtid, loathsome, disintegrated, deformed, apart from God. God is the beauty, the health, the salvation of the soul. We speak too exclusively of entering into Heaven, into life, into God; forgetting that the relation is truly— perhaps more truly—expressed by saying that God, and Heaven, and life, enter into us. We dwell in God, just because God dwells in us. The branch abides in the vine and the vine in the branch; but principally the vine in the branch. We feed upon Christ, He does not feed upon us. "The Kingdom of God is within you;" it is in your midst; therefore we pray: *Adveniat regnum tuum.* We speak of that Kingdom coming to us, not of our going to it.

Vegna vèr noi la pace del tuo regno
Ché noi ad essa non potem da noi,
S'ella non vien, con tutto nostro ingegno.[1]

Heaven, in its substance and apart from mere accessories, is simply the love of God perfected in the soul; the entire cleaving of the soul to God, whom she embraces with mind and heart—*Inveni quem diligit anima mea ; tenui nec dimittam.*[2] And again: *Mihi adhærere Deo bonum est*—My sovereign good, my heaven, consists in cleaving to God. And as eternal life is the love of God elevated and carried to its extreme perfection, so eternal death is the disease of sin worked out to its last consequences. Hell, in its substance and apart from all accessories, is in the soul, as truly as the soul is in Hell—perhaps more truly.

This answer alone explains man, and proves its own verity by its fitness. Were the soul a simple problem, chance might stumble on many an apparent solution ; but so complicated a riddle is past guesswork. A lock with a hundred intricate wards is the only possible explanation of the key which alone fits it, and which fits it alone. The soul, apart from God, is as meaningless, as useless as a stray key. Its whole structure and movement cries out for God. Who could understand the eye, with its lenses and mirrors and inexplicable mechanism, who knew nothing of light ? Everything in the eye has reference

[1] Thy Kingdom come, that peace with us may reign ;
   For if it come not of itself, in vain
   Our wit would toil that Kingdom to attain. (Dante, *Purg.* xi.)
[2] "I have found Him whom my soul loveth : I have laid hold on Him, and I will not let Him go."

to light, and everything in the soul has reference to
God. Everything in the ear is unintelligible to one
born deaf, and everything in the soul is incoherent
and senseless for one who is dead to God. When
we see the vine straggling over the ground, its
tendrils are unexplained; but when it climbs and
clings to the prop we know what they were made
for. God is the soul's prop. The soul is simply
and wholly a capacity for God, and nothing else;
just as the monstrance with all its golden rays and
gleaming jewels is simply and wholly a receptacle
for His Sacramental Presence—a crystal shrine
through which the faithful may see and adore the
Bread of Angels. Our soul is such a monstrance;
and its highest beauty and glory is from Him who
dwells in it, and shines through it. He is the light,
she is the lamp. On Protestant altars we some-
time see (or used to see) candles which are never to
be lighted. "How unmeaning!" is our first thought.
The soul is God's candle, on which He descends like
a flame and transforms her substance into His own
likeness. The candle was evidently made for the
flame which crowns it, beautifies it, quickens it.
God is not the soul, nor is the soul God; but
as the candle is for the flame, so is the soul for
God.

When Adam slumbered, God drew from his side
a help meet for him; a being altogether made for
him, soul and body, inexplicable without him. God
drew the soul of man from His own side, and she is
restless till she returns thither again. The soul is
God's spouse; made for His embrace, made to

bring forth in herself His Word, His Image, His Beloved Son. And the passion of the purest and noblest heart of man is but the far-removed symbol of the ardent love of God for His spouse. To Him her whole being cries out: Thou hast made me for Thyself, as the casket for the jewel, as the mirror for the sun, as the eye for light, as the ear for sound, as the harp for music. My mind craves for truth, and Thou art the Truth; my will for good, and Thou art the Good; my heart for love, and Thou art Love; mine eye for beauty, and Thou art the Beautiful; my ear for music, and Thou art Song; my soul for eternity, life, and salvation, and Thou art Eternity, Life, and Salvation.

We may say of the soul what is said of Divine Wisdom: *Thesaurus est infinitus quo qui usi sunt facti sunt amici Dei;* she is an unending treasure which few are aware they possess; a secret and unsuspected fount of perennial joy; a well of living water springing up unto life everlasting; a deep and difficult well for those who have not wherewith to draw. With most of us our soul is as a musical instrument in unskilled or half-skilled hands; but from which trained fingers can draw forth melody and sweetness. We are too slothful to go through the preliminary drudgery of practice. Impatient for some little present gratification, we pick out little tunes by ear, and never become masters in the art of spiritual music. Or it is like a great poem which to a child or a rude-minded person seems tiresome and overrated, because a certain amount of education is needed before the mind can

answer to its appeal, and enter into its joy; or it is
as one of the old masters whom the crowd hurries
by in our picture-galleries in order to pause en-
raptured before some flaring vulgarity, while the
true artist lingers over every line and shadow with
a pleasure which is accentuated and not blunted by
use. *Qui edunt me adhuc esurient*—"They that eat
me shall hunger for more," is true of God and of
every good that is Divine.

Plainly our chief care must be to learn to use
this treasure aright, to extract as much value out
each moment as we possibly can, to bring the
highest faculties of our soul into perfect play. For
"they who use it aright are made the friends of
God,"—not as though friendship were an added
reward, but because friendship with God is itself
that very use for which the soul was created, and in
which its best faculties reach their highest development. We know how wonderfully mere human
friendship opens up the soul and betrays to it depths
of which before it was all unconscious, how all that
is best in it slumbers and sleeps till it is wakened
to energy by the touch of love, by the cry in the
midnight of its darkness: "Behold, the Bridegroom
cometh." And herein every other love but shadows
forth some aspect of that one all-satisfying, all-
transforming love which is the soul's eternal life,
which alone immortalizes her—the love of the
Heavenly King and Bridegroom, to whom she is
drawn by every need of her spiritual nature; from
whose side she was taken that she might be a
spouse meet for Him, as it is written :

Virgins shall be drawn to the King in her train,
Her neighbours shall be brought unto thee,
They shall be brought in joy and exultation,
They shall be led into the temple of the King.[1]

These words are usually, and not unreasonably applied by Holy Church to our Blessed Lady as to the Queen of souls, through whom the souls of the elect are brought to Christ in one living mass, as it were, of swarming bees clustered round their queen. She is the very centre and heart of that great soul-world which God created and redeemed to be a Kingdom for Himself; to be subject to Him as the bride is subject in love to the bridegroom. Virgins shall be drawn in her train to the King; virgins of whom St. Paul writes, "I am jealous of you with the jealousy of God Himself, for I have espoused you to one Husband, to present you as a chaste virgin unto Christ." He speaks, indeed, of the entire Church, the whole congregation of elect souls; but what is true of all is true of each; each is a kingdom, each a chaste virgin to be presented spotless and undefiled to Christ, her Spouse and her King. "Glorious things are spoken of thee, O thou city of God, O thou soul of man, thou city of peace, thou city of the great King." Mary is indeed the Virgin of virgins, whose whole heart was His with a wholeness unsurpassable; but every soul, however soiled and sin-stained, recovers its virginity when it has been purified for God's embrace and taught through many tribulations to love God not only above all things, but alone. Therefore we are told

[1] Psalm xliv. 15, 16.

that the King proves His elect bride as gold is proved in fire seven times. And St. Paul, who like the holy Baptist, is the paranymph, the friend of the Bridegroom, who has His interests at heart and prefers them to his own, is jealous with the jealousy of God for those souls he is preparing for the King; jealous lest the purity of their affection should be tarnished by the least spot of any love not for God, or from God, or in God. And God Himself is jealous and says: "I, the Lord thy God, am a jealous God; thou shalt have none other gods but me;" thou shalt give Me all thy love, for I will have nothing less. He is jealous for that He knows that He alone is our Peace, our Life, our all-satisfying eternal Good.

And now see how souls are brought to God: "Virgins shall be drawn to the King in her wake;" drawn and not driven, drawn through their affections with the silken cords of love, willing captives to that most blessed tyranny. Drawn by the spell of the King's beauty, whom at first they behold, not face to face, but mirrored in His created reflex, yet nowhere so fully, so faultlessly as in the Queen of souls who stands at His right hand in her vesture of pure gold, fringed round with many-coloured broiderings. For if He is *Speciosus præ filiis hominum*—"fair before all the sons of men," she too is all-fair, and "grace is poured forth upon her lips." And as we turn from a sudden light to see the source whence it proceeds, so our eye travelling instinctively from the glory which flashes upon Mary's gold mantle, climbs to Heaven. It is as when we see one whose

eyes are fixed in rapture on something we cannot
see, and whose face is lit with a joy we cannot
understand; yet we fain would know that secret,
and are drawn to wonder, and seek, and knock till
it be opened to us.

Thus it is that God draws souls to Himself, one
through another. Thus it is that we are each to
draw souls to Him in the wake of our own, *Donec
occurramus omnes in unitatem fidei et agnitionis filii
Dei*—until we are all run together in oneness of faith
and knowledge of the Son of God, until we are all
made into one vast body centred round Mary and
wedded to Christ, our Head and Spouse.

Proximæ ejus afferentur tibi—" Her nearest shall
be brought unto Thee." It is those nearest to Mary
who are most quickly, most potently drawn; those
in whose souls there is the least alloy, whose mind
and affection has been purged in the fire from all
dross and impurity. As the soul nears Mary, it
also nears its own birth-place in the heart of its
Creator, and is drawn with an ever-quickening speed
to its final repose. It is drawn *in lætitia et exulta-
tione*—" in joy and exultation," which grows every
moment of its nearing. " In joy," for " though the
strife be sore, yet in His parting breath, Love
masters agony." Like all coming to birth, this
throwing off the bands of our narrower self, is
not without pain and anguish and cracking of
the heart-strings. If the soul is to come to the
King, she must forget her own people and her
father's house; yet, *labor ipse amatur*, the pain
itself is loved as the expression and the relief of

love. " In exultation," " leaping, and walking, and praising God," as the once-lame, glorying in his new-found, God-given strength, or as Mary herself who when carried to the Temple of the King, and being set down on the sacred steps from her mother's arms, " danced with her feet," as the old legend says. " I was glad when they said to me, Let us go into the house of the Lord ; our feet shall stand within thy courts, O City of Peace." And the thronging souls who are drawn after her to be presented to the King, they too have tasted the sweet bitterness of sacrifice and offering, and in joy and exultation have cried : " Lord, in the singleness of my heart, gladsome I offer Thee this day all, without reserve " —*Domine in simplicitate cordis mei lætus obtuli universa hodie.*

But what manner of King is this that the home to which His spouse is brought should be called a temple rather than a palace; that He should be loved with a love of adoration and worship; with sacrifice and offering and absolute self-surrender? *Ipse enim est Dominus Deus tuus,* says our Psalm, *et adorabunt eum*—" For He is the Lord thy God whom all shall adore." " Thy Maker is thy husband," says Isaias. His love and His absolute right of kingship is founded on His creator-ship, on the entire dependence of the soul upon His abiding thought and care, a dependence whereof that of the child upon the mother in whose womb it lives, is but a feeble hint, even as that mother's love is but a faint reflex of the love of the Creator for the soul ever new-born in His bosom.

And He rules as King in the soul when all her affections are so given to Him that she loves Him, not only above all things, in such sort that she would leave all else for Him, but alone, loving nothing else but in relation to Him, in the way that He loves it, and desires that she should love it; and for this consummation He moves her to long, and pray, and labour, and suffer, and cries out within her: *Adveniat regnum tuum.* " Oh, when will there be an end to these miseries; when shall I be delivered from the wretched bondage of these vices; when shall I be mindful of Thee, O Lord, alone; when shall I rejoice in Thee to the full; when shall I be without all let of true liberty, without burdening from mind or from body; when shall I contemplate the glory of Thy Kingdom; when wilt Thou be to me all in all; when shall I be with Thee in Thy Kingdom, which from eternity Thou hast been getting ready for Thy dear ones? "[1]

Of Mary, "the world's sad aspiration's one success," the one soul in which God has had His own way unimpeded, in which He has fully asserted His presence and shone forth as through a faultless crystal, of Mary it is said, " The Queen hath stood at Thy right hand in vesture of gold with many-coloured broiderings. Hearken, My daughter, behold, and incline thine ear. Forget thy own people and the house of thy father; and the King shall long after thy beauty; for He is the Lord thy God, whom all shall adore." For the soul is indeed a queen, when she is all glorious within, and when

[1] *Imitation*, iii. 48.

Christ rules over her with absolute unimpeded dominion. Subject to any other rule but His, she is so far a slave, nor has she yet perfect liberty, perfect self-mastery. But subject to Christ, she is by the very fact raised to a throne at His side and shares His rule over her every faculty and move-ment; thus dying to live, and losing to gain, and forsaking all to find a hundred-fold now, and ever-lasting liberty in the life to come. .For what is liberty but the perfect development and exercise of all our powers in due order. Thus, King and Queen, they reign side by side; God and His little creature. And she is His consort, *con-sors*, one who shares the same lot or portion. She is ever with Him at His right hand; whether by His Cross on Calvary or by His throne in Heaven. "If we suffer with Him," says St. Paul, "we shall also reign with Him." If His kingship over her was purchased with sorrow, her queenship is bought no cheaper; there is no way to His side but through thorns and brambles.

How is the queen clad? Like Mary, in her broidered vesture of gold; in her mantle of world-wide universal charity, big enough to shelter a thousand worlds-full of sinners who fly thither for refuge as chickens to their mother's wings; that mantle which enfolds the redeemed world as a sunlit sky thinly curtaining off the place Christ is preparing for us in secret, woven of gold purified seven times by her seven sorrows, for what love is so pure as the love we bear those for whom, and even from whom, we have suffered? And the many-coloured fringes with which this mantle is decked around, what are they but the virtues midst which charity rules as mother and mistress, which spring from her bosom, and draw their life from her; for love is the fulfilling of the law, the sum and substance of all its precepts.

Finally, the vocation of Mary is in some measure the vocation of every soul: "Hearken, My daughter, and forget thy own people and thy father's house," forget thyself and every other affection so far as it is debased by any undue infusion of self; lose thy life that thou mayest save it, give and it shall be given to thee, full measure, pressed down, shaken together, and running over; "leave all, and thou shall find all; quit thy desires, and thou shalt find rest." We Catholics need not to be told that the call to closer union with God, to love Him alone, far from deadening or quenching any right and healthy nature affection, or warping or maiming the soul; perfects, purifies, deepens, and exalts all that it regulates and restrains. None love father or mother or brother or friend so tenderly, truly, eternally, as they who love God more than all, and all for God's sake, as Jesus loved Mary or John or Lazarus, or the Magdalen, for Divine love is the myrrh which embalms all other love and saves it from taint and corruption. Ungoverned by that over-ruling affection, our other affections are a disorderly riotous mob, weak individually and collectively, and dangerous by reason of their very weakness and waywardness; but under that sway they are disciplined, strengthened, and welded together into the unity of an army with one mover, one action, one end, and licence and confusion give place to order and true liberty. This is that life bought at the cost of death and mortification, in which the self, forgotten in the remembrance and thought of God, is found again in Him, recognized almost as part of Him, and loved rightly for His sake and in sympathy with Him. Precious in the eyes of God is this death of the soul in which she is buried in Him and from which she rises to a new life—the death which Mary embraced when she elected to be the sorrowful Mother of the Man of Sorrows, and said, *Ecce ancilla Domini.*

Into the soul thus purified God looks as into a burnished mirror and sees there the reflex of His own beauty, "without spot or wrinkle," and longs for that soul and draws it to Himself with the impetuous ardour of the love He of necessity bears towards the very least shadow of His own Divine goodness; even as the earth draws back to her bosom whatever would vainly fly from her thrall. "The King shall then long for thy beauty, for He is the Lord thy God;" it is from His bosom thou wert taken; it is from Him thou wouldst vainly flee; it is to Him thou must return of necessity, in the measure that the mirror of thy soul is purged of selfishness and His nature and image shines out in thee. "Glorious things are spoken of thee," O thou soul of man, thou city of the great King.

THE HIDDEN LIFE.

" Il faut se bien persuader qu'il n'y-a absolument d'utile, de réel, d'interessant que ce qui se passe entre notre âme et Lui qui tout est là."—Mrs. Craven, *Meditations*.

As children our thoughts about God are childish of necessity, and are no more suited to our later years than the clothes and toys of our infancy. As men we must put away the thoughts of childhood unless our soul is to perish through nakedness and starvation. We must recognize that God is not one who made the world once for all and then retired from His labours to rest in the distant heavens and to survey His work from afar, but that whatever excellence is found in any creature is due to the image of God reflected there; and that as the image in a mirror is caused by the presence of him who stands in front of it, and stays while he stays and goes when he goes, so it is because God is most intimately present to all things, is permeating and penetrating their inmost substance, that they are what they are. For they depend for every instant of their being and every vibration of their activity on the continual, sustained exercise of God's conscious love. He radiates them into being as the flame radiates its light and heat. As the thoughts and images which we conjure up in our mind depend upon our will, so creation (whose reality compared with God's is but as a dream) hangs on the Divine will. Creatures are nothing more nor less than mirrors or crystals designed to show forth, to reflect and analyze the multiform beauty of the Divine Light, to split it up into its infinitely various components. Their beauty, their brightness, their colouring, is not their own, not from themselves, but from the Light that permeates them, from God who dwells in them. Yet while each is in some measure a temple of His presence, according to the degree in which it mirrors His goodness, it is in the soul of man, with its spiritual powers and activities, that His image is most perfectly and nobly displayed. Here, however, His indwelling is two-fold. In the indestructible nature of the soul and in those activities and perfections which are common to good and evil alike, nay, which are possessed in the most excellent degree even by the fallen spirits, in these He dwells in the measure that He wills, nor does His indwelling depend upon the consent of the creature. But if He would reflect and show forth those attributes which are essentially perfections, not of the mind alone, but also of the power of choice or of free-will, if He would dwell in us as sanctity, as truthfulness, as justice, as purity, as patience, as meekness, as love, still more, if He would crown these natural virtues and raise them to a Divine order by grace, and by His indwelling Spirit, if He would work Faith, Hope, and Charity in our hearts, then indeed He must wait upon our will; He must stand at the door and knock until we open and receive Him.

It **is of** this indwelling that St. Paul writes : " I
live, yet not I, but Christ liveth in me." For all
Christian sanctity is simply the presence of Christ,
of God Incarnate dwelling in the soul, uttering
Himself, asserting Himself there ; nor can we boast
of anything, save that we have not shut the door in
His face. All the glory of the temple is from Him
who dwells in it. Whatever sanctity or spiritual
beauty is found in the members of Christ's Mystical
Body, flows into them from the Head. It is the
life of Christ, extended and manifested in His
Church on earth, which continues the sacrifice of
praise and holiness inaugurated by Him in His own
person upon earth. The Church is the tree which
has grown out of that seed. Hence St. Paul writes:
" To Him (*i.e.*, to the Father) be glory *in the Church*
and in Christ for ever and ever ; " for Christ and the
Church are one thing.

We are sanctified, therefore, in proportion as
Christ lives and dwells in us. But our spiritual **life**
is a life of thoughts, words, and actions ; it has
its outward and its inward side. And ˇif we ask
ourselves which is the more important, the more·
fundamental, there can be but one answer. For
as the soul is to the body, so is the interior
to the exterior man ; and so is the inner life
of our thoughts and affections to the outer
life of our words and actions. Soul and body
alike are essential parts of humanity ; yet the
body is for the soul, not the soul for the
body. Christ must dwell in our outward and in
our inward life, but principally in the latter ; for

the outward is for the sake of the inward, and not conversely.

It is what we think about and what we love that matters most, and that makes us what we really are in God's eyes, as opposed to what we seem in the eyes of others. It is the secret life of our heart which is our highest, noblest life. It is in the theatre of our inmost soul that the great drama of our life is played. Men see but the shadows that flit across the curtain now and then, and overhear an odd word at times. God and our conscience are the sole spectators.

Our life for all eternity will be a life, not of speaking and doing, but of contemplating and loving—an interior life. "This is life eternal, that they should *know* Thee." Heaven is but the triumphant advent, the unimpeded reign of God in the soul. And so far as we here begin to enter into eternal life we must live principally at home in our own hearts, and regard that as the chief scene of our existence,—*Regnum Dei intra vos est.* In brief, eternal life is friendship with God—with a friend whom we find in our heart, whom we listen to in our conscience.

This is not the truism it sounds. For though we all admit as axiomatic that our inner life is of the highest importance, and that without it the outer life is only pretence and hypocrisy, yet in this pseudo-practical age we are likely to invert the right order of things, and to regard the importance of the heart's life as subordinate and relative to the life of our outward conduct; to consider it as a

means to that end, and not as a co-ordinate and far
nobler end in itself. We recognize that good actions
and fair words, if they are not merely hypocritical,
are the children of good thoughts and desires, and
that if we want to enjoy the fruit, we must cultivate
the seed. Yet it is this very analogy of seed and
fruit which is so fallacious, which leads us to regard
the inner life as valuable simply for the sake of its
outward effects, and to forget that the hidden activities of the soul are absolutely the highest. Truly
the greater includes the less, and if the heart is
right, it will not fail to overflow and betray itself in
our speech and conduct; for "from the fulness of
the heart the mouth speaketh." But it is the
fulness of the heart that God looks to and values,
and not the utterances of the mouth. The Catholic
religion has always been very plain on this point,
setting the contemplative life above the active in
dignity, as more conformable to that of the angels,
who for ever behold the face of God. And as it is
necessary for the Church's corporate perfection that
there should be always some members set apart for
such a life, as many, namely, as is compatible with
the Church's active ministrations, so it is needful in
the life of the individual that there should be times
set apart for the cultivation of those inner activities
in which our highest and best life consists.

Here the childhood of the race presents a
parallel to that of the individual. The Law was
before the Gospel. It was written on tables of stone;
it enjoined observances in word and deed. Excellent
and Divine, so far as it went, yet it brought nothing

to perfection till Christ came, not to destroy but fulfil, not to make light of outward sanctity, but to carry sanctification into the heart as well. For in order of genesis the imperfect is before the perfect, the animal before the spiritual, the earthly before the heavenly, although in the order of Divine intention that which is last to be realized is what is first and chiefest to be desired, and is the parent of all other desires. The Law forbade murder, but Christ forbade the angry and revengeful thought; the Law restrained deeds of selfish arrogance and violence, Christ taught men to be meek and humble in their hearts, to think gently, humbly, forgivingly of the weakness and sins of others. The Law said, "Thou shalt not commit adultery," Christ demanded purity of heart, cleanness of the imagination, and chastity of desire. It is out of the heart of man, according to Christ, that all lawlessness and wicked-ness proceed, and the external disorder caused by such violence and licence, is but an insignificant evil compared with the ruin of God's sanctuary within the heart itself, the profanation of His image in the soul of man, the darkening of the intellect, the enslaving of the will, the chaos of the affections and passions.

So it is with each of us individually. When we first turn to the service of God we are legalists, imbued with the spirit of the Law, and if not actually superstitious in our estimate of the import-ance of observances, yet incredulous of the extreme necessity and all-importance of the secret life and converse of the heart. We are careful, indeed, to check evil desires, because we soon learn that, as the smouldering spark gives birth to the flame, so desire kindles up into action. But it is long before we realize the simple fact that as our evil propensities—pride, anger, vanity, avarice, lust, and the rest—are strengthened every time we yield to them in outward act, so they can be fostered steadily, persistently, unnoticeably, by the mere unheeded dreamings of our imagination and wanderings of our fancy—apart from all desire or purpose of putting these fancies into effect. Nay, it is chiefly from this perennial source that our vices are fed and nurtured as by an insensible dew, so fine and subtle as to be imperceptible. And thus it comes to pass that our heart is overgrown with noxious weeds and tangling briars which we cannot account for, so silent and slow has been the growth, and yet so steady and constant.

What is true of our evil propensities is equally true of those that are pure and holy. It is by the continual stream of our thoughts and imaginings that they are insensibly nourished and strengthened, rather than by our outward actions, which are comparatively occasional and intermittent. We live more by the air we breathe, sleeping and waking, than by the food we take only from time to time.

Therefore St. Paul says:[1] " Whatsoever things are true, whatsoever things are pure, whatsoever

---

[1] " Quæcunque sunt vera quæcunque pudica, quæcunque justa, quæcunque sancta, quæcunque amabilia, quæcunque bonæ famæ, si qua virtus, si qua laus disciplinæ, hæc cogitate." (Philipp. iv. 8)

things are just, whatsoever things are holy, whatsoever things are lovable, whatsoever things are of
good report, if there be any virtue, if any praiseworthy discipline, *hæc cogitate;* think about these
things;" feed your heart on such food; meditate
on the things of God, on anything that is good and
beautiful or true in the works of God's hands, or in
the laws of His world, or in the thoughts and
doings and lives of men; on whatsoever is noblest
and best in human conduct. And though God
Himself, the source of all such goodness, should be
the chief food of our reflection, yet St. Paul knows
well that here we do not see God face to face, but
only in His works. Nor is it possible for our minds
always to be occupied directly and consciously about
the things of God, but it suffices that its theme be
something worthy and profitable, or in some way
referable to the service and glory of God, such as
our business or daily concerns, our lawful and
reasonable recreations, our converse with our
fellow-men. Still better it is for us to accustom our
mind to the higher thoughts that secular literature
and art furnish us with in such abundance; to
cultivate a certain orderliness, purity, and elevation
in our imaginings; not to disdain the grace that
God offers us in a good education, and in the
opportunities of refining our taste. All this helps
to bring order into the tangled wilderness of our
fancies, to strengthen the faculties of the soul, and
to give us a more perfect control over their workings;
so that when occasions offer we may use them more
effectually and faithfully in the direct service of God.

Speaking of the perfection of our outward conduct, St. James says, that he who offends not in tongue the same is a perfect man, for he is able to govern himself as with a bridle. For although in some sense the tongue has no movement of itself, but only that which it receives from our thought and will, yet it is so closely yoked with the imagination, so ready for instant use at all times, that it seems almost to share the automatic and semi-independent nature of that faculty, and to drag us along in its course, committing us to much that in no sense represents our matured and deliberate sentiments. In proportion as its movements are minute, rapid, multitudinous, they more easily evade our attention and self-control. Hence, since self-government is the precise point in which man differs from animals, he who can govern every movement of his tongue is indeed a perfect man and master of himself. Manifestly, he is perfect in his outward conduct; but more than this, he is also to some extent perfect in the control of his thoughts and affections; for without this, by reason of the close connection of word and thought, faultlessness in speech is not possible in any positive sense. For to master one's tongue is not to keep perpetual silence, but to say the right thing in the right place.

Yet there are hours when even the most restless energy must be still, and the busiest tongue must be silent, when there is no room for any other activity but that of the soul; and then he is indeed a perfect man who offends not; whose thoughts and approved feelings are faultless before God; in whose inner life Christ's image and indwelling is manifest; whose soul is united to the Divine Soul of our Saviour in all its imaginings, reasonings, aspirations, sentiments, through the indwelling of that same Spirit which sanctified His Soul and the soul of His Mother and of all His saints.

This is, indeed, the highest point of perfection; the most difficult, and therefore the last to be attained in its fulness. The Law was our pedagogue which led us to Christ; the exterior life is the scaffolding preparatory to the never-finished task of building up the inner sanctuary of God's presence.

If our tongue seems to run away with us, far truer is this of our thought, which may be compared to an endless stream, springing from the hidden depths of our memory, which rolls past us, bearing on its bosom all manner of odds and ends, the litter and *débris* of our past experiences and reflections; nor is it in our power to do much more than to stand on the bank and watch, and with our attention fix and arrest what is profitable for our spiritual food, suffering all else to float by, or even hastening it on its way. True, it depends largely (not altogether) upon our previous choice what this stream of subjective time shall find in the storehouse of our memory to carry past us in its current. We are not immediately answerable for all the fancies that flit across our brain, except so far as by deliberate approval we make them virtually our own act. But the general character and tone of our involuntary memories and fancies is to a great extent chargeable to our past conduct, exterior and interior. Moreover, those who watch over their hearts, gradually acquire a knowledge of the laws which bind together our fancies into chains and groups; they know what leads to what; and therefore they can in some measure determine the particular channel in which the stream shall flow; and so they can advance indefinitely nearer to that perfect inner self-mastery which is never absolutely attainable by mortal man in this life.

Perhaps this interior life was never more difficult, never more apt to be underrated, neglected, forgotten than in these days, when knowledge is multiplied to the hurt of wisdom, and the means of mental subsistence is exalted into an end. There is so much to be known now-a-days if we would pass muster as people of even ordinary education, so much of the experiences and thoughts of other men to be stored away in our memories, that life in most cases is not long enough for the process and no margin of leisure remains for digesting and assimilating the food with which we have been surfeited. We deal it out to others as we ourselves received it, crude and unchanged; as it were, so much coin that passes from hand to hand and bears no other stamp than that of the nation.

And with the multiplication of knowledge and information the evil increases daily, and thought and reflection becomes the province of a dwindling number of specialists, to whom the minds of the millions are enslaved, for it is the tyranny of capitalism in another sphere. We no longer have

time to think for ourselves, but our thinking is done
for us wholesale, and distributed to us through the
press, and the very faculty of meditation has grown
paralyzed from disuse.

This fault of modern education cannot but make
itself felt in the spiritual life of the faithful at large
in a decay of the ability and habit of reflection.
Not to speak of a narrow and exaggerated idea of
practical piety which would (if it dared, in the face
of Catholic tradition) make the service of God
chiefly consist in everlasting fussiness and external
activity, in " Church-work," and parish-work, and
controversy, in the corporal works of mercy, which
is secretly impatient of contemplative orders, contemplative saints, and contemplation in general,
which is puzzled how to defend the eremitical life or
the life of mere suffering and solitude that certain
saints have chosen ;—not to speak of all this, it is to
be feared that in regard even to our spiritual needs,
information and knowledge are apt to be mistaken
for that vital thought, that meditative wisdom which
is the true life of the soul, the quickening flame, of
which knowledge and information and experience is
but the fuel. We store our mind with the recorded
experiences and reflections of others, but we do not
compare these things and ponder them in our heart;
we do not assimilate and digest. We gather manna
ourselves and we distribute it to others ; but we
forget that it is given to us for food ; to be eaten,
not to be gazed on—and all because the leisure,
the practice, the habit, and therefore the ability of
tranquil reflection tends to become the privilege

of the few, and because there is so much to be devoured that there is no time to ruminate.

However difficult the interior life may be, yet it is all-important. " Except you eat the Flesh of the Son of Man and drink His Blood ye have no life in you." If the first sense of these words refers to sacramental communion, it cannot be doubted but they are also verified of the spiritual communion in which Christ dwells in our hearts through faith. Spiritual communion is not merely a substitute for that which is sacramental, but it is the usual condition for the fruitfulness of the sacrament; nay, in some sort, it is the end to which the sacramental eating of Christ is directed, the grace it is designed to produce. In the Eucharist we receive the seed of that supernatural life which ordinarily manifests itself in our heart and in our conduct, but without meditation the seed lies idle and uncultivated—the force may be there, but it is latent. Christ, and Christ Crucified, is the food of our soul, the daily bread of our eternal life, the fuel of Divine love in our heart. He is the Word Incarnate, the Divine " Saying," which we must keep and ponder in our heart; in whom whatsoever things are true, pure, lovely, of good report, and praiseworthy, are summed up and gathered together as in their source and end.

In all this matter Mary must be our model of the interior life; Mary, in whom Christ dwelt as He dwelt in no other, in whose heart alone He had His own way from the very first; in whose life He asserted Himself unimpeded. Her words and actions, however full of sublime significance, were few. But the whole record of her life of stupendous fruitfulness and activity is epitomized for us in one brief sentence: Mary kept all these sayings and pondered them in her heart. " Blessed is the womb that bore Thee," cries a voice in the crowd, "and blessed the paps which Thou hast sucked." " Yea, rather," says our Lord, " blessed are they that hear the Word of God and keep it." Blessed was Mary above all women in that she was Mother of God; yet more blessed in that she was full of grace and had found favour with God; blessed, in that Christ dwelt in her womb, yet rather blessed, in that Christ " dwelt in her heart by faith."

THE PRESENCE OF GOD.

Quo ibo a spiritu tuo et quo a facie tua fugiam.
"Whither shall I fly from Thy Spirit, whither escape from
Thy presence?"—Psalm cxxxviii.

WE are always told before entering on prayer to
"put ourselves in the presence of God;" and at all
times to endeavour "to live in the presence of God."
Indeed, it may be said that sanctification lies in a
practical realizing of the presence of God. For
Heaven is the state in which we see God face to
face and stand in His presence continually; and
sanctity is but Heaven begun upon earth. In proportion, therefore, as we live in God's presence, do
we enter into the lot of the saints in light. Plainly,
if God is omnipresent, if all things are naked and
open to His sight, whether we like it or not we are
always equally in His presence; that is, we are
equally present to Him. But local or physical
presence is one thing, and conscious presence is
another. Two trees are physically present one to
another in the same garden, and this relation is
necessarily mutual. But while a tree is present to
the touch or sight or consciousness of an observer,
the observer is not present to the consciousness of
the tree, for it has none. So too, one person may
be present to the consciousness of another who is

thinking of him, or looking at him, or listening to
him, and yet that other may not be present to him.

To live in God's presence, or to put ourselves in
His presence, means to become actually conscious
of God as present; or at least so to live as though
we were thus actually conscious.   For at times the
presence of others will act as a check upon us even
when we are not positively thinking about them at
all; because we have a sort of latent sense, or sub-
consciousness of being watched and observed.   I
suppose it may be explained by saying that there is
a certain line of conduct and converse, a certain
pitch or tone, which we take according as we are
alone or in company, and, again, according to the
nature of our company; and that when once the
consciousness of our surroundings has started us on
one of these lines, we persevere in it after we have
ceased to attend to the reason, unless something
diverts us altogether.

As children we must of necessity think of God
under the somewhat magnified figure of our earthly
parents and rulers.   He lives, we know not how,
above the clouds, beyond the stars—wherever that
may be; He surveys the earth and its dwellers from
afar, with an eagle-vision of surpassing keenness;
He rules it by some mysterious *actio in distans*,
except when He sends angels to execute His will,
as it were, in His absence.   Religious art and
symbolism, nay, the enacted symbolism by which
Christ ascended, and was lifted up with the clouds,
or by which the clouds were parted for the descent
of the Dove, all tends to press this picture of

the absent God still deeper into our imagination, so that even when reason rises to the truth of God's omnipresence, fancy ever gives it the lie and hinders the practical realization of the fact. We lift up our eyes and hands in prayer as to a God outside us and above us; and herein we follow the practice, not merely of the rude and simple, but of all the saints and of Christ Himself. The appearances under which God has revealed Himself; the terms and figures in which the inspired writings speak of Him, all alike tend to set our imagination at variance with our reason, nay, with our faith, which tells us distinctly that God is a Spirit to be worshipped neither on Sion nor on Garizim, but in spirit and in truth; that He dwells not in temples made with hands; that the Heaven of heavens cannot contain Him; that if we go up into Heaven, He is there; if we descend into Hell, He is there; that His eyes are everywhere beholding the evil and the good.

Herein our quarrel is with the necessary limitations of our finite nature, which require that spiritual truths should be presented to our childish mind, not in their naked purity, but in the swaddling-bands of sensuous imagery,—God permitting or not hindering the admixture of error, for the sake of the golden grains of truth which cannot be otherwise conveyed. But it is for us as we grow, to put away the thoughts of childhood, as we put away its clothes or its toys to adopt those more suitable to our years. Unfortunately, while we educate and develop our mind in every other direction, we are

content to remain babes all our lives in the things
of God and our soul—"the things that belong to
our peace." But as the clothes of our infancy are
too strait for comfort and decency in our maturity,
so our first conceptions of God and spiritual things
are too crude and grotesque to be taken seriously
by our formed intelligence, or to exercise any
influence over our heart and will. Custom and
reverence may prevent our casting them aside
altogether; but they have ceased to be a reality to
us. We are as those who having done a little Latin
and Greek in their boyhood before going into
business, wonder secretly what pleasure, still more
what use, some can profess to find in classical
literature; and regard such enthusiasm as a craze
or affectation. Perhaps they remember a line or
two from Horace, or an aphorism from the Delectus
which they quote on occasion, to show a certain
respect for conventional ideas of education. So
we find many whose religion consists of a few
platitudes remembered from childhood, seeds still
lying by the wayside, which have never struck
root so as to become a living growth developing
pari passu with the growth of the soul. Human
respect may seal their lips, but in their hearts they
wonder what others can find in religion, and why
they speak of it as a necessity of life. Such minds
are an easy prey to the shallow sophist who has no
difficulty in persuading them of the untenableness
of their religious notions; nor it is with much of a
wrench that they part from the faith which they
have never understood and never loved.

" Why does God hide Himself? Why can I not see Him or hear Him? Why does He let things run their course, and do so little to show His power over Nature? " These are some of the first difficulties which rise in our minds as we emerge from childhood, suggesting to us that there are some common features to be found in theology and in fairy tales, and inclining us to put them into one category. Figuring God as corporeal and human, we unconsciously suppose that He makes Himself invisible by some miraculous power; that He forbears to make Himself heard for some capricious reason; that whereas we make our power over Nature felt every moment, He chooses to be inert, lest His presence should be detected. Perhaps our ill-informed teachers tell us that God affects this secrecy in order to try our faith; and if we ask why God should try us by faith, we are told that we may not ask, but must take things as we find them—a sort of answer which can silence but cannot satisfy.

Plainly, what we have failed to recognize is, that God does not by some magic make Himself invisible, but that He is naturally invisible to bodily eyes, and that if He makes Himself seen or heard, it is by a miracle; that in such cases the form we see is not God, nor are the words we hear His words, as though He had voice and lips and tongue as we have. Nor does God enter into conflict with Nature and overcome it as we do, or turn aside the orderly course of events as by some foreign external agency; for it is He who moves in all Nature, and the orderly course of events is but the expression of

D

His mind and will. It is in the language of His creatures, in the workings of His providence, in the voice of our conscience, that God is heard and seen. He is not secret or hidden, if we search for Him with the right faculty, namely, our intelligence. Sound is not the object of sight, nor colour of hearing; nor is God the object of my sense, but only of reason and intelligence. We are not aggrieved because we cannot see electricity, since it is naturally not visible. God is as naturally invisible; nor is it caprice but necessity which makes faith—in the wide sense of holding to invisible realities—a condition for salvation. Indeed, that which marks the progress of man from savagery to perfect humanity, is the practical apprehension and realization of invisible realities, shown in a tendency to look beneath appearances to the underlying substance of things, to pass from effects to their hidden causes, to live more in the past and the future by memory and foresight, and not as mere animals on the apex of the present instant: in a word, to be governed by reasons, ideas, principles, rather than by sensations, impressions, impulses. So that, even in the natural order, there is no salvation without faith, which in this wide sense is the substance of things hoped for, the evidence of things not seen.

Let us now determine a little more closely and clearly what it is to live in the presence of God. We are told that the angels and blessed always behold the face of our Father who is in Heaven; that they see the very substance of God with the eye of their intelligence; conceiving Him not merely as the cause of some special effect which manifests His presence; but conceiving Him directly in Himself. If I hear a great crash, I form a distinct conception of it, by which I should recognize a similar crash as belonging to the same class, and should say: "There's another!" I also know at once that it has a cause; but what the cause is, an explosion, or a train, or an earthquake, I have no idea; or rather, I know the cause simply as the cause of this noise, and nothing more; and I want to know something more about it as well. I want to know it as directly as I know the noise which it has caused. So in this life we know a great deal about God as the cause of creation, but we want to know Him as directly as we know creation; to know not merely what He is in relation to His creatures, but also what He is in Himself. For God is not merely a creator; just as a poet is not merely a poet, but a man with a personality of his own, of which his poesy is but a fragmentary manifestation.

But God is no more the proper object of any created intelligence, than the blinding brightness of the sun intensified a thousand-fold is of the vision of some dark-loving animal, an owl or a bat. Raised by grace to powers above all their natural exigencies, the saints 'and angels face that brightness boldly, without the medium of any darkened glass; they see God and yet live. And that vision fascinates their gaze and holds them spell-bound, so that they can never for an instant cease to behold the face of the Father.

And whatever else they do or think is the result of
that vision; is consciously caused by it, and no
more interrupts it than an object seen in the light
interrupts my consciousness of the light. It is in
God as in a mirror, it is in the mind of God and in
the heart of God, that our angels always behold us.
They do not turn away from God to look at us; but
rather they see us with the Divine eyes in consequence of their union with God. It is through
God, moreover, that they act upon us and minister
to us; their will being altogether merged in His;
even as love makes us one thing, having one thought,
one operation with those we love.

The blessed are thus continually conscious of
God's face; and that, with a full and direct consciousness; not as we are conscious of the light or
of the air, in an indirect manner, as of one of
numerous elements in our present experience; but
as of the principal and central object of their attention to which everything else is secondary and
subordinate.

As we cannot enjoy this face to face vision, so
neither is it possible for us during our mortal life to
be continually conscious even of God's veiled
presence. For, in the first place, whereas the
brightness of His face draws the eyes of the blessed
so irresistibly that they are absolutely unable to
avert their gaze, the contemplation of His hidden
presence needs an exertion of the attention.

In the former case, as far as attention is concerned, the mind is passive; it is difficult, nay,
impossible not to attend; but in the latter, the

mind is active, and not to attend is easier. It is well to observe this difference between passive and active attention. Abstraction may be either a power or a weakness, a matter of self-control, or of want of self-control. In the latter case, when it diverts the attention from something else, wholly or in part, it should rather be called distraction. Albeit the blessed are passive in their enrapt abstraction, yet the rapture is not of defective weakness, since no finite will can resist the draw of infinite beauty.

But in this life we have to seek God if we would find Him; we have, to some little degree, to exert ourselves, to open our eyes and keep them open; to watch and to listen; to school ourselves to a greater delicacy and readiness of perception.

There have been indeed men of holiness and deep thought, who have maintained that God is always confusedly present to our consciousness, that He is mingled in our every momentary experience as the central strand round which the rest are woven; that as we are always conscious of our own weight, though normally it makes no separate impression on our memory but only in states of weakness and weariness, or as we are always conscious of the air we breathe or of the light in which we walk, or of the health which we enjoy, although no disturbance of these conditions concentrates our attention upon them as upon a principal object, so God is the most universal, constant, and essential condition of all our experiences, the spiritual light without which we can see nothing; and yet just because of this unbroken regularity, evenness, matter-of-courseness, it is impossible for us to separate this light from the objects which it reveals to us, or to attend to it as to a distinct and principal object. As all the colours which we see with our bodily eyes are but various limitations of the colourless light under which we behold them; so (they conceive) all finite being is but a limitation of one infinite Being, in which it lives, moves, and exists; and is intelligible just so far and no further. God is, as it were, the intellectual light, by sharing which all these finite things become visible to the eye of the mind. We do not see that light apart, in its purity; but only in combination with the object which it illumines, and which shows off, so to say, some one or other of its infinite potentialities. As open to misunderstanding, through want of sufficient accuracy of expression, this teaching has been authoritatively condemned. For indeed it would seem to imply that God, or the Divine substance, in some way actually entered into the constitution of creatures or received into Himself those limitations whereby they differ from one another in kind; whereas this can only be said of a certain abstraction of all finite being which we call " Being-in-general," which is in a wholly different and infinitely lower plane than the Divine being. This " Being-in-general" is a mere chimera of the mind whereby we give consistency to God's creative activity after it has issued from the Divine will and before it has been determined to any specified effect; as though God said *Fiat,* leaving the object undetermined. It is of this

"being" only that every creature is rightly conceived as partaking, or as limiting it to some one
phase of its infinitely various potentiality, even as
everything we see with our bodily eyes singles out
and reflects some one ray of those splendours of
which the seven-stranded sunlight is woven. Now,
in truth, God is the Sun from which the light of
finite being proceeds; but He is the cause of that
light, not the light itself. It is through His presence
and His influence that all creatures have existence
and intelligibility; but what they partake is not
divinity, but an effect of divinity.

Close as He is to all things, intimately as He
permeates all finite existences; yet He is a Light
infinitely different in kind from the light which He
imparts to them; to us, unthinkable, ineffable. We
can at most touch the hem of His garment, but we
dare not face Him in our infirmity and littleness,
until He call us and bid us come: "Thou shalt call
me and I will answer Thee."

Still it must be our chief aim and study to live
as much as possible in His veiled presence. If we
cannot see His form, we can see His shadow; if we
cannot hear His voice, we can hear His footfall; if
we cannot touch His hands and side, we can touch
His vesture. We are surrounded by the signs of
His presence; and we must learn to read them
quickly, to pass swiftly from the sign to that which
it signifies, so as at last to forget the sign and dwell
wholly on God. For a sign is first something
absolute in itself and afterwards something relative,
carrying the mind on to that which it points to;

and therefore it is possible for the mind to rest in
the sign finally without passing on at all. And this
is more true of those signs which are not entirely
designed and intended to lead our thought elsewhere. Smoke betrays the presence of fire; and
a red light betrays the presence of danger on the
line; but in the latter case the betrayal is designed,
which it is not in the former. God's works are in
some true sense designed and intended to reveal His
presence to us; but still it is not their only end;
and therefore it is most possible and easy for us to
think of them without thinking of Him, to rest in
the sign without passing on to the thing signified.

As children we read books without taking any
interest in the personality of the author; but the
cultured and matured mind cares for literature
chiefly as a revelation of the soul from which it
sprang. Similarly with regard to music or painting,
which are loved best when they are loved as forms
of expression, as utterances of a spirit like our own.
How absolutely uninteresting, because soulless, is
all manner of machine-music and mock art, just
for the reason that the connection with the originat-
ing mind is so remote, so much more than second-
hand. It is not a sign of the *presence* of the artist.
We applaud the violinist or the pianist himself, and
not the instrument nor even the music regarded in
its own perfection. We pass straight from the
excellence of the product to the greater excellence
of the producer. But who would ever dream of
applauding the most finished performance on a
musical-box or a piano-organ? The distance from

effect to cause is too great; and we rest simply in the effect. Now, if we cleave to our childish pictures of God, if we take what might irreverently be called a "clock-maker" view of the Deity, according to which He is conceived to have made the world once for all, and wound it up, and set it a-going, and to have retired to rest in an infinitely distant Heaven; then indeed we shall never be able to cultivate a sense of the Divine presence. But if we hold firmly to the truth of reason and faith, and reflect on it, time after time, until it becomes not only a truism of the mind, but also well worked into our imagination; if we remind ourselves repeatedly that all the play of nature and the play of our own being, body and soul, is the effect of God's most intimate presence; who, if He is not the Soul of Nature, nor part of Nature, yet is more intimate to all nature and more necessary to its being and movement than our soul is to our body; then we shall gradually find ourselves passing easily from the creature to God, with ever lessening effort, and at last spontaneously with no effort at all. And certainly love will accelerate the growth of this habit. For where the treasure is, there will the heart be also. We dwell most easily on that which is most interesting. As has just been said, our childish interest, unlike that of our riper thought, is in the performance rather than the performer; but when we have realized that there is nothing really interesting on earth but the human soul, then we are carried from the lesser to the stronger attraction. Who cares, of all on board, what hand has kindled the lighthouse-lamp, save one perchance who knows that it has been kindled by the loving hand of wife or mother, and who while others cry, "There it is!" whispers in his heart, "She is there!" Such is the different mind with which men view the world according as they have not or have learnt to read God's presence everywhere. *Dominus est*—"It is the Lord," says the keen-sighted love of St. John. For as the sensual by a selective sympathy find sensuality in a thousand places where the pure-minded pass by untainted; or as the suspicious and resentful are quick, too quick, to detect an affront; so those whose eyes are sharpened by love find God lurking everywhere.

Let us not look on this exercise of the presence of God as an affair of the imagination, as though it consisted in a certain fictitious picturing of God ever beside us, or before us, or behind us. Such efforts tire the head and give a sense of unreality to religion. It is really a question of opening the sealed eyes of our reason and seeing what is everywhere to be seen, within us and without us, above and below, on the right hand and on the left; in all being, and life, and movement; in Heaven and earth; on sea and on land, and in everything they contain; in all beauty and grace and strength; in all loveliness of form and colour; in all sweetness of melody and harmony, in all delicacy of fragrance and flavour; in all sensation, and reason, and intelligence; in all love, and tenderness, and affection; in the fruit of man's mind and hand; in the utilities of industrial art; in the elegancies of culture and refinement; in the spirituality of liberal arts; in the discoveries of science; in the high dreamings of philosophy. Still more is God to be seen in the moral attributes of the soul, in what-soever things are pure, true, lovely, virtuous, praiseworthy. Above all, is He to be seen and heard in that highest point of our soul, where our being runs into His as the stalk which buries itself in the earth that begets, supports, and nourishes it, namely, in conscience, which cries to us, "Cleave to the right," with a voice that is in us, but not of us; the voice of one who is with us yet over us.

For we walk not alone, but ever side by side with God, whose arm is round us, whose lips are at our ear, even when we are deaf to His whisper: *Læva ejus sub capite meo et dextra illius amplexabitur me*—"His left hand is under my head and His right hand embraceth me." So it is the soul walks through the desert of life leaning on her Beloved. *Etsi ambulavero in medio umbræ mortis, non timebit cor meum quia tu mecum es; virga tua et baculus tuus ipsa me consolata sunt*—"Though I walk in the midst of death's shadow my heart will not fear, for Thou art with me, Thy rod and the staff have consoled me." Conscience is the rod and staff of our gentle Shepherd, who thereby checks and stimulates us alternately that we may not run forward or lag behind, or in any way be parted from His side; and if we have not grown callous to this salutary sting and discipline, what greater consolation can we have than such evidence of the presence and care of the Shepherd and Lover of our souls? "Thy crook and Thy staff are my consolation."

"Enoch walked with God; and was not; for God took him." Such is the history of those souls who listen to the voice of the Shepherd, who are conscious continually of a sort of double personality, of being God's yoke-fellows, one of a twain, of suffering and acting with God, thus splitting up the simple "I" of their unreflecting thought into "we," and finding another personality intertwined with their own.

Finally, God is to be seen by those whose eyes are open, in all the workings and dispositions of His providence, from the least to the greatest; and when the unenlightened cry out: "It is fate; it is fortune; it is necessity of nature," faith and reason say, "It is the Lord; let Him do what seemeth good unto Him;" and: "Into Thy hand I commend my spirit," and, "My lots are in Thy hand."

Let us not then look on this practice of the presence of God as one of many devotions which we are at liberty to take or leave; for it is the great work we have come into this world to do. To see God is eternal life, both here and hereafter; here, through a glass darkly; there, face to face. We are here for a while that our weak eyes may be gradually accustomed to that dim but growing light which heralds the sunrise of eternity; that we may not be blinded by the brightness of His coming.

GOD IN CONSCIENCE.

"Conscience is the aboriginal Vicar of Christ, a prophet in its informations, a monarch in its peremptoriness, a priest in its blessings and anathemas, and even though the eternal priesthood throughout the Church should cease to be, in it the sacerdotal principle would remain and have a sway."
—*Newman*.

It is much to be regretted that the word "conscience" or "dictate of conscience" has come to be used indiscriminately for two very distinct acts or utterances of the mind—for the moral judgment which indicates to us what is right or wrong in human conduct; and for the command which bids us follow that indication. In either sense conscience may be called the "voice of God," though more properly in the latter.

In our moral judgments God speaks to us no otherwise than in any ordinary utterance of our understanding or our reason. Inasmuch as He has created our mind to be in some finite way a mirror of His own, and co-operates with all its vitality and movement, and tries, so far as we will permit Him, to flood and permeate it with His light, it follows that whatever truth it tells us, He may be said to tell us indirectly, and through the instrumentality of the mind: indirectly—for in every judgment the mind truly speaks, and is not a mere passive instrument of conveyance. It

originates in itself, not indeed without Divine assistance, the word of truth which falls upon our inward
ear.   But except with regard to a few first principles,
which are in a certain qualified sense inborn and
irresistibly evident, the mind is subject to much
contingency in its inferences and deductions about
right and wrong; in which there is room for endless
deviation and error.   So far as the mirror of our
reason is flawed or flaws itself, and thereby distorts
and perverts the Divine Reason which it is made to
reflect, it can in no sense be said to speak to us with
the voice of God.   It is indeed, in virtue of its office,
God's appointed messenger, delivering to us the
determinations of His will respecting our conduct
and happiness, but it is a fallible messenger, whose
ear, whose memory, whose tongue may be often at
fault; and who thus may convey to us a very garbled
version of the Divine message or command.   Yet.
conscience, in the sense of our moral judgment, is
not so absolutely untrustworthy as might seem.
There are tests and rules to be applied here, as well
as in the case of human witnesses, whose testimony,
under due conditions and restrictions, is a source of
certainty.   There are occasions without number
where it is intellectually possible to doubt the
verdict of our conscience, yet where it would be
culpably imprudent to pay any practical heed to
such doubt; and there are other cases in which the
message is so palpably ambiguous and obscure as
to leave our liberty of action intact.

It is not our purpose here to examine the notion
of moral rightness in conduct, which all know by

intuition to be so distinct from any other kind of rightness. Men wrangle over the analysis and state-ment of the idea, but as to its existence and separate character all are agreed. Like every other rightness, it implies an end to be reached, and an order to be observed in reaching it. A right action is one which preserves or promotes a certain desirable order in our conduct, that is, in our words and outward behaviour, or in the inner working of our mind and heart, so far as they are under our free government. And a wrong action, contrariwise, is one which induces a disorder in our conduct.

The end with reference to which our conduct is said to be morally right or wrong, is that chief and supreme end which God has created us to attain, namely, the salvation of our soul here and hereafter in the exercise of the highest and most ideal love. This end is in a strict sense obligatory and morally necessary, and therefore such conduct as is required to secure it has a corresponding and dependent necessity. But this necessity and obligation is made up of two very distinct factors; of two forces which exert a sort of compulsion upon our will. Of these one is our irresistible attraction towards our ulti-mate and complete happiness, and all that we conceive to be inseparably connected therewith; the other is the urgency of the Divine will brought to bear upon us in the dictate of conscience.

First then there is this implanted desire for our own fulness of joy, our true well-being, our ideal of rest and happiness—a desire which we cannot resist or put aside in any moment of our conscious activity.

When once we recognize any action as inseparably bound up with the realization of that desire, the thought of that action begins to exercise a sort of dominion over us, nor can we resist its power until by some reversion or perversion of judgment we divest it of that connection with our happiness which was the secret of its sway.

"If you will enter into life," says Reason, "keep the commandments." It is not possible for us to deny our wish to enter into eternal life, and to attain the solid joy that attends that life; but we can shut our eyes to the necessity of keeping the commandments, and in this way we can resist the pressure and obligation which rightness exerts upon our will. Nature obliges us to desire happiness, but does not oblige us to desire any one method of life, except so far and so long as we judge it to be requisite to our happiness. Whatever necessity and obligation there is, is from Nature; that is, from God as the author of the soul's essence. To eat and drink is a necessity of our nature, but to eat or drink this rather than that is left largely to our choice.

Yet all this necessity and pressure is from ourselves, from that implanted appetite which is part of our being. So far, wrong-doing is only shown to be high treason against our own truest interest, an offence against self. But we cannot subvert any designed and established order without offending him who has established and willed it. If while I am waiting in the library for a friend whom I am visiting I amuse myself by deliberately disarranging

and mixing up the books which I see he has carefully set in order, I cannot but be aware that besides
the material disorder and mischief I am producing,
there is another evil of a totally different and more
serious kind for which I am responsible, namely,
the ruffling of my friend's temper. There is nothing
we should value so much as the reasonable esteem
and affection of others; and therefore the thing we
should dread most is the just censure and anger of
those whom we love and reverence. Whatever
servility there may sometimes be in the dread of the
consequences òf their anger, yet there is nothing
servile in the dread of the anger itself. Children
playing at keeping school will patiently accept
punishments, which inflicted in anger by their
parents or teachers would be received with passionate
tears; showing that it is the implied censure and
displeasure which gives the punishment its worst
sting. Hence, the annoyance of my friend is the
worst consequence of my wanton mischief; compared with which the disarrangement of the books
is small and remediable. I can put the books in
order again, or can make some equivalent restitution; but I cannot force my friend to be towards
me as before.

Every thinking creature is sensible, at least dimly
and confusedly, of being dependent on some personal
power which has put him into this world among his
fellow-men, and has given him a definite nature
with a definite work and a definite end, however
imperfectly recognized; and therefore that the
ascertaining and carrying out of that purpose is

E

not merely his own concern, but a duty which he
owes to another to whom he belongs ineffably and
absolutely. He finds, moreover, in his awakened
reason an instinctive love and desire for the objective
interests of reason and right order, quite irrespective
of his private and personal interests, which have at
times to give way to the more universal and imperative good. He finds himself angry against injustices,
which touch neither him nor his belongings, and
aglow for the cause of right and truth and order,
where no egoistic bias is assignable. And the growth
of this objective, disinterested love of rightness is
checked or accelerated in the measure in which the
God-given instinct is yielded to or resisted. All this
points to the fact that his reason and will are given
him only to be instruments of the will of the
personal, subsistent Reason of God Himself, who
presses continually on the created spirit, guiding it
to an end of which it can have at most a partial and
instinctive perception, such as a horse may have of
the purpose of his rider.

Recognizing, therefore, that the order which
reason demands in our conduct with respect to
ourselves and to others is something dependent on
the nature of things established and willed by the
Supreme Reason, it is impossible for us to disturb
that order without being aware, at least in some
dim way, that we are incurring the anger and displeasure of that personal Reason whose creatures
and instruments we are. And if the just censure
and anger of our parents and rulers is something we
should dread as a great evil, how far greater an evil

is it to incur the anger of our Father who is in
Heaven, in whom we live and move and have our
being, on the breath of whose love our soul hangs
for every instant of its existence and movement,
who should be the supreme object of our love and
reverence and praise, in friendship with whom our
final happiness consists. To have made God angry,
this is the greatest evil of sin. The disorder we
have caused in God's work, in our own soul, in
human society, however evil in itself, however
hateful to God, is a finite evil, for which a reparation is conceivable. But by what means shall we
force God to turn to us again with favour, and to
restore to us the priceless treasure of His love?

Here then is a new pressure brought to bear
upon us of quite a distinct order; an appeal to our
need of being loved by God, to our dread of being
hated by God; or, if we are still servile and selfish,
to our desire of the consequences of being loved;
to our dread of the consequences of being hated.
It is the pressure of will against will, and person
against person. It is no longer a question of treason
against self, but of treason against God. No man
can really sin against himself, except in a meta-
phorical sense, which splits his personality in two;
or which treats his lower and higher will as two
distinct persons. But conscience puts him *en rapport*
with a personality other than his own, and thus
deprives him of his falsely imagined liberty and
independence. It tells him he is chained fast to
another who is in a certain sense affected for good
or evil by his every movement, and that that other

is no less than his God and Lord; that he must no
longer think of himself as *I*, but rather as *we;* since
no act of his soul bears upon self alone, but upon
self and God.

It is in this sense of the pressure of God's will
upon ours that the obligation of conscience chiefly
consists. Whatever imperfect pressure may be put
upon us by our innate self-regard, it is as nothing
compared with that which is exerted upon us by our
equally natural regard for the Divine favour.

Let us then carefully distinguish *conscience* as the
sense of what is right, from *conscience* as the sense
of obligation or of a pressure exerted upon our will.
In the former case God speaks to us indirectly and
often fallibly through our reason, and tells us " This
is right, that is wrong." In the latter God reveals
to us infallibly *His own will,* and says, " Do what
you believe to be right; do not, what you believe to
be wrong;" and by this revelation our will is brought
into immediate contact with His, whether to yield
to its pressure or to resist it. Who does not know
from human intercourse, the difference between a
mere communication and exchange of ideas in con-
versation, and the far closer shock of soul with soul
when anger or love is excited, and will meets with
will in conflict or in embrace? It is as bringing
us into will-relations with God that conscience
differs so generically from any other act of our
mind.

But why, it may be asked, should we treat the
impulse of conscience as the voice of God, rather
than the impulse of passion or of any lower instinct

which is as certainly indicative of the will of Nature, whose will is no other than the will of God? The fallacy of this objection lies in taking some one part of our nature, some single spring of action, and treating it as though it were the whole. Human excellence is not the perfection of this faculty or of that, but of all united under the rule of conscience. Virtue for man means the subjection of the lower to the higher, their harmonious blending. Meekness, for example, or chastity, could not exist were there not strong passions to curb, a self-centred attraction to combat. All indeed is from God—the force that is curbed, and the force that curbs; but it is for man to see that the thought of God's mind and love, the Divine intention or ideal is fully, not partially, uttered in his own conduct. The speech may be marred and broken in the utterance, and convey a distorted sense. No natural desire is wrong or evil so long as it is shaped and modified according to the pattern present to conscience; but when suffered to run riot, though the wasted force is God's gift, yet its lawlessness is the fault of man.

We have different duties with regard to our conscience, according as we mean by "conscience" the sum total of our moral judgments, or the pressure of God's will upon ours urging us to follow those moral judgments. The very same imperative obligation which forces us to do what we believe to be right, forces us no less, and as it were inclusively, to find out what is right, to correct, perfect, and develop our moral judgment by all means in our power. It will not hear of that moral "indiffer-

entism " which considers it but little matter what
we do, so long as we do it *bonâ fide,* believing it to
be right. He is no sincere friend of Right and
Truth, no sincere friend of God, who cares little
what offence he commits, what pain he gives, so
long as it is unintentional, who is indifferent to
"material" sin. True, the chief guilt, which
consists in the conflict of will with will, is absent,
if the fault be committed in blameless ignorance;
but the lesser harm is not inconsiderable; nor can
it be a matter of indifference to one whose soul is
in sympathy with God and His ways. Such a soul
will make it its first duty and most earnest desire
to learn the will of God in the minutest detail. Its
whole aspiration will be that of the 118th Psalm:
"Oh, let my ways be directed to the observance of
Thy justifications; then shall I not be ashamed
when I shall have looked into all Thy command•
ments. In my heart have I hid Thy Word that
I might not sin against Thee. Blessed art Thou,
O Lord, teach me Thy justifications; unveil
my eyes that I may behold the wonders of Thy
law."

In all other matters we are to some extent
bound to secure that our mind and reason shall
be, in its measure, a faithful mirror of the mind of
God, without flaw or tarnish; but we are bound,
without any qualification, to a like care, where the
truth to be attained concerns the imperative will of
God touching the hourly conduct of our lives. It
is therefore our first duty to educate and instruct
our moral judgment continually; to observe, to

listen, to read, to ponder, to examine, to compare, that by all means we enjoy the fullest attainable light in a matter so paramount. Our sources of information are the first principles of morality and their legitimate consequences, applied to our own experience and the experience of others; the traditions of society, the examples of the good and great; the advice of those whose wisdom and experience give weight to their words; and then for us Christians there is the revealed law of God, the teaching and example of Christ and His saints, the guidance of the Catholic Church in the consensus of her approved writers, and in the private direction whereby her priests apply and modify general principles to individual cases.

Obviously, as long as life lasts, our mind will be capable of further perfection and exactitude in this as in other matters. Never shall we be so skilled as not at times to experience perplexities and to need the counsel of others. Yet our progress should ever be towards a greater self-helpfulness and independence of judgment in the affairs of our own conscience. There is no doubt a false independence which despises the ordinary means of light and information, and strives to weave *à priori* cobwebs for its own use. But there is also a false dependence which springs from a certain mental laziness and timidity, and which seeks to throw the whole burden of one's decisions on other shoulders. As in the practical affairs of every-day life, so in the problems of conscience and self-government our aim should be to profit in every way by the experience

and wisdom of others in order to advance beyond
it, and to form a power of judging for ourselves.
While we are yet without experience, and while our
reasoning faculty is as yet rudimentary, we must
submit to the direction of others who know better.
But if the child's hand is always held and guided by
the teacher, if he is never told that the end of such
help is to enable him eventually to dispense with it,
he will never learn how to write. Similarly those
who make the voice of their spiritual director a
substitute for their own conscience, who never use
the light that God has given them in their own
reason and in the information they already possess,
become crippled and paralyzed as far as the faculty
of moral judgment is concerned. For the difference
between death and life is the difference between
that which is moved passively by another from
outside, and that which moves itself in virtue of
some inward principle which is part of itself.
Doubtless, as has been said, there are crises and
problems where the wisest and most experienced
are at a loss, and then it becomes a duty to have
recourse to those who are in a position to help us
to see for ourselves—which is the best kind of
direction—or else to command our faith and confidence in their claim to see what we cannot see.
But short of such extremes, it is the part of the
good educator and adviser not to help those who
can help themselves, and who in so doing advance
themselves towards a more perfect self-helpfulness.

Perhaps there is no more essential condition to
our growth in clearness of moral discernment, than

that of practical fidelity to the light that is in us. Nor is the reason far to seek. It is repugnant to our natural and almost laudable pride, to sin in the full face of our better knowledge; whence comes the inevitable tendency to justify our faults both before and after we commit them—a process which involves a certain violent twisting or at least an obscuring of our moral judgments about right and wrong. Let these perversions be sufficiently frequent and grievous and we soon fall under the natural penalty of "judicial blindness," a state in which we are culpably but really incapable of seeing the truth, and rush blindfold to our own spiritual ruin. Nay, even in smaller matters of counsel and higher perfection, we are all continually tarnishing the clear surface of that mirror wherein the pure of heart see God and the will of God, as the sky is seen in smooth water. The edge of our spiritual discernment is ever being blunted by rough usage, and needing to be refined by self-examination and correction.

Moreover, if mere intellectualism sometimes makes us skilful casuists and gives us a sort of delicacy of touch in dealing with the niceties of conscience, yet practical fidelity to the right, and an earnest desire to live up to our ideals, will give us a far surer guide in that instinct wherewith love feels and apprehends what will be most pleasing to the Beloved. Not that the act is purely blind and instinctive, but so swift is the inference, so minute and complex the data from which it is drawn, so prompt the following up of the will, that memory has no time to record the process, and leaves us with the impression that we have been inspired or impelled from without. This "taste" or "tact," which love begets in us, is certainly a far safer and more useful guide than any power of reflex reasoning, however highly cultivated. The latter is not only more fallible in its process, but also is confined to problems where the data can be fully and distinctly grouped as the premises of a formal argument—a condition hardly ever realized in the concrete. The way in which we recognize the character of our own actions as right or wrong, is something like the way a child discerns its mother's pleasure or displeasure. It is done at a glance, and with infallible certitude, but who shall give a satisfactory statement of the process, or answer all the difficulties another might bring against the inadequate reasons given for the decision? For our mind apprehends an action not under some one or more of its formal aspects, but in its concrete entirety, in the full clothing of its circumstances, amongst which are our own character, personality, and antecedents, the sum total of our innumerable and complex motives, the clearness or unclearness of our vision at the instant of action, the fulness or the imperfection of our deliberation, the precise degree of attraction or repugnance we experienced. This is what we can never convey to another, what we can never fully express to ourselves, so as to make any formal and logical inference available against the certainty of our intuitive judgment.

It is then by fidelity to the light which is in us,

and by availing ourselves of the means of instruction provided for us, that we may hope ever to progress towards a greater refinement in our power of moral judgment. And upon this refinement our religious faith largely depends. For the more we see in God, and the more sensitive we are to His beauty, the stronger is the bond which enslaves us to Him. But it is in proportion as we ourselves are just and merciful and patient and pure, that the purity, justice, and meekness of God and of His Church is appreciated and loved by us. Without that, no dialectic founded on prophecy and miracle, no "natural theology," will be of any service to us, either to win us, or to preserve us, or to recover us. On the other hand, fidelity to conscience must infallibly bring with it sufficient faith for salvation, and moreover will change the dry stick of barren orthodoxy into an ever-growing intelligence of the things of God. "If thy heart were right, then would every creature be unto thee a mirror of life and a book of sacred lore; for there is no creature how small and mean soever, but reflects some ray of God's goodness. Wert thou but inwardly good and pure, thou wouldst see everything easily and understand it clearly. A pure heart pierces Heaven and Hell with its gaze. According to what we ourselves are inside, so do we judge of that which is outside."[1]

Moreover, faith rests on and springs from an abiding sense of the *duty* of belief, from a permanent recognition of God's will and command that we

[1] A Kempis, ii. 4.

should hold on blindly in the hour of darkness and
obscurity to the truths we were convinced of in the
hour of light and of clear intuition. For faith is a
hearing and an obeying. But the conscience which
has grown deaf to God's voice in other matters, is
in danger of this last degree of deafness, when
the soul no longer recognizes the voice of the
Shepherd; nor hears, nor follows, but wanders into
the darkness.

Up to this we have been dealing with our duty to
" conscience " regarded as the faculty of moral judgment; and we have seen how this department of
our reason demands special care and cultivation,
that it may become to its utmost capacity a reflex
of the mind of God, of that ideal which God desires
to realize in us if we will but suffer Him to show
us His will and to help us to follow it.

But conscience stands even more properly for
the pressure and inclination exerted upon our will
by the will of God, which is brought to bear upon
it as soon as the mind recognizes " right " to be the
term and expression of a Will. This pressure is a
reverential fear of God's anger as in itself the worst
of evils and a self-regarding fear of the consequences
of that anger; and also a love of God's good-will
and favour as in itself our chief good, besides a
desire for the resulting advantages of His favour.
Here, again, we owe a duty to our conscience,
regarded now, not as a judgment of the understanding, but as an inclination or bent of the will.
Every time we yield to this Divine stimulus, we
not only maintain, but increase our sensitiveness to

its influence. We become more and more filled with a reverential fear of God's expressed will. Contrariwise, if we resist we grow callous and unimpressionable. Every time we brave God's anger we fear it less, till at last we lose all fear, and become stone deaf to that still small voice whose whisper is caught by those only who are on the alert.

Let us notice how distinct these two forms of "conscientiousness" are one from another. For we may find a great delicacy of moral judgment combined with a certain callousness of the will; and, on the other hand, a remarkable sensitiveness of will where the judgment is very ignorant and erroneous. So, too, the words, *lax, rigorous, scrupulous, wide,* and the like, are open to the same ambiguity. Given the same moral judgment as to the malice of a lie, one man will shrink from it far less than another; and given equal reverence for the Divine will, one will judge that to be grievous, or at least sinful, which another thinks little or nothing of.

It is precisely in conscience viewed as an inclination of the will, that the soul comes in contact with God as the author of its moral life. In our physical and psychical life, and to a large extent in our intellectual life, God enters into us and displays His attributes in us in spite of ourselves. His power, His wisdom, His spiritual attributes, are declared in the existence and operations of our nature, in which He utters Himself in a finite manner. But if He would display His moral attributes—those, namely, which are essentially perfections of the free-will, perfect ways of choosing, He must stand at the door and knock until by consent we draw the bolt and let Him in. Then indeed He enters in to sup with us, to permeate our soul with His light and love, to fill her with a beauty not her own save so far as she has not hindered the entrance of Him whose presence is her sole beauty. *Nigra sum sed formosa*—she is of herself dark, but in virtue of her Spouse she is full of beauty and brightness.

Conscience is then, as it were, the little stalk by which the soul is united to God as to the parent of its moral life; hanging upon Him as the fruit hangs on the tree. Through that narrow channel the Divine life is poured into our spiritual veins, and gives us our vigour and expansion, and full development; and all that hinders that quickening inflow impoverishes and weakens our soul. Through conscience God's ideal of our individual destiny, of that final state which each one of us is capable of rising to, is gradually transferred to our moral judgment, wherein His thought is more or less imperfectly reflected; through conscience again, our will is urged to realize the ideal thus set before us, and to suffer God to assert Himself within us.

It is in recognizing God's will and presence in the urgency of conscience that interior life consists. Union and peace with God is but union and peace with conscience viewed in a higher and truer light. Here it is that God speaks to us; not indeed as man to man, but with a far closer and more intimate communing, whereby without words or symbols we are directly made conscious of His will. To the unreflecting, conscience seems part of themselves; its voice seems their own—so closely are God's workings intertwined with those of their will and reason. But reflection tells us that we cannot in any true sense command ourselves, or disobey ourselves, or fear our own anger, no more than we can run after ourselves, or tell lies to ourselves, or steal from ourselves.

The "otherness" of God from ourselves, and of the voice of conscience from the voice of our own free resolves, needs but be clearly stated in order to be clearly recognized; and when once recognized, our solitude is gone. "It is not good for man to be alone," is only so far true that, short of some exempting condition or higher vocation, man is fashioned and designed for the married state. But of man's spiritual being it is absolutely and essentially true that he is not made to be alone, or to live alone for one moment of his conscious life. He is by his whole nature and destiny an instrument in the hand of God, even as the pen I write with is wholly and altogether an instrument in my hand designed to express my thought. Conscience is the point of contact where God lays hold of this instrument, and inclines it to His own purpose. "Inclines" it, for it is free; and herein is not like the pen, which has no self-perverting, self-destroying power. And He inclines it not by a blind instinct, but by an intelligent whisper, gentle in expression, but strong and terrible in authority. And the resulting action is of us twain, whether in agreement or in disagreement; we are tied together—God and myself, the

Creator and the created instrument which He chooses to wield; we are joint principles of one and the same act by which He seeks to express Himself in my conduct and life. While God is to us " He," or even "Thou," we have not yet realized that intimacy which excludes all sense of distance and separateness other than personal, and which dares to couple together in thought as "we" and "us," God and the soul which He has wedded.

The sense of God's nearness and inseparable intimacy to the hidden roots of our spiritual life has been prominent in good men of all times, places, and religions, who in one form or another have re-echoed David's sentiments where he likens himself to a sheep whom God leads forth to green pastures and beside still waters, checking him with His crook, or urging him with His staff, so as to keep him ever close to His side. "Though I walk through the valley of death's shadow I will fear no evil, for Thou art with me, Thy crook and Thy staff are my consolation." It is precisely in conscience that we feel these alternative checks and urgings, and find therein an assurance of the presence and careful watchfulness of "the Great Shepherd and Bishop of our souls." It is in the obedient following of conscience that we arrive at the green pastures, and lie down in peace by the waters of rest, and lack for nothing. It is the sense that God is with him that enables the conscientious man to bear calmly all manner of temptations and persecutions and injustices. "A good man prides himself only in the witness of a good conscience. Have a good conscience

and you will have an abiding joy. A good conscience can stand a great deal, and be very cheerful
in spite of troubles. A bad conscience is always
timid and fidgetty. You will rest very sweetly if your
heart reproach you not. Never be glad except when
you have done the right thing."

If there is a false independence savouring of
selfish arrogance, there is also a certain true independence and " scorn of consequence," which has
characterized the really great and good of all ages ;
and this is due mainly to the sense of yielding
obedience to no creature but to conscience alone, or
else for conscience's sake. The Christian (explicit or
implicit) can never yield to wealth or position, or
force or numbers ; he is no respecter of persons ; to
God alone will he bend ; and thus he is fearless
when conscience justifies him, and he bears himself
towards all unjust usurpation with the pride of a
free son of God : *Gloria justorum in conscientia sua et
non in ore hominum*—" The pride of the just is in
their own conscience, not in the prate of men."

We have compared conscience to a little stalk
which ties us to God, the source of our spiritual
life, as the fruit is tied to the parent tree. To push
this illustration, we may notice that this bond may
be wholly severed, so that the fruit falls to earth
and loses vital connection with the branch ; or else
it may be merely weakened ; or, finally, it may be
strengthened indefinitely. Here we have a picture
of the bearing of our actions upon our vital union
with God through conscience. There is a fatal
disobedience which separates us wholly from Him ;

and a lesser disobedience which disposes us for a fall; and then there is a close following of the mere wishes and suggestions of conscience, whereby we are knit ever more firmly to God, and the channel of communication between the soul and her Spouse grows ever wider and freer. But whether in matters of command or of counsel and suggestion, the voice of conscience unheeded grows fainter and fainter, and sounds as from a great distance, until at last it dies away altogether. The change is in us and not in God. He has not gone far from us, but we have gone far from Him, "into a far country," where we seek freedom from the restraint of His presence, and find slavery among the swine. And if there He finds us out and pities and calls us, and puts it into our heart to arise and return to Him, still we have a long and painful journey before us. We came downhill in the fulness of our. strength, we return uphill in the extremity of our exhaustion. What hope is there for us, unless He see us yet a long way off and run to meet us and to cut short our weary labour? In other words, to recover the lost sensitiveness to conscience is a slow and difficult task, impossible without God's grace. The restoration of our perverted moral judgment is comparatively easy. It is not hard to recognize the fact that God was right and that we were wrong; that the result of our "private judgment" is that we are perishing with hunger, while the mere hirelings of Heaven abound with bread. This *Peccavi*, which is but the sentence of our own reason upon our own folly, is the very first dawn of a conversion (be it in small matters or in great), which is perfected in that *Peccavi* uttered in the bosom of God.

But it is hard to quicken a sentiment that has once been killed by resistance. It is hard to feel at will a fear of what we have schooled ourselves to brave. We seem to need some new and far stronger stimulus, if our heart is to be stirred. If God should break the silence around us, and speak to us with human voice and human words, we should doubtless fall down terror-stricken and cry: "What wouldst Thou have me to do?" Yet the same God, heard in the far closer voice of conscience, has no terrors for us,—so dependent are we on habit and wont.

It is therefore to preserve us from this callousness, and in some measure perhaps to restore or increase our reverential fear of conscience, that the practice of examining our conscience is of such vital importance. Plainly this does not mean comparing our moral judgments (as manifested in our conduct) with received standards, such as the Decalogue or the teaching of moralists. This is a duty and an important one, as we have already insisted; but is quite distinct in its object and end from that of examining our relation of obedience or disobedience to that voice which says: "Do what you believe to be right, here and now." It is one thing to inquire: Did I do what was objectively right? another: Did I do what I sincerely believed to be right? The first inquiry concerns the truth of our moral judgments; the second, the reverential

submission of our will to God's. This latter is the
all-important inquiry which should be made, not
merely at stated times, which is well, but at all
times. Am I strictly conscientious? Am I afraid
of my conscience; afraid of God? Or am I
growing callous and indifferent, and to what extent?

Often, indeed, when the substance of the transgression is comparatively light, yet the harm done
to ourselves by violating conscience is considerable
and not easily undone; just as in the matter of
perseverance, an offence which its isolation is trivial,
is most serious when viewed as a breach in that
chain of virtuous acts by which a good habit is
generated.

To *notice* an infidelity will not undo the harm
inflicted upon the will,—there, indeed, it seems that
God's medicinal skill is needed,—but it will stimulate
us to turn to God for forgiveness; to beg restitution
to our former state or to a better; to make reparation to His Divine Majesty; and, above all, to arrest
further downward progress. The wholesale and
persistent neglect of this natural duty is to induce
eventually that blindness and hardness of heart
through which a man comes at last to crucify his God
without knowing what he is doing. This is the
natural result, but it is no less, on that account, a
divinely inflicted punishment, since all natural
laws are but the expression of the necessary will
of God.

SIN JUDGED BY FAITH.

"He was a murderer from the beginning, and he stood not in the truth; because truth is not in him. When he speaketh a lie, he speaketh of his own, for he is a liar and the father thereof. But if I say the truth you believe Me not."
—St. John viii. 44.

"CUT it down, why doth it cumber the ground?" says the master of the vineyard to his husbandman; speaking of the fig-elm which had disappointed him year after year. "Nay," says the other, "let me dig about the roots and nourish them; and if then it is still fruitless, let it fall." It is the work of meditation to dig about the roots of our spiritual life and to nourish them, to go deep into first principles and strengthen our grasp of them,—not very attractive or easy work, nor productive of any very sudden or sensibly violent moral revolution; yet in the long run, slowly and surely bearing abundant and lasting fruit. Nor is it enough to review, examine, and deepen our principles. We must also judge ourselves by them; contrasting with them our practice; clearing the mirror of conscience and setting it before our face; convincing ourselves of sinfulness and of sin. But especially will it conduce to that penitential spirit which is the very root of self-reform, to clear and deepen our notion of the nature and malice of sin, whether regarded in itself and its effects, or as an offence against the fear and reverence and worship we owe to God; still more, against that absolute love and devotion which is His due.

And here revelation comes in largely to aid the insufficiency of reason and to secure that, what otherwise would be known only with difficulty and hesitation by a few, may be known easily, certainly, and universally; and though we may never say that revelation is a strict exigency of human nature, yet in this matter it is almost evident that if revelation were denied to us, some substitute would need to have been provided if our race was to rise from barbarism to any sort of higher moral development.

Children, having no experience and only the rudiments of reason, are not expected to know what is good and expedient for them in conduct, or what is hurtful and dangerous. They must therefore believe and obey those who do know. We assign sanctions to their conduct, we threaten them with penalties and hold out rewards which will appeal to them, and will supply the place of intrinsic reasons until such time as they shall be able to see for themselves, and to justify the judgments which now seem to them arbitrary and severe. But are we not all far less than children in respect to God? Surely the babe just born knows as much of the world and its ways as the wisest of us can know of the ways of God, whose sway stretches over heaven and earth, time and eternity. How can one whose eye rests but on the surface of things,

and ranges within the narrowest of circles for the
briefest of moments, pretend to join issue with Him
whose thought penetrates all things, and estimates
the bearing of the first instant of created time upon
the last? What definite notion can we possibly
have of that final result to which we and all other
creatures are being moved as instruments in His
hand, guided by a thought which is in His mind
and not in ours? What likelihood is there of our
clearly divining the meaning and scope of the
primary instincts of our conscience, of those inexplicable yet irresistible impulses in the interests
of right and truth and order, even at the expense
of our private and separate gain; of those unselfish
sympathies with objective goodness dimly recognized
as the will of Him who creates us, whose we are,
and whom we serve? Nor are we more likely to
grasp adequately the end and purpose of those
Divine commands and prohibitions which only revelation makes known to us. If nowhere else, at
least in the direction of our life to that end for
which God has given it to us, we need faith, the
simple obedient faith of little children. Our first
parents failed in this very point. They would be
as God, knowing good and evil, judging right and
wrong for themselves; they, from the level of earth,
would equal their view to His who is enthroned
above the highest Heaven. They would know the
why and *wherefore* of this arbitrary and irksome
prohibition and of this threat of death; or else they
would take no notice of it, as being a violation of
their dignity as intelligent and self-governing agents.

That this spirit of private judgment and unbelief enters into every formal sin is what we shall see a little later, when we come to consider sin in the light of reason, as a disorder in itself and as a personal offence against God. But reason is useful in this matter rather as testing and verifying the teaching of revelation, than as a guide or exponent of the full truth. After it has told us all it can tell, there still remains a large residue of mystery which we must accept on faith; nor is the grasp of reason sufficiently firm and unfaltering to offer a purchase for the will when under the pressure of acute temptation and blinding passion. In such crises our reason is soon dazed and bewildered, and if we cannot hold fast to God's Word we are lost. Even could we reason correctly, from the fullest data, on the subject of sin, yet we cannot always be reasoning, least of all in the hour of temptation.. Besides this, our data are hopelessly inadequate, while few care to face the trouble of thought and reflection, and fewer still can think successfully and fruitfully. Obviously, therefore, faith is God's appointed means for our guidance; we must receive the Kingdom of God into our soul as little children, or not at all.

It is certainly the weak point of modern Christianity that there is so little of this faith in us, filled as we are with the narrow rationalizing spirit of protestant self-sufficiency. It is in the air, and we inhale the poison at every breath. We are disposed to make, each of us, a god for himself, accommodated to the subjective peculiarities of his understanding, who shall be entirely comprehensible and free from mystery, whose commands and prohibitions shall be perfectly explicable by the principles of human conduct and government; but the notion of receiving God as He has revealed Himself objectively, of taking difficulties as an indication, not of error in that revelation, but of error in our own mind, is far from us. In this spirit we argue, as Eve did, not from the revealed punishment of sin to its internal and natural malice; but conversely we examine sin itself, weighing it in our faulty balance, and then rise up in rebellion and declare we will not believe that it can ever merit eternal punishment. We do not see what harm can come of our transgression; and hence we boldly pass to unbelief: " Hath God said ye shall surely die? Ye shall not surely die."

Now it is the nature of our finite intellect to judge the seed by its fruits, and not by an intuition of its hidden capacities. We argue from effects to causes; from appearances to their parent realities; from shadows and consequences to substances and antecedents. We cannot see directly into the heart of a thing as God can, but we have to wait until it unfolds itself. And therefore, that we might not have to learn the nature of sin by bitter experience, and when perhaps it was too late, God gave us a revelation of the ultimate fruits and consequences of sin. He showed us how, of its own nature, it led to eternal death, so that believing His word we might be assured that sin is a far greater evil than we can ever expect to understand for

ourselves. So it is that a good Catholic should
view the question, and in the same day that we
cease to be guided herein as little children, and
insist on judging for ourselves, "we shall surely
die"—*Morte moriemini.*

It is, then, by meditating on these revealed consequences of sin that we shall most solidly establish
in ourselves that spirit of holy fear in which we are
so wanting in these days.

Yet fear, like hope, has a double object, one
direct and impersonal, the other indirect and
personal. I hope for eternal happiness; and it is
to God I look for the realization of this hope.
Again, I fear eternal death, and it is before God I
tremble as the Just Judge who will inflict this
punishment on the unrepentant sinner. Here, for
the moment, it is our aim to cultivate a fear of the
person rather than of the thing; of the anger of
God rather than of the consequences of that anger.
For as it is essential to our happiness to be loved
of God, so it is destructive of the same to be the
object of God's hatred and anger. In other words,
God's anger is a greater evil to us than any of its
consequences; though when we are utterly hardened
and indifferent as to how God regards us, the fear
of the consequences of His wrath will sometimes
prevent us from falling, or will recall us to repentance. The fear of God is therefore a higher motive
than the fear of Hell.

Either fear, however, is rightly said to be the
"beginning of wisdom," or of that perfect love
which casts out fear. St. Augustine likens it to the

needle which passes through the texture, but leaves the thread behind it. For when fear is wakened in the sinner, he begins forthwith to cast about for a road of escape from the consequences of his sin, whereby he may "flee from the wrath to come." And there is but one road open. "If thou wilt enter into life, keep the Commandments;" and these Commandments can be reduced to one—the sovereign law of love: "Thou shalt love the Lord thy God with thy whole heart and soul and strength." Hence by recourse to prayer and to the sacraments he seeks to kindle in his heart once more the flame of Divine love.

And while this love is yet feeble and imperfect, it needs often to be backed up and supplemented by fear; not being of itself strong enough to withstand the more violent assaults of temptation.

But when love is mature and perfect, then fear is said to be cast out; "for," says St. John, "fear hath torment," *i.e.*, he who needs the spur of fear always acts with repugnance and unwillingly, as one who chooses the less of two evils and finds no joy in his choice. Whereas he who endures out of love alone, counts the suffering as nothing.

Yet, as Aquinas explains, it is not strictly fear, but the servility of fear, which is cast out by perfect love. It is called servile, because it is the motive of a slave who obeys because he must, and not of a son who obeys with love and has one common interest with his father, or of a free soldier who obeys his captain for love of their common country. When we obey and serve God for love of His glory, and out of sympathy with Him and His cause—the cause of Truth and Love and Justice and Holiness and Order—then our obedience is filial and not servile. But as long and as far as we need the lash of fear, we are slaves. Yet even when love is perfect and fear can afford to be idle and rest from active co-operation in our life, we must not suppose that the motives of fear have been in any way weakened, or that, like a disused organ, it becomes atrophied and withers away. It is there all the time, as an inner barrier, ready to come into use, should the outworks give way through any misfortune. Thus St. Ignatius, in his Book of the Exercises, bids me pray that if at any time, through my fault, the love of God should grow cold in my heart, at least the fear of Hell may check me in my downward path, and turn my steps upward once more.

In truth, the fear and the love of God must grow step by step together, because fear is the very back-bone and strength of that love. It is not something to which love is added and superimposed, but is a constitutive element of love. For love is not excited by some of the Divine attributes, as fear is by others, but by the whole *complexus*, by the Divine character in its entirety. Servile fear, indeed, is begotten of a partial and imperfect view of God's face; it sees only the severer attributes—justice, might, majesty, wrath; it hears only the lower notes of the chord, but is deaf to the higher and sweeter tones which combine with them into a perfect harmony. Those who do not know the greatness of God do not know His condescension; those who have no conception of His justice have no conception of His mercy. We must tremble at His wrath, before we can marvel at His patience and gentleness; we must be deafened by the thunders of Sinai, before we can be subdued by the still small voice of conscience. And all that nourishes love, nourishes fear also; for indeed, who were more alive to the severity of God's judgments, and the heinousness of sin, than those who were furthest removed from the servility of fear—the saints and the Blessed Mother of God herself? Let us be assured that no tenderness of emotion, no thrills of ecstatic ardour, are any proof of Divine love if the spirit of fear is absent. The Seraphim, who are on fire with love, veil their faces before God; and when St. John saw Him he fell at His feet as one dead. Now-a-days men have made themselves a god who is all indulgence, softness, weakness, fashioned in their own image and likeness; a god who is as agnostic, as indifferent to truth and right as they are themselves; whose love is as unrestrained by self-denial as their own. But we worship a Father who chastens those whom He loves and scourges every son whom He receives;[1] who is a fierce fire, consuming utterly whatever it cannot convert into its own nature; who is an invincible force, crushing to powder whatever it cannot carry along with it. It is either a blessed thing or a fearful thing "to fall into the hands of the living God"—a blessed thing to fall into the hands of His

[1] Hebrews xii.

love; a fearful thing to fall into the hands of His anger. For anger and hatred of all evil is but another dimension of the love and desire of all good; and where this latter is absolute, irresistible, infinite, the former must be no less so.

In his Exercise on Sin, St. Ignatius[1] would have us dwell first of all upon the fall of the apostate angels, of which we have no obscure statement in revelation, albeit the details are not given to us. It is commonly and very reasonably believed that whereas man, the lowest spiritual creature, comes to his fulness of knowledge gradually, and through a process of alternate blunders and rectifications, the unembodied spirits receive the full measure of their natural light in the first instant of their creation. Existing out of time, free from the slow successions of natural change, they have no infancy or adolescence, but are produced in their perfect maturity. Thus, the good and the true is presented to their choice fully and clearly in the first instant of their being, to accept or to reject; nor does there await them any new aspect of the question which might alter their judgment. Whereas to every man, the good and the true is offered under a thousand inadequate aspects, time after time, until the appointed measure of light by which he is to be judged has been accorded to him—a measure manifestly differing for different individuals.

Hence it is accepted usually that the fall of the angels was the work of one sin, accomplished in

---

[1] This and the following discourse are developments of the first two exercises of the " First Week."

one instant. The precise nature of that sin, or
how temptation could originate in a purely spiritual
being where bodily concupiscence and mental infirmity found no place, does not directly concern us
here. They are rightly said to have fallen through
pride. For pride is nothing else than the rebellion
of the member against.the head; the desire to be
absolute and independent instead of subject; the
preference of one's separate and solitary advantage
to the good of the whole whereof one is but a part.
It is the self-centralizing, self-exalting tendency let
loose from the yoke of reason to run its course, and
not restrained to the service of God, and by the
higher law of universal good.

Nor must we confound the conflict between
nature and grace, between the higher and the
lower will, between truth and error, between
reason and disorder, with the struggle of mind
against matter, of spirit against sense, which goes
on in our human nature, compounded as it is of
soul and body. In the worst of men we may at
times, not often perhaps, find the flesh subdued to
the spirit, or at least not rebellious. There may
be a complete control of the passions and feelings
induced by pride, ambition, or even diabolic malice.
There is such a thing as a *victoria vitiosa,* when one
vice dominates over all the rest and subdues them
in its own interest. But where passion is absent or
subdued, there may still be sin in the spirit; for its
tendency is not simple but complex. And so in the
disembodied spirit, merely because it is a creature and
finite, there is not a simple, but a double appetite or

tendency—a resultant of two forces, one making for self-preservation, self-preference, self-development; the other, using this force, checking it and directing it to the universal and objective good, that is, to the glory of God, whereof every creature is before all else an instrument. I do not say two appetites, but one complex appetite, which sin can resolve ·into discordant elements. For the good or "end" of every being corresponds exactly to its nature. Every finite being is primarily for God, secondarily for itself in order to God. Were these two ends wholly disconnected, there would be two appetites. But since one is subordinate to the other, they harmonize into one complex appetite. If there is discord through sin, then as death is the severence of body and soul, neither being complete without the other, so here also severance is moral death. And it is in approving or in disturbing the due· balance of these component forces that free-choice is exercised. Pride consents to the claims of self and turns a deaf ear to the claims of God and Truth.

It is our love that is free. It is not enough to see the truth and to see it clearly; we must also love it. The angels saw with perfect clearness their true position as creatures of God. They saw that their own good should be subordinate to the universal good; that they were intended and designed primarily for God and secondarily for themselves. They recognized clearly in themselves fundamental instinctive tendencies in harmony with this double nature and destiny of theirs. And yet being free to know and love this plan, and throw themselves into it, they chose otherwise.

And now we have to pause and see the terrible ruin wrought by one sin in these the most glorious of God's creatures, and then learn what a deadly poison sin must be. As was the excellence of their nature, the height to which they were called, such was the depth to which they fell, and the vileness of their corruption. Human nature, falling from a lesser height, was not so irreparably shattered to pieces, nor can any lost soul of man know the full anguish of that " fire prepared for the devil and his angels." For the capacity of suffering, like the capacity of joy, is in proportion to the fineness and delicacy of the spiritual nature. What are the pains and pleasures of some sluggish reptile compared with those of the highly organized frame of man? Similarly the angelic intellect suffers a perversion in such sort that they who are by nature full of intelligence and understanding, and ministers of light, are now changed into powers of darkness—" the rulers of the darkness of this world." This is notoriously the effect of sin, to induce a judicial blindness, so that they who *will* not see when they can, *cannot* see when they will. Once bring a false principle into any mind, and in proportion as that mind is more active and vigorous it will be reduced to a completer and more utter confusion. A torpid mind will hold the poison of a lie unassimilated long enough; but where reason works actively, either the false principle must be thrown out, or else the whole mind brought into conformity with it. Now

G

what is effected in the human mind by a gradual
process of leavening, is effected instantaneously in
minds unfettered by time and cerebral limitation,
such as those of the angels.   Hence we can imagine
the total and radical revolution caused by sin in the
angelic intellect, inducing a confusion like that of a
panic-stricken army in retreat.   Nor does this mean
a change in their essential nature; but only a state
induced by their irrevocable free choice of a lie, to
which they must cleave for ever, having passed into
their eternal and unchanging condition.

What tastes sweet to a healthy palate tastes
bitter to one which is disordered.   God, who is the
final perfection, the supreme desire and the joy of
the sound and healthy will, is the torment and horror
and death of the will perverted by sin.   For it is at
once violently drawn towards Him by the fundamental and ineradicable instinct of its nature, and
yet driven back in consequence of its self-induced
antagonism to truth and goodness; and thus it is
racked and straitened unceasingly.   It is as when
one whose eyes are weak with disease is compelled
to endure a glare of light tolerable to none but the
strongest vision.   Thus the whole force of the angelic
will is turned from love to hatred; and there is no
hatred so bitter as that of what we once loved most
ardently.   To the fallen angels, God, and man (the
image of God), and love, truth, justice, holiness,
order, beauty, harmony (the cause and interest of
God), are all as hateful as they are dear to the saints
and unfallen angels.   And all this ruin is in a true
sense the natural effect of sin; of trying to stand in

stiff opposition against the irresistible onrush of
God's will and God's love. And when we say it is
the natural effect, we do not deny that such penalties
of sin are inflicted by the will of God. For all
natural effects result from the will or inclination of
nature, which is in truth the will of Him on whose
nature all natural laws depend. For it is indeed
the personal will of God which moves in all nature,
physical and spiritual, and is expressed in the laws
of nature. There are certain unessential determinations of the law of sin's penal consequences which
may depend on God's free-will, but the substance of
the law is from His necessary will, from the very
nature of things in themselves, that is, of God in
Himself. If a man leaps over a precipice, he cannot
blame the rocks below for dashing him to pieces;
nor can we blame God if, when we wilfully fling
ourselves against the immoveable rock of His truth
and love, we are shattered to atoms and eternally
destroyed. We can only blame ourselves, our own
free choice.

But how can a God of love entrust His creatures
with such a power of self-destruction? Here again
we are complaining of the necessary will of God, as
though it were His free-will. The power of choice,
like every other grace, is given *in resurrectionem ;* for
our help, not for our hurt—it is intended for use, not
for abuse. If it is used for our hurt, *in ruinam,* that
is no part of God's will or design. Yet from the
very nature of the gift it must be capable of abuse in
those who are yet in a state of imperfection and
probation.

Self-formation, self-movement is the very idea of
life.   An animal is not a machine moved by God as
by an outside force; but it forms and moves itself
in virtue of internal principles which obey God's
will, and God's will is no physical or mechanical
force.

It is also the dignity and privilege of the created
spirit and of intelligent life, to be self-forming.   We
become what we love; we are true and good and
great by freely loving and choosing goodness and
truth and greatness; we become divine by choosing
God.   He puts before our eyes as an end to be
reached, as an ideal to be realized, a true self as
opposed to a false self.   He offers us life and death,
sweet and bitter, and leaves us free to enter into
one heritage or the other.

The human spirit determines and forms itself to
some degree in its every free choice.   Each act is of
its own nature a step taken in the right direction or
the wrong. .It is implicitly a choice of an ideal
happiness in which God holds, either the sole
place, or at least the first place, or else in which
something takes precedence of God. But the angels
formed or misformed themselves finally and irrevocably in their first choice made in the full light
of all the knowledge of which they were capable.

The contemplation of this ruin which the fallen
spirits wrought in themselves by their sin ought to
breed in us that double fear of which we spoke
above; first, a fear of those evil consequences themselves, which is altogether prudential and self-
regarding; secondly, a great personal fear of God,

from whose necessary will and law all these terrors
proceed, and of whose past anger they are the effect
and expression. For indeed that anger itself is
more to be dreaded than any of its consequences,
since our greatest good is to be loved by God; and
our greatest evil to be hated by Him.

We must therefore look back over our life of
continual rebellion against the voice of our conscience
and of our better self, against the voice of God
within us, and think how great a weight of indignation we have been storing up against ourselves,
albeit God's mercy has so far restrained the storm
from bursting upon us. No man ever violates the
laws of nature with impunity. The vengeance may
be slow, but it is sure. And the law of conscience
is just as inexorable, being no less an expression of
the same invincible will and love.

Yet in both orders there is room for miracle;
for the intervention of God's free-will, which can
supplement and determine, without contradicting
the natural and necessary course of things. He
who can heal the sick and raise the dead with His
word, can call the soul back from corruption; He
who made a way through the Red Sea, can hold
back the billows of wrath already curving over the
sinner, ere they break and overwhelm him.

If we now turn to the story of the fall of our
first parents, the same lesson of sin's deadly character
is brought home to us again. We must dwell upon
the world as it would have been had Adam never
sinned nor forfeited all those preternatural pre-
rogatives and conditions of nature by which God

designed to raise this earth to a paradise, to make it the vestibule of Heaven itself. We must eliminate sin, and concupiscence, and ignorance, and sickness, and death from this world, and people it with inhabitants who in happiness and holiness would be more akin to angels than to men such as we are. And with all this we have to contrast, not the present world, whose corruption is mitigated with the leaven of Christianity, whose despair is quelled by the hope of redemption, but rather with such a world as this would have been without the Gospel and without all that light and grace by which it was and is educated and prepared, so to say, for the Gospel.

And this contrast presents us with a measure of the evil of sin and of the vehemence of God's abhorrence of sin, of His natural and necessary antagonism to wickedness and pride. He had in Adam raised man from the dust of his unassisted frail humanity, to set him with the princes of his people, almost on a level with the angels in respect of light, and self-control, and immortality; their equal in point of supernatural grace; their superior in virtue of the prospective Incarnation of God and His alliance with our family. He had made him little less than a god, crowning him with glory and honour. But being in honour man had no under-standing. He would not be less than a god, but equal to God in the discernment of good and evil; and thus in the pride of knowledge he became as the beasts that perish. He would clamber to a yet higher eminence than God had allowed to him, and in the very act fell headlong to earth again, maimed and crippled.

Finally, we may consider the revealed conse-quences of one single unrepented deadly sin. And by a deadly sin we mean an act whereby the will aims at an ideal of ultimate happiness in which the possession of God and submission to Him does not hold the first place, but is sacrificed to something else. For in every free act, as has already been said, we implicitly make for some such ideal. If the act of its own nature and tendency is incom-patible with God's supremacy among the objects of our final bliss, it is a mortal or deadly sin. If it is compatible with that supremacy and yet is directed to some final object which is not itself referred and subordinated to God, but loved besides and together with God, in such sort that it makes for an ultimate state of bliss whereof God is the chief, but not the only factor—then the sin is venial.

"He who loves father or mother more than Me is not worthy of Me," says God. It may be that such a man loves God very tenderly and sincerely. But he does not love Him with the love due to God if God holds the second place to any creature or to all creatures put together. If, however, God does hold the first and supreme place in his scheme of happiness, then the welfare of his parents or children may be an object of desire in two ways. First, in such sort that he loves his child just in the way God wishes him to love it, in sympathy with God's mind and will in the matter; recognizing his own affection as God-given and as indicating God's will;

seeing God in the creature and the creature in God.
And such love is only an extension of the love of
God; and its object is in a way united with God
into one complex object, and loved in harmony with
God. When all creatures are so loved, then a man
loves God not only supremely, but solely, with his
whole heart. And this is the perfection of sanctity;
a state which we have to strive to attain. Secondly,
loving God supremely, and being willing if necessary
to make the sacrifice of Abraham, a man may love
his child or his reputation or some other creature
ultimately and for its own sake, and in some way
co-ordinately with God, albeit in no sense supremely.
He may be willing for the sake of that creature, not
indeed to break with God, but to sacrifice God's
lesser interests in certain matters, just as a man who
would die for his country may shirk paying taxes and
other small duties of a good citizen. And such sins
are venial; incompatible with perfect love, but not
incompatible with sufficient and substantial love.
God preponderates in the affections, but He does
not satisfy and absorb them entirely.[1]

---

[1] As the difference between venial sin and imperfection is a
source of difficulty to many, it may be well to note that "imperfection" is used positively and negatively. Positively, for a
deficiency of some perfection that is due and obligatory, as *e g.*, we
speak of an imperfectly formed letter, meaning a misformed letter.
It implies, however, that the defect is slight and not substantial. So
used, an imperfection in our moral conduct is the same as a venial sin.
Negatively, the term is used to denote the absence of some perfection which is in no way due or obligatory, but which would add a
certain fulness and richness to the good action in question, and is a
matter perhaps of counsel. God is pleased if I am generous to the
poor: more pleased if I am more generous; but not displeased if I

Our Saviour reveals to us the natural consequences of deadly sin when He says, "I say unto
you, My friends: Fear not them that can kill the
body, and after that have nothing more that they
can do. But I will tell you whom you shall fear:
fear Him who, after He hath killed, hath power to
cast both soul and body into Hell, yea, I say unto
you, fear Him." And here notice that He speaks
to His friends; to those whose hearts are now full
of loyal love for their Master. Yet neither they, nor
any of us, however fervent and devoted, can afford
to dispense with this safeguard of holy fear. And
who is it that speaks? Jesus Christ, the very

am not more generous. If in some sense the more perfect act is
also the more reasonable, it does not mean that the less perfect is
positively unreasonable, but merely less reasonable, provided it be
entirely good, so far as it goes, and contain no positive disorder.
To make the better course always obligatory, to deny that an
action is good because it might be better, to exclude all possibility
of exercising free generosity by works of counsel and supererogation,
is also to open the door to interminable scrupulosity and to make
our every action sinful—as Luther would have it.

Thus when we speak of "perfect love" as a matter of precept,
and when we imply that in some sense it is necessary and obligatory
that God should entirely satisfy and absorb our affections, we mean
that to love ourselves or any creature with a love which is not
referable and at least implicitly referred to the love of God, is,
however venial, a positive imperfection. Such love is "perfect"
because it lacks nothing due to it. But that we should love God
with an heroic intensity of fervour, that we should explicitly and
frequently refer all our affections and interests to Him, that we
should be devoted and enthusiastic in His service, that we should
embrace the counsels as well as fulfil the precepts—all this adds a
perfection and fulness to our love which, however reasonable, is in
no way due or obligatory, and the withholding of which, though
less reasonable, is in no positive way unreasonable, imperfect, or
inordinate; but only in a negative way.

Truth; so calm and moderate and faithful in all His utterances; the same God who made man and who made Hell; who became Man and died that He might save man from Hell. He does not think it a sordid thing to stand in awe of Him who is a "consuming fire." He knows that such fear is the very foundation and fibre of the tenderest and only enduring filial love and self-forgetful devotion. "Fear Him; yea, I say to you, fear Him." How He insists upon it! Nor are we to forget that the body is to bear its share in the soul's destiny for evil as well as for good; and that the fire prepared for fallen spirits will contain all the virtuality of bodily fire.

And again He says, "If thy right hand or right foot cause thee to stumble, cut it off and cast it from thee;" that is, if your chief means of helpfulness or of livelihood should be to you an occasion of deadly sin; or if that on which your pre-eminence and success in the race of life depends should separate you from your allegiance to God, "cut it off"—a sharp, decisive, painful sacrifice—"and cast it from you;" put it as far from you as you can; shake it off like a poisonous viper; no regrets, no looking back to the city of sin! "And if thy right eye offend thee, pluck it out and cast it from thee;" if father, mother, child, spouse, or friend, if one who is dear to you as the apple of your eye, dearer far than life itself, even if such a one should stand between you and salvation, "pluck it out and cast it from you;" no compromise, no quarter. Surely "this is a hard saying: who can bear it?" Yet it is only what is said elsewhere: "He that loveth father, or mother, or child more than Me is not worthy of Me." It is only what the conscience of great and good men, pagan or Christian, in all ages have told them, that the claims of truth and justice are paramount; that he who refuses if need be to sacrifice his only son rather than lie, is not worthy of the truth; that death is a less evil than merited dishonour.

And why am I to nerve myself to such anguish? "It is *better* for thee," says our Lord. He does not appeal to His own goodness, which claims my entire love and service, but simply to my prudential self-regard. And He assures me, as one who knows and sees the Hell He is speaking of, that all I can suffer in this life through loss of livelihood, through failure, through poverty and contempt, through loneliness and separation and the rending of my heart-strings, is not worth a thought compared with the misery and anguish of that eternal, unchanging state of destruction and spiritual death, that "gehenna of fire where the worm dieth not and the fire is not quenched." And if that is what mortal sin means; if that is the measure of its hidden malice and of its vehement antagonism to God's goodness, and, therefore, the measure of the Divine anger and indignation which it necessarily excites, have I not great reason to feel shame and confusion at the thought of myself as I must appear in the eyes of God, seeing what my past life has been, and how persistently I have opposed God's almighty will and love, constraining me through my

conscience, urging me ever onward and upward,
yet ever repulsed or at best unheeded.

And so I betake myself to the Cross whereon
God is dying in torments to save me from Hell; and
I marvel and wonder why it is He has singled me
out for so much mercy, and patience, and forgiveness.
I think what He might have done to me a thousand
times over, in all justice, leaving me to the natural
consequences of my madness and folly; and I look up
to His bleeding brow and wounded hands and feet and
pierced Heart, and see what He has done instead.
O mira circa nos tuæ pietatis dignatio! O inestimabilis
dilectio caritatis, ut servum redimeres Filium tradidisti!
—"O wondrous condescension of Thy pity in our
regard! O unspeakable tenderness of charity! to
ransom Thy slave Thou didst deliver up Thy
Son!" And if the thought of His merited wrath
and indignation filled me with shame and confusion,
my shame is multiplied a hundred-fold when I
contemplate His patience and love. And then at
His feet with Mary Magdalene and in the presence
of His Blessed Mother weeping for my sins, I ask
myself what have I done for Christ in the past; or
rather what have I not done against Him? What
am I doing for Christ now? What am I going to
do for Christ in the future? And then I offer
myself to be His for ever. *Domine, quid me vis*
facere?—"Lord, what wouldst Thou have me to
do?"

SIN JUDGED BY REASON.

"We have never been slaves to any man: how sayest thou: You shall be free? Jesus answered them: Amen, amen, I say unto you, that whosoever committeth sin is the servant of sin."—St. John viii. 33.

WE have now to ask ourselves what mere reason can tell us about the nature of sin. Not that reason unassisted could ever have got as far as it can now get since faith has gone before and pointed out the way. Faith tells us many things that are well within the compass of reason; but reason would never have thought of them if faith had not suggested them.

There are times and moods for all of us—all who are human, and not wanting in that frailty which, mingling with the higher and nobler elements of our nature, gives it its characteristic pathos—there are times when we think that if there were no God, no future life, no restrictions and prohibitions, life would be aimless indeed, inexplicable, unmeaning, yet for its brief span so much easier, more painless, more enjoyable, that we almost regret our high destiny as sons of God, and envy those whose consciences have grown callous to scruples and remorse. The constant peace and blessedness of God's service makes but a slight dint in our memory, compared with the occasional crosses and restraints which are the small price we pay for it. To our ingratitude it seems that all that is right is hard, all that is wrong is easy, that God's ways are perversely uphill and narrow, and the ways of sin broad and downhill; and we never look to the fruit and issue of one and the other.

It is the policy of Satan to represent our loving Father as an arbitrary tyrant, ruling us as slaves in His own interest, or as an austere Master, reaping where He has not sown and gleaning where He has not scattered; as one delighting in restrictions and prohibitions for their own sake, and, as it were, in order to find new occasions for the exercise and display of authority. So it was that the tempter argued with our first parents in Paradise, and so it is that he tempts us all daily by whispered insinuations to that same effect. Well does St. Ignatius speak of him as the "enemy of human nature." Hating God, he necessarily hates God's image and likeness and all that God loves; and his one aim is to obliterate and defile the likeness, since his malice is impotent against the original. Still more, ever since God in Christ has wed to Himself the human family, and thus raised man above the highest angels, does the "enemy of human nature" long to degrade and profane what God has so exalted and sanctified.

No, God is not arbitrary; and if His commandment and discipline is grievous to us in our present state, it is only because *all* growth and development is necessarily attended with pain—moral growth no less than physical. It involves the death of the old, and the birth of the new, a continual process of ceasing and becoming. It must be so in finite creatures drawn forth from nothing and reaching their last perfection in process of time. It is the nature of time itself, which is but the dying and passing away of the present to give place to the future. "Except a grain of wheat fall into the ground and die, it remaineth alone; but if it die it beareth much fruit." Wherefore if God afflicts and chastens us, it is not willingly (that is, with pleasure), but reluctantly; it is not merely because He chooses, but because He must. It is not because He forbids sin that it is evil; but because it is hurtful to us, therefore He forbids it. As necessarily and as vehemently as He loves His own nature, so **necessarily**, does He love man, the image of His nature, and hate all that profanes and defiles that image; so that God's absolute detestation and abhorrence of sin is only another aspect and dimension of that infinite love, wherewith He necessarily loves His own Divine goodness. Nor even are the sanctions with which He enforces His necessary laws altogether arbitrary. Hell itself is as much the fruit and outcome of sin as death is of starvation or of mortal disease; it is as much a natural law as the sequence of poverty upon prodigality; it is dependent indeed upon the will of God, but not upon His freewill. Men are not sent to Hell, but they go there. That he who walks over a precipice should fall to the bottom, or that he who plucks out his eyes should be blind, is necessarily the will of God—as are all natural sequences—but it is not a result of His free choice and arbitrary decree. " Concupis-cence when it is conceived bringeth forth sin, and sin when it is finished generates death," — by a natural and necessary process.

However, it is not merely because it leads to the everlasting torments of Hell that the path of sin is thorny and perilous. Hell is the natural issue of sin, just because sin is so bad in itself; it is the evil fruit of an evil tree; it is sin worked out to its full and unimpeded consequences, and given unrestrained dominion over us. And, in like manner, it is not simply because the steep and narrow way leads to Eternal Life that it is to be preferred and followed, but because it is the right way, the best way, and really the happiest way; because, notwithstanding a certain amount of surface suffering, the yoke of Christ is easy, and the burden of His Cross is light, compared with the yoke and burden of sin ; because Wisdom's ways are ways of pleasantness, and all her paths are peace.

Limited as our point of view must be, and feeble as are our powers of intuition and reasoning, yet we can, to some little extent, see for ourselves that what God forbids is really bad for us in the long run, however pleasant it may seem at first. If we cannot always understand the evil of one solitary sinful act itself, and apart from all its consequences, yet we can form such an estimate of those consequences, both to the individual and to human society at large, as to understand why God, who loves us so vehemently and irresistibly, must be so inexorably opposed to the first beginnings of such harm; so keen to stamp out the first spark of so destructive a conflagration. "Behold," says St. James, "how great a matter a little fire kindleth." We ourselves hate the very name or even the suggestion of those things which we have cause to know to be evil and hurtful; and similarly God's love for us leads Him to a proportional hate of all that is even remotely connected with our spiritual misery and destruction.

If we want to know what sin is and what it leads to, we must not judge it merely by those effects which fall under our eyes every day. For no one is so thoroughly depraved as to give way to any sin without the least attempt at restraint; much less to give way to all sins. Far less likely is it that society at large or any great part of society should throw off every yoke and abandon itself freely to evil inclinations of every description. Yet it is only by making some such supposition that we can form any adequate idea of the hurtfulness of sin. Let a man give way to laziness and sloth without any restraint, and at once we see life becomes impossible for him. One such example of inertness is enough at times to destroy a whole family and bring it to poverty and misery. What if the whole family were made up of such members? What if all society were so constituted? Plainly this vice alone—whose seed is in every one of us—would involve the speedy extinction of the human race were it let have its own way.

How soon and how utterly the habit of telling lies ruins the moral character of its victims! how quickly it extends, and how deeply its roots reach.

H

down into the soul! How incurable it is! How it
paralyzes the gift of speech, whose purpose is to
mirror the soul. And when the disease becomes
epidemic, how ruinous it is to mutual trust and
charity and reverence! Yet perhaps we have seldom
met an wholly unmitigated liar who made no pretence whatever of veracity; and even the most
degraded populations have offered some kind of
resistance to the spread of the practice. Perhaps
one lie in itself may at times seem utterly harmless;
not only free from all hurtful consequences, but
fruitful in good consequences, conducive to peace,
and charity, and justice. But there is an infinite
distance between the man who has never lied, whose
veracity is still "virgin," and him who has crossed
the line, and who has given proof that his allegiance
to truth is not absolute, but qualified. It may be a
little thing, but like so many other little things, it
involves a great principle. A lie, as such, is an
apostasy from the cause of God; a concession to
the cause of darkness and deception. "It is only a
venial sin," one may say. Yes, but God would
rather see you blind, halt, and maimed than that
you should commit a venial sin; so differently does
He judge of what is hurtful to you. A lie, how
harmless soever, how helpful soever, is in His eyes
like to the first plague-spot of a disease which has
swept nations off the face of the earth; it is a little
germ full of the most virulent poison, and with
unlimited powers of self-dissemination.

We may consider anger in the same way; the
suffering it causes to its victims and to all those

around them; what crimes it leads to—blasphemy, cruelty, violence, injury; yet rarely is it wholly unrestrained. What then if it had full play; if it were indulged in universally? Who could live in such a hell upon earth? And so of resentment, peevishness, discontent, sarcasm, ill-nature, pride, arrogance, boasting, meanness, avarice, selfishness, fraud, dishonesty; not to speak of coarser vices like drunkenness and impurity. Let any one of them run its course unimpeded, and it stands to reason that it will destroy the happiness of mankind, and make life, individual and social, altogether unbear-able and impossible.

It is, then, with the nature of things that our quarrel is, and not with God. We want to be free from the necessary consequences of our own actions; to keep what we have thrown away; we barter our birthright for a mess of potage, and account our-selves wronged because we are held to our bargain.

We see clearly that it is by the repetition of single acts that habits are formed and customs become general; and that though no one act can produce the effect, yet unless single acts are forbidden absolutely, each man will dispense himself on every occasion. And notwithstanding we act as the improvident spendthrift who, regarding each indi-vidual economy as insignificant, saves nothing, and ends in beggary.

Again, our reason and intuition tell us that our whole nature is so designed and intended, that the spirit should have dominion over the flesh; that we should never be swayed by mere feelings, passions, and emotions, except so far as they have first been summoned before the tribunal of conscience and there approved. This is what we call self-control, or being master of oneself; and every virtue or moral strength is some particular form of self-mastery, while every vice is some particular form of self-slavery. Now, though we feel a sort of shame about merely physical infirmities, to which we are necessarily subjected, yet it is quite distinct in character from that shame we experience in being convicted of moral weakness, of want of self-control where such control is both possible and due, *e.g.*, in being detected in greediness, or meanness, or untruthfulness, or dishonesty. We recognize that our nature is thereby perverted and distorted, nay, rather inverted, since what should be under is uppermost; the flesh leads and the spirit follows: *Servi dominati sunt nostri*—" Those who should be our slaves, are our masters." We feel the unmanliness of sin and vice. Indeed, we are wont to characterize this lack of self-mastery as effeminate, brutal, savage—words which all confess that developed humanity implies perfect self-control. Hence even when we sin we invariably try to deceive ourselves and others by finding *reasons* to justify our conduct, as though we scorned to act on mere inclination or otherwise than on principle, thereby tacitly confessing that we are thoroughly ashamed of ourselves for having acted otherwise.

And together with this natural shame at our moral nakedness, there is a more or less explicit sense of guilt or of offence committed against that necessary will of God made known to us in the ordinations of nature and in the design of our own spiritual constitution; a sense that we have not only marred ourselves, but angered Him whose work and image we are. All this, be it noted, is something quite distinct from the sense of having merited the censure of our fellow-men, or the censure that our own mind tells us we should pass upon another who acted similarly. It is distinct, moreover, from the apprehension of any pains or punishments our sin may bring upon us, of any pleasures and rewards it may deprive us of. These apprehensions may co-exist with the sense of guilt and moral shame, and even predominate in our thought where conscience has grown enfeebled, but they are merely prudential and self-regarding motives, born of a love, right in itself, but no way akin to that unselfish love of objective rightness and of the Divine will which finds utterance in the dictates of conscience.

But besides all the positive harm which sin works in us, we must remember that it excludes and deprives us of that Divine goodness and happiness for which we were created, namely, the unselfish love of our God and Maker and of our fellow-men in God and for God. It ties us down to what is sordid and transitory; it founds our happiness on the shifting sand, and not on the eternal rock. Pride is incompatible with the praise of God; self-sufficiency with reverence; self-seeking with service. In every sense, therefore, sin is our ruin and destruction; it is the death and corruption of our soul; and it is only because at present we can drug ourselves with the narcotic of pleasure, or of distracting excitement, and because the spirit is not alone with itself but can pour itself out on creatures, that we do not already somewhat experience the torments of the damned by a faint foretaste.

Yet all this objective harm and disorder, this hurt to ourselves and to others, is the least evil of sin, even as reason considers the matter. For our conscience testifies not only to a violation of order, but to a defiance of the will of the ordainer; it tells us that sin is an opposition of person to person, and of will to will; an unjust opposition of the creature to its God and Creator; of the feeble and finite will to the omnipotent and irresistible will of the Divine Goodness and Love. We feel that we have made ourselves hateful to the All-holy and All-mighty. To be loved, no less than to love, is our last end or beatitude—for all personal love is im•perfect and restless till it is mutual. We seek, not God's gifts, but Himself, just as nothing we give Him and do for Him will suffice if we withhold our very self. *Sicut non sufficeret tibi, omnibus habitis, præter me; ita nec mihi placere poterit quidquid dederis, te non oblato*—"As the whole creation could not satisfy thee without Me, so neither can all thy gifts satisfy Me if thou give not thyself."[1] As it is by loving Him that we give ourselves to God and He possesses us, so it is by loving us that He gives Himself to us and we possess Him. To be hated by God, to be the object of His anger and dislike, is in itself, apart from all other evil consequences in

[1] *Imitation,* iv. 8.

the way of punishment, the greatest evil that can befall us.

And it is precisely as involving a resistance of will to will that sin generates anger, like the steel which strikes fire from the flint. We know this from ourselves. However grieved we may be for the hurt done to us, or the opposition offered to our wishes by some inanimate or irresponsible cause, we are not angry as with a person. But voluntary opposition, especially if we conceive it to be unjust, excites first annoyance, then indignation, which grows and gathers like an angry storm-cloud, and bursts at last in a fury of vengeance and reprisal. So it is that by opposing the will and determination of omnipotent Love, sin stores up Divine indignation against the sinner, which when let loose from the restraining hand of mercy, will drive him from the presence and favour of God as chaff is driven before the face of the tempest.

And here St. Ignatius would have me contrast myself with God, person with person; and to this end first to dwell upon the absolute insignificance of my own personality, as but one of the almost infinite multitudes of men which have peopled the earth. A man may be somebody in his own household and family; though even there he is soon forgotten—but what is he in a great crowd or assembly? what as one of a nation? what as one of a race?—and yet what is that race compared with the numberless orders of spiritual personalities which belong to the other world? My moral and personal insignificance therefore is hardly less than

my physical insignificance as an atom of this
material universe, or as a solitary ripple on the
endless sea of time.   And then I am to contrast
my frailty and weakness with the Divine strength
and endurance, my fleeting life with God's
eternity; what am I but an autumn leaf that
trembles on the bough and is caught away by
the first breeze—*Folium quod vento rapitur*, as Job
says; on what a slender thread I hang! What is
my physical force compared with the forces of
nature; what stand could I make against the rage
of the ocean, or against the earthquake, or the
thunderbolt; what resistance could I offer to the
impetus of a planet; what to all the forces of
the universe leagued against me?   And yet God
moves them with His finger, nay, with the least
breath of His Love, of His Holy Spirit—the *Digitus
Dei*.   And it is against the infinite impetus of that·
Love, against the omnipotence of that subsistent
Will, that I set myself when I sin. I defy the laws
not only of the universe, but of the Builder of the
universe; I endeavour not only to turn aside the
course of Nature, but to change that Divine Nature
whence created Nature derives all her force and
necessity. Is it wonderful if sin issues sooner or
later in the destruction of the sinner?

Further, in every sin I set up my judgment
against God's judgment; my wisdom against His;
I pretend to know better than He what is good for
me, what I ought to do. Or I refuse to obey
because I do not see the why and the wherefore.
I, from my little corner of this darkened cave of a

universe, guessing from passing shadows and gleams
as to what is going on above and beyond, pretend
to an equality with Him whose eyes are over all
the earth, and see from end to end of time. Yet
what do I know compared with so many around
me? What, compared with the collective knowledge of the race? And what is this, compared
with what is knowable to man and may yet be
known? And this again is to God's wisdom and
knowledge as the light of a glow-worm to the light
of the sun. How sickening and irritating is the
scepticism or the dogmatism of the half-educated
mind inflated with its modicum of late-acquired,
ill-digested knowledge! Yet is it anything like as
disgusting as must be the self-sufficiency and vain
intellectual conceit involved in every sin?

And then I am to contrast the Divine goodness with my own vileness and poverty of body
and soul; dwelling on this *corpus humilitatis*—"this
body of humiliation," this burden of corruptible
flesh, with all its infirmities normal and morbid,
designed to be a perpetual *Memento* of our derivation from the slime of the earth. *Memento homo,*
says the Church to us year by year, *quia pulvis es
et in pulverem reverteris*—"Remember, O man, that
dust thou art and unto dust thou shalt return."
Yet how little do men seem to remember it when
they strut about with their heads in the air, as
though they were not at best whited sepulchres; as
though they did not need continual tending and
cleansing in order not to be altogether loathsome and
horrible; as though they were not at every turn liable

to be seized upon by one of those legion diseases
which lie in ambush round our path in the service
of inevitable death and decay. In making man, in
yoking the lowest grade of spiritual substance to an
animal carcase, God's wisdom seemed to have devised
a being to whom pride should be impossible and
ridiculous, in whom it should find no food to feed
on, no cleft or cranny to lurk in. Even under the
most favourable conditions, if God has endowed me
with perfect health, vigour, strength, and beauty,
how perishable and transitory it is; how slight and
common an excellence it is; above all, how entirely
a gift of God through natural and necessary causes!
When I think of all the beauty and grace and
wisdom displayed in physical nature which has
inspired so much joy and worship in hearts of
kindred beauty, and when I remember that all
this, together with that of countless worlds as fair
and wonderful, is but a hint at that undreamt-of
Beauty which is God, surely I must be in straits
for something to pride myself on if I can find aught
in my body. Yet it cannot be denied that perfect
bodily health and beauty often breed a spirit of
independence, an insolence of pride, which leads to
sin.

If I turn from my body to my soul, there I find
still less to boast of. Doubtless as it leaves God's
hands, the soul of man, however lowly its rank in
the spiritual order, is immeasurably greater and
nobler than anything in the world of matter. Yet
as there is no animal born so feeble and unprotected
as man, so urgently in need of assistance and nurture

and education, depending as he does on the family and on society for his proper development, in like manner his soul's greatness is all potential and in capacity, and depends for its development on union and association with God. It is by nature a receptacle or dwelling-place of God's light and love, and derives all its goodness and beauty from His indwelling. For as the body when the soul is withdrawn becomes so much carrion and rottenness, so the soul when it ceases to "lean on her beloved," to cling to Him as the vine to the elm, becomes corrupt and abominable beyond all measure. What brightness has the mirror apart from the sun, and what greatness or goodness has the soul which casts off God? If this is true of all created spirits, it is truest of man's soul, the least and feeblest, albeit the dearest of all God's dear children. And when the corruption of spiritual death once sets in, then indeed, as St. Ignatius says, the soul becomes no better than a centre of pestilential infection streaming out on all sides.

We can perhaps never sufficiently realize how sin ramifies in its harmful consequences as long as the world lasts; how it is a little spore which of its own nature tends to multiply with fearful rapidity long after the act has been forgiven by God and forgotten by us. And this gives another point of sharp contrast between the vileness of my own soul and the goodness of God, whom I offend so easily. From Him as from its source flows out all that is good in this world, whether in Nature or the soul of man; all the light and glory of creation radiates

from this Sun, all darkness and death is only a name
for His absence; while the only absolute and unqualified evil which mars His work is sin, and sin
flows from the perverse will of man to "increase
and multiply and replenish the earth," and to change
it from Paradise into Hell.

Vile as I am, however, soul and body, by sin I
put myself on an equality with God; as though
I were as good as He. I refuse to accept a position
of subjection and inferiority. It is so with every
rebel and his liege-lord; he is always a leveller and
an upstart. We smile now superciliously at the
old Ptolemaic astronomy, which represented the sun
as whirled round the earth once a day. We show
how absurd it would be to suppose a body so vast
should sweep through a circle with a radius of
ninety million miles in twenty-four hours; how
much easier it is to suppose the daily revolution of
the earth on its axis; especially when the fixed
stars, whose mass and distance we now can conjecture less inadequately, offer each of them a similar
and greater difficulty. And yet, when we sin we are
guilty of an immeasurably greater absurdity. We
make self the centre round which God and everything else is to revolve; our will is to rule, and
God's is to be ruled. This is surely the worst part
of sin, the personal opposition of the creature to its
Creator, of will to will; of our self-love to the love
of God; the objective harm, which is the matter of
prohibition, is a little evil compared with this;
though viewed in another aspect this too is an
objective disorder beyond all other. For obedience

is itself a virtue, as much as any other virtue which we practise under obedience; and if reason is violated by a disturbance of the due relation between men, or by faults against temperance or self-control, so most of all when man sets his will against the will of God.

Here St. Ignatius would have me pause and gather up the results of my recent reflections; look back on that long indictment I brought home to myself in the review of my past life; weighing well the severity of the Divine justice revealed to me in Holy Writ; seeing finally how all this harmonizes with the dictates of my natural reason, which is forced to cry out: *Justus es, Domine, et rectum judicium tuum*—"Just art Thou, O God, and right in Thy judgments." And if God has opened my eyes and touched my heart, I shall surely break out into a cry of astonishment at God's goodness and mercy, which has borne with me so long and so patiently. For when He might most justly over and over again have cut me off in the midst of my sins, or withdrawn all His richer graces, and suffered me to run my own perverse course from bad to worse, He has instead pursued me, and overwhelmed me with forgiveness and generosity; He has served me in all His creatures, has fed and supported me; He has given me all my life, movement, thought, and will—nay, the very acts and energies I turned against Him were the gifts and evidences of His present love. He might well have sent His angels to destroy me, but instead, He gave them special charge over me to keep me in all my ways. Instead

of turning a deaf ear to the prayers of His Blessed
Mother and of His saints, and forbidding them so
much as to mention my name, He not only harkened,
but longed to be entreated in my behalf. In a word,
when every claim to His forbearance was forfeited,
when He might have loathed me in my degradation,
He pitied me instead, and secretly drew me to a
better mind, to a desire for His service; and when
I was yet afar off He could bear the separation no
longer, but ran out to meet me, and silenced my
confession with a kiss of peace.

And so I betake myself once more to the foot of
His Cross, and marvel what there can be in my
miserable soul that God can so love; what has
enslaved Him to this degree of self-abasement. And
from marvelling I pass to love and adoration, and
thence to the sorrow of a broken and contrite heart.

SIN AND SUFFERING.

"Amen I say to thee, thou shalt not go out from thence till thou repay the last farthing."—St. Matt. v. 26.

IN the preceding considerations we have spoken of sin chiefly as of a personal offence and estrangement from God. But how does this offence re-act upon our own soul? We know that God is the life of the soul here and hereafter. The mind is made for truth, as the eye is for colour or the ear for sound. Knowledge is the life of the mind; colour is the life of the eye; music is the life of the ear; God is the life of the whole soul, mind and heart. As the ear is dead till music strikes it into life; so the soul, till God breaks upon its vision. Without God, it is dead.

Yet there is the negative death of inaction, and the positive death of destruction. To hate is more than not to love. When the soul hates what is lovable; when it loves what is hateful, then it is dead with the death of conscious destruction. This is the "eternal death" which the Gospel opposes to "eternal life." As the exercise of any faculty concerning its fitting and proper object is attended with joy, so pain results from its application to a wrong object. It is like forcing a lock with a wrong key. By **sin** we do **not** merely cease to be

God's friends, but we become His enemies; and this with a mutual enmity. If it is the greatest of spiritual consolations to be at one with God; it is the greatest of miseries to be driven from His face. A stone is not drawn more necessarily to the centre of the earth than is the created spirit to the bosom of God. Were the stone conscious of being held back from its goal, still more of being driven from it by some contrary violence, this consciousness would mean misery. To continue the metaphor: the nearer it approaches the centre, the more forcibly and impetuously is it borne on. So when the soul shakes off the fetters of matter, space, and time, and enters its proper spiritual ether, its flight towards God is as that of a bird, no longer wearying itself with futile flutterings upwards, but freed from the snare of the fowler, and steered to its home by an unerring, God-given instinct. What then, if opposed to this fundamental attraction of our whole spiritual being, this blind restless craving for God, there be found an overmastering repulsion, so that we are at once driven and drawn; drawn, by the deep-down, ineradicable instinct of our spiritual nature and constitution; driven, in virtue of the self-induced distortion of that nature; driven, by those same forces and energies which we were left free either to bring into harmony with our primary impulse or else into conflict and discord with it. The pain of conscious loss[1] is no mere negation, but a sharp

---

[1] There is conscious and unconscious loss; and there is the consciousness of a loss apprehended distinctly (as when one has lost his sight), and that of a loss vaguely guessed at (as in one born blind).

agony, whose poignancy, no doubt, is proportioned
to the clearness and deliberateness of the soul's
aversion from God. The same impetus of Divine
love which hurries along to their bliss those souls
that yield themselves to its sway, crushes to
powder those who dare to oppose it, or stand stiff
against it; the same light which fills the eyes of the
saints with glory, dazzles and darkens and withers
the eyes unanointed by grace; the same fire which
warms and gladdens and comforts God's friends,
scorches, torments, and consumes His enemies.
God is the life of the soul, and God is the death of
the soul, "for our God is a consuming fire."[1] No
one, save those to whom it is given, can see Him
and live. When the unpardoned soul passes "from
out the bourne of time and space" into the changeless instant of eternity, where longer and shorter
have no meaning, and joy and sorrow no divisible
dimension of duration, it finds itself for ever fixed
in a state of destruction; "for ever shattered, and
the same for ever." In that first eternal pang its
punishment is complete, for it is not more shattered
because it is longer shattered. "As the tree falls
there shall it lie."

And now we turn to the other element of sin—
the *material* element, as it used to be called. We
must view it as a disarrangement of God's plans; a
spoiling of His designs; a disturbance of the order

---

[1] We do not mean, of course, that God is to be identified with
the "fire which is not quenched," but that the thought of God's
goodness torments the soul of the wicked as much as it gladdens
the soul of the saint.

of creation; an interference with God's created glory. For God in His goodness has willed to surround Himself with creation as with a halo of glory which in no way indeed can add to His own uncreated brightness and beauty, but of which glory He is truly the subject, even as a king receives an extrinsic glory from his retinue and the pageantry of his royal Court. Here it is that God can in a true sense be said to be dependent upon us; we can further or hinder His designs; we can make reparation for our own transgressions and the transgressions of others.

When we examine most of God's precepts and prohibitions we find, as far as our poor reason carries us, that they are all directed by His loving wisdom to the good of creation in general and of man in particular; and we can often see how sin is naturally fraught with mischievous consequences for the individual and for society. Yet until we can mount up to God's throne and view things with the eyes of Him "whose wisdom reaches from end to end, and disposes of all things sweetly," we can never hope to see more than an infinitesimal fraction of the consequences of any single human act. For example, a man tells a lewd story—a little sin perhaps for him. He may mention it in confession or he may forget it. It is passed from mouth to mouth as time goes on, and gives birth to a foul thought here and there; and this springs up in the fancy unbidden a thousand times, and draws others in its train; and perchance the thought fructifies in deeds and actions, themselves fruitful of others. Who can compute the harm or tell where it will stop, if ever? And so of many a lie; many a harsh and unkind word; many a slander and calumny; many a theft or injustice; many a negligence and omission. How terrible it would be were God to disclose to us the sum total of that harm in the world which shall eventually be traceable to our faults! I think we should be driven to despair at once. Still more when we consider that a blemish is more hateful according as the beauty which it mars is greater. Could we but enter into the grandeur and glory of God's design, we should be utterly confounded to see how stupendous a work we had spoilt and profaned. Of course, when we sin we **do** not know all this; nor do we always think very explicitly of what we do know. Yet we are justly blamed and held accountable, like little children who are told not to meddle with the clock or with some other piece of machinery which they don't understand. We know very well that sin is forbidden for good reasons, by God, whose providence is over all; and that we ourselves are not likely to form any adequate notion of those reasons, since they are as wide-reaching as creation. But in our littleness we want to be as God, knowing good and evil for ourselves and measuring it by our own ken.

This disorder which sin produces in creation, great as it may be, is yet a finite evil. It is an injury done to God's garment, but not touching His Person. As forbidden by Him, it cannot be committed without an accompanying personal

offence. But the two elements must not be
confounded. If I annoy my friend by upset-
ting his house and furniture, I cannot undo his
annoyance. That is for him to do in his free
forgiveness. But if after I am forgiven I neglect to
re-arrange his affairs so far as I can, I tacitly
reiterate my offence. Similarly, after God has
forgiven us, if we neglect to set right, as far as we
can, what we have set wrong; if we fail to restore
the order which we have destroyed, or to make any
compensation that is in our power, we thereby
relapse into our former offence. And by harm done
we must not understand the mere social effects of
sin, but the disturbance of that moral order which
requires the subjection of our own passions to the
rational will, and of the rational will to God. For
this too is a finite disorder, to be compensated by a
corresponding repression of the same rebellious
faculties; in a word, by their punishment—for we
all feel at once that indulgence is balanced by
restriction, and over-feeding by a fast.

And this is what we mean by the temporal punishment due to sin. We say "temporal," because it is
finite, and we express finitude in terms of time. For
those who die in deadly sin, the temporal punishment
is said to become eternal. Not that it lasts time
without end, nor yet does it cease after a time—for
time is no more; but because, as Aquinas points
out, the state of the departed is unchangeable,
unprogressive. They are stayed, and, as it were,
petrified in their first conscious instant of other-
world existence. And over and above the pain of

personal antagonism and opposition to God—their lost treasure—there recoils upon them all the evil that they have caused in God's creation, in themselves and in others, so that the balance of the moral order is restored, and truth and right are triumphant — *Deposuit potentes de sede, et exaltavit humiles*—The lofty are brought low, and the lowly uplifted. Yet compared with the anguish of antagonism to God, which is the very death of the soul, this penalty for the disorder of sin is finite. As to the precise nature of that timeless torment it is vain for us to speculate. In a modified sense we may say of it: " Eye hath not seen, nor ear heard, nor heart conceived." For although it is not a supernatural mystery like the Beatific Vision, yet it belongs to that spirit world outside time and space, whereof we have at best remotely analogical conceptions. Our Saviour speaks of a " fire unquenchable; " and Holy Church forbids us to confine the torments simply to remorse, or to deny that it will penetrate to every corner of our conscious being, so that the senses shall expiate their unlawful indulgence by a consciousness of sense suffering.

The more we learn to look upon the whole physical and visible world as the self-expression and symbol of that world which is spiritual and invisible, and to regard this frail body of our humiliation as not merely the earthly tenement of our immortal part, but as in some sense its creation and its sacrament—even as the whole world is God's creation and sacrament—the easier does it become to conceive that the element whose infusion transforms and spiritualizes the risen bodies of the saints, releasing them from the fetters of time and space, is no other than the sanctified soul transfused with the fulness of the Divine indwelling; and that as the natural soul fashions to itself a fitting garment of flesh and blood, and communicates its own nature and idea for the time being to the matter which it stealthily draws from its environment, so the same soul transfigured and glorified, glorifies and transfigures that which it assumes and subdues to itself. If this be so, it is not incongruous to believe that when eternal death is perfected in the soul, its sting should send its poison into every fibre of our double nature. But in all this we are simply groping after some less inadequate statement of truths belonging to a world wholly unimaginable, and are safe only in holding to the words of the Gospel and of the Church, to those divinely authorized expressions of a mystery which is above and beyond our adequate apprehension, which can never be exactly translated into the language of the senses. "It belongeth to the royal lordship of God," says Mother Julian of Norwich, "to have His privy counsels in peace, and it belongeth to His servants for obedience and reverence not to will to know His counsels. Our Lord hath pity and compassion on us for that some creatures make themselves so busy therein; and I am sure if we wist how greatly we should please Him and ease ourselves to leave it, we would. The saints in Heaven they will nothing wit but what our Lord will show them."

There is yet another consequence of sin, that is, of repeated sin, which we must take notice of; namely, vice. Vice is a propension or inclination towards sinful actions; begotten chiefly by our own sins, though perhaps to some extent inherited from our sinful ancestors. There are also propensions to sin which in no way owe their origin to personal fault, but are merely constitutional. Now, as virtue is an adornment of the soul—for we all feel that a good disposition is a spiritual charm distinct from that of good conduct, and that good conduct is better if it proceeds from good inclination and does not need to be forced—so vice is undoubtedly a blemish which unfits the soul for the presence of God; not, indeed, a blemish comparable to the stain of actual sin, but still a deformity and disfigurement in point of disposition. It was the error of Pelagianism to rate men by their disposition rather than by their actual conduct, to fix their eternal destiny by the consideration of what they would have done in hypothetical circumstances, and not by what they did in their actual circumstances. It is by our works that we have to be judged, by our deliberate thoughts, and resolves, and words, and actions; not by our habits, inclinations, and dispositions. These latter are indeed important, but wholly for the sake of the actions to which they give birth. But so far as morality stands for virtues, good habits, and inclinations, it may be said that our whole moral evolution consists in the gradual elimination of all evil inclinations, and in the cultivation of contrary dispositions. Sin not only retards but undoes our progress in this respect. However rich the repentant soul may be in grace, yet until it is purged of all vicious tendencies it is not fit for God's presence.   For flesh and blood shall not inherit that Kingdom ; nor corruption incorruption.   Our mortality and frailty must put on strength and immortality.   And as all birth and growth and refinement is, for us earth-bound limited creatures, at the cost of much suffering and tribulation—*per multas tribulationes*—so the purification of our soul from vice and infirmity is a bitter and laborious task.

It has been disputed[1] whether the purgatorial fire is merely expiatory of the pains due to forgiven sins, or is also perfective of the heart and mind of the sufferer.   But in truth the difference of view is more apparent than real.   It is certain that nothing

---

[1] *sc* , Between Bellarmine and Suarez.   The former thinks that even the guilt of venial sin is remitted in Purgatory : the latter holds that such guilt, together with all vicious tendencies, is burnt out of the soul at the Particular Judgment by an act of sovereign love, leaving nothing but temporal debts for the purgatorial fire.   Plainly it is largely a matter of words.   Both agree that these three things—venial guilt, vicious inclination, and temporal debt—need to be purged away, the two former by some intense act of love (whose natural language is suffering or contrition), the third by pain.   Bellarmine views the three processes as simultaneous, and calls it all Purgatory ; Suarez regards the third as subsequent to the two first, and reserves to it the name of Purgatory.   We know too little about duration in the spirit world to make the controversy very profitable.   St. Catherine of Genoa seems to take a middle position and to apply the term " Purgatory " to the second and third processes.   Needless to say, this discourse of ours is founded on her classical treatise : *In us quæ de Purgatorio determinata non sunt ab Ecclesia, standum est us quæ sunt magis conformia dictis et revelationibus sanctorum.* (Aquinas, in 4 *Sent.* d. 21. q. 1. a. 1.)

defiled can enter Heaven, and that this refers not only to the defilement of sin or to the debt of temporal pain, but also to those vicious habits and tendencies of the soul which remain after the fullest absolution and indulgence, and are called the *reliquiæ peccati.* These spiritual diseases and indispositions must be cured before the soul can see God; and they are cured as soon as the medicine of grace, already received, works its full effect; that is, when by strong, painful acts of love the soul has corresponded to and utilized the secret forces conveyed to it through the sacraments, and has thus been perfected through suffering. Now, when we say that temporal pain is due to forgiven sin— that justice requires it, it is not to be thought that pain as such can satisfy justice; but rather pain as atoning for that lack of reverence and love involved in sin; pain, as an expression and embodiment of love and reverence. It is because there is no love or reverence in the lost, because all they suffer is against their will, that their pains cannot in the strict sense satisfy justice, even as in this world the wicked who rebel against God's lash rather increase than remedy their guilt.

It is only love that can expiate the unjust withholding of love; and therefore the temporal punishment due to forgiven sin is really in the long run medicinal, or at all events nutritive in respect to the soul of the sufferer, whether on earth or in Purgatory.

As it is but a superficial and utilitarian view of Christianity which regards it principally as a system

of morality whose end is social and political peace
and prosperity, and which therefore looks on the
life to come as a mere sanction subordinated to the
securing of those temporal effects; (whereas, in truth,
Christianity wholly subordinates this life to the
next, making it little better than a pre-natal
existence, a time of secret moulding and fashioning)
so it is a mistake to regard Purgatory as a sort of
accidental stage, a mere finishing process by which
the last touches are put upon a work which has
been substantially completed on earth.   Truly in
some sense it is in this life that the foundation of
our salvation is laid, that its lines and dimensions
are determined and fixed, that our free-will accepts,
or rejects, or modifies the plans and ideals of the
Divine mind in our regard.   But if the seed is sown
here, it is only in the glow of suffering that it
germinates and sends up its stalk; and if in some
few exceptional cases that work of development is
to a great extent completed in the furnace of
earthly tribulation, yet for the most, and as a
general law, it is in Purgatory that the causes here
freely set in motion, find due conditions in which to
work out their necessary effects in the soul.   Doubtless the love of the martyrs, which, like that of their
Master, finds expression in absolute self-sacrifice
and in the bearing of unspeakable torments, perfects
the labour of many years in a little space; but
though such extreme suffering is not for all men the
price of grace and salvation, yet it does not seem
likely that grace can yield its full fruit or that the
soul, already saved, can be fitted for the King's

embrace short of an equal purification by pain. The martyrs and confessors are those who to some extent received here that purgatory which we all must receive sooner or later. But the many are too weak to purchase grace at such a cost, and God condescends to their frailty by veiling from them the full burden they have taken upon themselves till such times as they shall be able to bear it willingly.

We are now in a better position to appreciate the sufferings of the blessed souls in Purgatory. When the pardoned soul passes out of this life it is ushered into the presence of our Saviour,

> And with the intemperate energy of love
> Flies to the dear feet of Emmanuel :
> But ere it reach them, the keen sanctity
> Which with its effluence, like a glory, clothes
> And circles round the Crucified, has seized
> And scorched and shrivelled it ; and now it lies
> Passive, and still, before the awful throne.
> O happy, suffering soul ! for it is safe ;
> Consumed, yet quickened by the glance of God.[1]

For it is thrust through with the sharp and fiery sword of contrite love. Who has not at times been filled with self-hatred, with a passion for self-inflicted suffering, on the sudden conviction of baseness and ingratitude towards some noble and loving soul ! What then must be the anguish, the thirst for self-vengeance, when the whole lovableness of God and the whole extent and depth of its own sinfulness is first flashed upon the soul—a pain that is saved from being remorse, and yet is increased

[1] Newman's *Dream of Gerontius.*

by the knowledge that in spite of all God loves it still, loves it infinitely. And proportioned to the awful force with which the disembodied and pardoned soul is drawn towards the bosom of God, is the strain and agony of that violent separation which must last till it is perfected and purified.

This then is the first and chiefest pain of Purgatory, the pain of bitter, though love-born sorrow for past unlovingness; the agony of violent present separation from an embrace just missed. I do not know if in the nature of things this suffering can be alleviated by our prayers; or that the Holy Souls would willingly be spared a pang of that sweet saving sorrow whereby every vice is burnt out by the roots and every virtue burnt in.[1] We do not know if this process be measurable in terms of time, or if it be, as Suarez seems to have thought, the work of an instant. It is, indeed, a fiery trial, whereby the gold is freed from its dross in the scorching flame of Divine love, and as long as there is dross and impurity there will be sharp agonizing suffering.

But the same light which discloses to us our sin as a treason against our Eternal Lover, also shows it to us as to its intrinsic malice. There for the first time we are set face to face with God's fair plan of creation; and we see what it is we have helped to spoil, and to what extent. We trace the ramifications of our guilty acts like ugly black lines spreading

---

[1] Not that this involves any increase of sanctifying grace; but only that the grace and love already there should work its effect and spread itself to every corner of the spiritual frame.

out on all sides, and stretching forward to the last syllable of recorded time. And if now our memory leaves us conscious of only a big blot here and there, then the whole story will stand out clear as to its minutest detail; and half-smothered motives that we refused to admit to ourselves will be dragged forth into clear light; and we shall see ourselves contrasted not only with what our inmost conscience told us, but with what it might have told us if we had used our opportunities of knowing better. And our rectified will, in full sympathy with God's, will be shocked and horrified at the hideous moral ruin we have worked; and it will be ardent and restless in its desire to compensate and atone by its own suffering and submission, for the disorder caused by its past indulgence and rebellion. But how measureless and all but infinite a task will this appear! And will it not be the earnest desire of such a soul that all should by love and patient suffering make reparation to God in every possible way for this great dishonour He has received; and especially that for the harm whereof it has itself been the author, it may, by its own sufferings, or by those of others near and dear to it, make due restitution. If I see my friend's house on fire, I will get all I have any claim on, to help me to put it out—still more, if it is on fire through my carelessness; or through some past fault that I am now sorry for. In this it is that the souls in Purgatory so earnestly desire our help, that we may hasten the day when God's honour shall be satisfied; and when they will no longer feel the intolerable pain of responsibility for a disorder not remedied, for a debt still unpaid; and when they will at last be able to enter into the joy of God's presence purified, not only from the relics of sin, from evil or imperfect inclinations, but also from that debt of personal penalty whereof they shall then have paid the last farthing.

Against the practice of assisting the souls in Purgatory our laziness suggests, with some ingenuity, that after all they are happy and blessed: *Beati mortui*—"Happy are the dead." They are safe in port; out of all risk and danger. Would God we were as well off! Let us therefore pray and work for those who are still storm-tossed and uncertain of salvation. What comparison can there be between the two needs?

First of all, this objection is not usually urged by those who are very earnest in their intercession for the living; or who have, in consequence, no moment of time left for the needs of the dead. On the contrary, the charity which urges to the one form of intercession, usually urges to the other. Then, it is true that the souls in Purgatory are happy substantially, fundamentally. But, as these words suggest, our happiness lies in layers and is divisible. Fundamental happiness is compatible with superficial or less fundamental misery. The saints on earth had this fundamental happiness of being right with God; but they also had great sufferings and tribulations of soul and body to endure. And these sufferings were very real; and very worthy of pity. I know there is a spirituality which despises—in the case of others—any trouble that is not spiritual;

which is so impressed with the advantages of trials and pains for other people, that it can see nothing in them to pity. " If a man has the grace of God, he has a treasure of infinite worth. Why should we pity him because he has got all the sorrows of Job on his head; because he has lost his home, and children, and influence, and health? These are but temporal sorrows; these but the thorns of a heavenly crown. Why pluck them out?" This is not God's way, who made body and soul, and redeemed both alike; who desires not our fundamental happiness alone, but our entire happiness; who afflicts always with regret, and only "for greater gain of after-bliss;" who feels the least of our pains far more than we feel it ourselves, being "afflicted in all our afflictions;" who pities the pitiful, and blesses the man who has consideration for the poor and needy, and smoothes his pillow for him in his sickness; who calls a man a liar if he pretends to bewail invisible and supernatural evils, and yet has no pity for those that are visible and natural.[1] The same reasons which forbid us to neglect the temporal and bodily needs of the living under pain of reprobation, forbid us to neglect the sufferings of the blessed dead. Nay, because they are blessed and dearer to God, we owe them a special care and service. St. Paul tells us that our charity, which is due to all, is first due to those that are of the household of the faith. And are not the blessed dead more truly in God's household than the living? If God wants us to visit Him in the prisons of earthly justice, much

---

[1] 1 St. John iv.

more does He wait for our consolation in the
debtor's prison of heavenly justice. "Remember
the poor debtors," for they cry out to us day and
night with their endless *Miseremini mei!* Let us
make friends with them now, that when our time
comes they may help us, and at last welcome us into
everlasting habitations. For they will not be like
Pharao's butler, who, when released from prison,
no longer remembered Joseph his helper, but forgot
him.

This, indeed, is the least of all motives, though
a good one. Still better, is the thought that alms-
giving, if it be the child of real charity and pitying
love of others, cleanses our soul from all sin and
wins us a heritage of mercy. Also, whatever unselfs
us, and takes us out of our narrowness, and makes
us live for others and in others, and dwell, not upon
our own wounds, but on those of Christ's Mystic
Body, is an incalculable good.

Again, charity to the dead is in some way more
beneficial to our faith than charity to the living.
For faith means a realization of the invisible world;
and one reason why this devotion flags is because
we are more alive to pains we can see and imagine,
than to those of the mysterious spirit-world. Humani-
tarian charity, important as it is, involves no great
exercise of faith in the invisible.

But beyond all these reasons and motives there
is one which appeals to our love of God, and of
His Blessed Mother, and of the saints, His friends
and courtiers. We have often heard of miners
being buried alive in the bowels of the earth,

while their parents and friends were standing above their living grave, broken-hearted and terrified, listening anxiously for some sound or sign from the depths, to sustain and quicken their languishing hopes. So may we figure to ourselves, God and His Blessed Mother and the saints, standing on high above the abyss of Purgatory, where the Holy Souls are buried under a vast depth of incumbrances and debts of punishment to be worked out, through which their faint cries for assistance scarce penetrate : " From the depths have I cried to Thee, O Lord. Let Thy ears be attentive to the voice of my supplication."

God is in some sense powerless, and dependent on our co-operation for the deliverance of His dear children, whom He afflicts not willingly but of necessity; His wisdom and justice tie His hands, and bid Him wait for the payment of the last farthing. And Mary longs to welcome them home to her Mother's heart, with all their sufferings and sorrows past, their tears wiped away, and their cup of joy filled to the brim—even as she is said to have waited with restless longing by the tomb through the vigil of Easter to clasp to her breast the first-fruits of the dead, the first-born of her many children. And the saints are also athirst for the deliverance of the blessed dead ; for every new-comer to their festival increases the joy of all the rest—a joy that grows and feeds on sympathy, a fire that burns more fierce and bright for every new faggot that is cast upon it.

And so, as usual, the instinct of the Catholic

religion is found to be true and right and faithful as soon as we look into it carefully and devoutly.   Our faith is everywhere seen to be an exquisite harmony, so delicate, so exact in composition, that no element can be removed or disturbed without destruction to the whole.   The devotion to the Holy Souls might, to a superficial thinker, seem an arbitrary accretion to the body of Catholic teaching, something stuck on from without, that could be removed without hurt.   But closer examination proves it a true vital outgrowth whose veins and fibres reach down through the whole plant to the very earth itself, whence it draws its life.   You cannot touch it or tear it without injury to every other article of belief, to the doctrine of sin and its consequences—which again involves the doctrine of God as Creator and Redeemer—to the doctrines of vicarious suffering, of the communion of saints, of charity, of mercy, and of all the doctrines which they depend upon and involve.

THE GOSPEL OF PAIN.

Aut pati, aut mori—" Let me either suffer or die."

WE are told in the Breviary lesson for the feast of St. Teresa[1] that, not content with the passive, patient, and loving endurance of the many crosses and afflictions whereby in the ordinary course of His providence God purified and chastened her affections, and prepared her soul for an eternal union with Himself, for the everlasting embrace of the Heavenly Spouse, she was wont, in obedience to the inspiration of Divine love, to go out of her way in search of further sufferings, to regard them as pearls of great price to be earnestly sought for, and carefully hoarded when found; that she was restless, uneasy, fretful, if ever she were wholly free from pain or sorrow or humiliation, from the Cross in one form or another. For her, life without suffering was not worth living; it was death, worse than death: *Aut pati, aut mori*—" Let me either suffer or die."

Her earliest manifestation of this strange passion was when as a mere child she fled from home, hand in hand with her little brother, to seek martyrdom among the Moors. That indeed was the greedy

---

[1] This is the development of a sermon preached on her feast in 1896 in the Carmelite Church, Kensington, London.

improvidence of childhood, which would have sacri-
fieed the unknown treasures of suffering, hidden in
the womb of futurity, for one short, sharp ecstasy
of present pain ; which would have driven the pierc-
ing sword home at a blow, rather than inch by
inch, with protracted lingerings and loving delays.

But God saved her from herself and from her
folly, as He always does those who love Him ;
thwarting her present good desire that He might
fulfil it a hundred-fold in due season. He had in
reserve for her a baptism, not of blood, but of sorrow,
a far deeper chalice of suffering than that which her
infant greed had thirsted for, a glorious chalice full
to the brim, overflowing, inebriating with heavenly
joy and ecstasy. *Aut pati, aut mori :* she was not to
die, but to suffer. *Non moriar sed vivam*—" You
shall not die, Teresa, but you shall live and suffer
and declare the wonderful works of God."   •

A strange answer, indeed, to the problem of life's
value, in these days when it is so generally assumed
as a first and self-evident principle that suffering is
the one unmitigated evil, and that to escape it
ourselves, or to lessen it for others, is the only
reasonable and worthy end we can put before us.

Here both egoist and altruist, he who lives for
himself and he who lives for others, are at one in their
estimate of good and evil. The former, indeed, by
cutting the cords which would bind him by affection
to his fellow-men and make him a sharer of their
sufferings, narrows the area in which Sorrow can
lodge the arrows she directs against him ; the latter
going out of himself by sympathy, makes, together

with the many with whom he is bound up, an easy mark for her most casual dart. Yet what they fly from, and what they fight against in both cases, is one and the same thing—pain, suffering, sorrow.

None, however, are so short-sighted as not to see that, however undesirable pain may be in itself, it is, nevertheless, in the established order of things very often a necessary condition of life and enjoyment; that it must be faced firmly and frequently by those who wish to extract the full value from a finite and limited existence; so that their very horror of pain should lead them to bear it, nay, even to seek it, in their own interest or in that of others for whose happiness they live. They recognize that all creation is groaning and travailing, expecting its deliverance; that pain is the inevitable condition of growth and expansion; that life feeds upon death; that the present must die in giving birth to the future. *Aut pati, aut mori;* no life but at the cost of suffering, seems the universal law of evolution. To survive is to struggle; to struggle is to suffer, and to cause suffering. And this law they extend from the physical into the moral and social world, and they tell us that those who, shrinking from its seeming cruelty, would by some vain utopian scheme end this struggle between man and man, with its attendant suffering, would in reality be courting social death and decay, would be multiplying for posterity those very evils they seek to avoid for themselves.

Thus those who hold most firmly that a pleasureable life, free from pain, sorrow, and affliction, is

the one thing to aim at, are willing to allow that
only through many tribulations can we enter into
such a kingdom of enjoyment. *Aut pati, aut mori;*
those who flee the Cross cannot grasp even the
perishable crown of pleasure.

The most selfish and shameless of pleasure-
seekers, if he be not led blindly by his feelings from
moment to moment, if he exercise any foresight or
human prudence in the conduct of life, sees clearly
that he must suffer for pleasure's sake; that he
must deny himself and practise judicious self-
restraint; that he must be a miser in economizing
the enjoyments of life in the present, for the sake
of greater eventual gain of enjoyment. Reflection
and experience alike tell him that the pleasures
of life stand out more brightly against a dark
background of pain. The most acute pleasure,
if continuously sustained at the same pitch, soon
ceases to affect our consciousness in any way;
i.e., ceases to be pleasure; for pleasure springs from
the consciousness of an agreeable state, and consciousness is like a drugged sleeper kept awake only
by incessant rousings and changes of position.
Without going so far as those who say (with
Schopenhauer), that pleasure is only the consciousness of a cessation or mitigation of pain, every
pleasure-seeker must allow that pain is the very
tonic of the sensitive faculty, whereby the dulled
appetite for pleasure is sharpened anew. Without
suffering, life, even for such a one, were not
worth living, but would quickly exhaust itself
and become flat, stale, and unprofitable. *Aut pati,*

aut mori; if pleasure be life, one must either suffer or die.

If we turn to the philanthropist, *i.e.*, to him who, in obedience to a God-given instinct for which most modern philosophy vainly seeks any coherent justification, strives to communicate to others what he himself esteems the truest happiness—we find the same inevitable condition accepted. Positivism, which includes in its scheme of benevolence all sentient creation from man down to the meanest insect, decks itself out in the blood-stained garment of Christian asceticism. It breathes everywhere the spirit of self-sacrifice, it speaks the language of charity, it vaunts the Cross upon its brow. Nay, it has rediscovered Christ; it has raised from the dead Him whom the Churches have slain. *Aut pati, aut mori,* it says; the greatest amount of enjoyment for the many can only be secured by the self-sacrifice of the few who devote their lives to a crusade against pain, the arch-enemy, who suffer more, that others may suffer less, and yet by sympathy with the joy of others, find their own unselfish sorrow turned into joy. In all this there is something so analogous to Christian fraternal charity, that the very elect themselves are often deceived. For here too—so far as there is any definite positivist morality or law—love to our neighbour is the fulfilling of that law.

Christian and positivist alike live and suffer for the common happiness. It is, however, in their estimate, not only of what true happiness consists in, but of the relation between pain and happiness, that they are as antagonistic one to another, as light to darkness. Too often, indeed, the kind-hearted, good-natured philanthropist makes little profession of any definite theory of life and happiness, but busies himself incessantly "going about and doing good" as his momentary instinct or feeling prompts him. He does not delay to go minutely into the remote or possible consequences of his benevolent activity, or to search keenly into his motives, but wherever he is pained by the sufferings of others in any form, he at once seeks to relieve his own pain by relieving theirs. And by yielding to this kindly impulse and indulging it, it becomes more and more tyrannical in its demand for gratification, so that eventually he is simply dominated altogether and indiscriminately by his abhorrence of every form of suffering. Were suffering really the ultimate evil, and were enjoyment the ultimate good, such a tyranny of benevolence would be simply the fulness and perfection of Divine charity.

Yet let such a one be reduced by poverty, sickness, or other causes to long years of helpless suffering in which he can no longer minister to the happiness of others, and let him be set face to face with the problem as to what that happiness is which he sought for them and which they should now minister to him, and he will be forced to see that he has hitherto been as a physician going about dispensing drugs and remedies of which he knows nothing, for the cure of diseases of which he knows as little; that he was healing others while he knew not how to heal himself; that he was a blind leader of the blind; plucking motes from his neighbour's eye, all unconscious of the beam in his own. An indiscriminate pain-shirker himself, he dealt with others as he himself would have wished to be dealt with.

Nay, in bearing the burdens of others he far surpassed any Christian saint. For the Christian may never, for the love of others, himself forego one particle of that final happiness which he desires to secure for them, nor incur the slightest taint of that ultimate evil from which it is his supreme endeavour to preserve them. He may never sin, even a little, that others may sin less, or stand for an instant in his own light that others may enjoy a fuller view of God's face. Whereas the philanthropist, viewing pain as the last and unqualified evil, will endure it himself that others may escape it; thus sacrificing what he deems his own highest good as a means to the highest good of others.

This self-care is sometimes objected to Christians as indicating a lower altruism, a less absolute unselfishness than obtains, at all events in theory, among the disciples of Comte. Yet unjustly. For though the Christian must love himself *before* his neighbour, and though "charity begins at home," yet his self-care and self-love is subordinated as a means to the care and love of others for God's sake, that "he may have wherewith to give to him that is in need." It is only in the measure that he has found and tasted happiness himself that he will feel the desire to impart it to others.

Flammescat igne caritas,
Accendat ardor proximos,[1]

is the Catholic principle.   If, then, a man must love
his own soul *before* his neighbour's, it is a "before-
ness" of time rather than of affection.   The Christian
conception of humanity as an organism, as a many-
branched tree rooted in God and drawing life from
Him, demands that each part be animated and
moved towards the general good of the whole
organism as its all-dominating aim; and yet it is in
perfecting and strengthening itself that it contributes
most effectively towards this universal and unselfish
end.   It never could possibly be for the happiness,
that is, for the true well-being, of others that
a man should neglect his own highest life; but
rather, the stronger, the higher he is, the more
effectively can he raise and strengthen others.
The mother must feed herself for the sake of the
child at her breast.   It is, therefore, the motive from
which it springs, the end to which it is directed,
that turns what would otherwise be spiritual selfishness into that truest altruism which regards God
and self and neighbour as one thing—vine and
branches—with one life, one movement, one interest.

Most of the kindness of modern humanitarians,
however well meant, is really as spurious as that of
the father who weakly yields to every wish and
whim of his children, who will never inflict the least
pain upon them that can by any possibility be
avoided, who takes it for granted that suffering is

---

[1] Kindle the flame of good desire
Till all around be set on fire.

never a good, is never to be endured save by way of economy as a condition of less eventual suffering. Yet even this end should make the development of the pain-bearing faculty a far more important feature of education than it is at the present day.

The whole aim of humanitarians is to lessen the amount of pain in the world, but in no wise to teach men to bear pain, much less to value it, to court it, to be in love with it, as St. Teresa was. They seek to raise the standard, not of happiness (which, indeed, they lower), but of *comfort;* thus implicitly making comfort, or freedom from hardships and bodily sufferings, if not the essence, at least an essential condition of happiness. They strive to make men less accustomed to privations and inconvenience, and therefore more impatient and intolerant of such as are inevitable, to make the conditions of contentment ever more manifold and complex, and therefore more rarely realized, more easily disturbed.

Nay, the very sympathy extended to suffering, the tone, so to say, in which it is pitied, makes it much harder to endure. How often do we not bear up against trouble until we find ourselves pitied; how often is it not pity which first suggests to us the misery of our plight? Suffering would be bearable enough were it not for reflection, which magnifies it and joins its several pangs into one chain of woe, and brings those that are past and even those that are future to bear upon the present, and crushes us with pain of which nine-tenths belong to the world of ideas. But this phantom grows to a Brocken-spectre when we see it reflected in the eyes of all around us. Our estimate of good and evil is largely taken from those with whom we dwell, and our enjoyment and suffering depend on that estimate. Thus we marvel at what our fore-fathers put up with in the way of discomfort; we admire their patient endurance of various incon-veniences, injustices, oppressions, which to us would be quite unbearable; and forgetting that the con-ditions of contentment are far more subjective than objective, we fancy that our ancestors must have been as miserable as we should now be in the same circumstances. Instead of inuring men to the rough climate of this mortal life, humanitarianism has accustomed them to wraps and muffles, and rendered them susceptible to every little change of temperature—poor, frail, pain-fearing creatures.

Indeed, there are no greater enemies of human happiness than those who substitute pleasure and pain for good and evil. Pleasure is coy and will not be sought directly. She is found by those who seek her not, and flies, as does their shadow, from those who hotly pursue her. And pain is terrible chiefly to those who have learnt to view it as the ultimate evil. So that in pursuing the one phantom and flying from the other, they are not only diverted from the quest of true and solid happiness, but inevitably fail to secure even that which they seek.

As far as this modern philanthropy understands itself, it is simply "positivist;" it is indifferent to belief in God or in the life to come. It finds its motive largely in a sense of pity springing from the very decay of faith, pity for human life so short, so full of misery, so void of hope, and thence it conceives a desire to sweeten the bitterness of that lot, to crowd all possible enjoyment into life's brief span, to exclude all avoidable suffering and sorrow, and in every other way to minister anodynes and narcotics which will mitigate the sadness of existence, and foster the illusion that life, without God, without immortality, is still a prize worth having. And this same pity for temporal pain and suffering, as the evil of evils, is naturally extended to the whole of sentient creation, to all our fellow-mortals, from whom we are thought to be divided by no very certain line; whence the extravagances of zoophilist. fanaticism, and the growing tenderness for animal suffering which, though beautiful in itself when resting on a rational foundation, is altogether reprehensible when raised to the rank of a supreme rule of action to the prejudice of higher principles. The Buddhist has at least an apparent religious justification for his attitude in the matter, but the modern positivist (unlike the Catholic Christian) can offer no basis for his zoophilism save the tyranny of a sentiment, good in itself, but pampered into a mania by indiscriminate indulgence, and which by its very extravagances hurts the cause he would help. For there is no affection, passion, or instinct, however natural, or useful, or admirable in due season and measure, that may be always and everywhere indulged without reference and subjection to the higher rule of reason whose minister it is.

It is not surprising that those who estimate the evil of the world in terms of pain and sorrow should descant in no measured language on the cruelty of Nature, and should refuse to believe that behind all there is a personal God who could prevent all this misery and yet will not. If He *could* not, say they, how is He almighty? If He *will* not, how is He all-loving? In either case how is He infinite; how is He God? Nor would the objection be without weight, were temporal enjoyment the final good of man; were there no higher good with which the lower has no common measure, being, so to say, in a different plane or category. "If in this life only we have hope," says St. Paul, "then are we of all men the most miserable"—a pessimism no less applicable to life viewed merely in the light of reason; if the present enjoyment of sentient creation be indeed the ultimate good, then it is hard to see the finger of the All-Mighty, the All-Loving God in such a result as is evident to our limited view. And therefore we find many pure, unselfish souls, bewildered with this disheartening philosophy, devoting all their energies to a fruitless contest with the inexorable laws of this seemingly cruel world, if perchance they may even by a single drop lessen the vast ocean of misery and pain, seeking no other happiness than that of procuring the happiness of others, though scarce knowing what happiness means. Their instinct of benevolence, ill-instructed though it be, is from God, the Author of all charity and unselfish love. In living for the good of others they are at one with the Christian, but in their estimate of what that good consists in, they are diametrically opposed to a religion which regards pain or sorrow, not merely as an inevitable and regrettable condition of good, to be minimized as far as possible, but as a positive means to good, something to be sought out and willingly embraced in due season and measure ; not merely as a bitterness incidental to the medicine of life, but as itself a medicinal bitterness;—a religion which says: Blessed are the poor, blessed are the mourners, blessed are the persecuted, blessed are the dead ; which commends to us the example, not of one who was merely a martyr to inevitable violence, but of one who could have descended from the Cross, yet would not.

Still, with all its short-sighted horror of suffering, modern philanthropy is well aware that it is only through much suffering that its aspirations can be realized, that it is only at the cost of endless labour and self-sacrifice that the sum of human misery can be in any way lessened, or the sum of enjoyment increased, that if such social and collective felicity be life, then the law holds good : *Aut pati, aut mori—* "Either suffer or perish." Still more evident is it that if one's individual happiness is found only in self-forgetful devotion to the vaguely conceived welfare of others, such devotion involves continual suffering, and that the life of altruism is a life of pain. *Aut pati, aut mori ;* if selfishness be death, if unselfishness be life, we must either suffer or die.

If now we turn from these who lay such

exaggerated stress on material comfort, and on freedom from bodily·pain and from pain of the merely
sensitive affections and instincts, who reduce all
moral duties to the one universal duty of an unselfish
regard for the almost animal happiness of others;
and if we turn to those who in all ages, guided
by the mere light of reason, have taken a higher
and nobler view of man's nature and capacities for
happiness, who find the value of life, in whatsoever
things are true, whatsoever things are pure, whatsoever things are just, whatsoever things are holy,
whatsoever things are lovable, who scorn to make
pleasure an object of direct pursuit, whose single
aim is objective truth and right, whether it bring
pleasure or pain in its wake, who define good as
that which ought to *be* and which they desire should
be; not as that which they would like to *feel;*
who (at least confusedly) recognize the interests of
reason and conscience as the universal interests of
God, to which they but minister as servants and
instruments in His hands; if we turn to these
and question them, we receive again the same
merciless sentence: *Aut pati, aut mori*—"Either
suffer or die."

They know well that restraint and suffering is
essential to the formation, the growth, the maintenance of every virtue—suffering in the mind, in
the will, in the heart, in the affections, in the
senses.

For does not the mind rebel against the yoke
not only of faith but of reason? Does it not play
into the hands of the imagination and of the senti-

ments, and betray us at all points? And is not the natural will a rebel to all obedience and law? And are not the affections prone to selfishness and narrowness, and hostile to the wide spirit of charity and brotherly love? And are not the senses and passions stubborn against the control of temperance and fortitude, and of all the other virtues included under these? Are they not all so many infidels who have gained possession of God's holy land, that is, of the sacred territory of the human soul— infidels, in their blindness to the principles of faith and reason, in their spirit of boundless self-assertion at the expense of God's glory and man's happiness, infidels who are to be, not slain, but chastised and subdued and pressed into servitude in the interests of Divine Wisdom, their conqueror? Can all this disorder be checked, all these wild forces be kept in hand, can the sweet yoke and light burden of Heavenly Wisdom be imposed and borne without suffering and pain? *Aut pati, aut mori.* Life without suffering is impossible; if truth, if holiness, if virtue, if friendship, if purity be life, we must make up our mind either to suffer or to perish.

And this, all the more, when we remember that there are hours of special combat and fierce temptation to be prepared for, when the rain descends and the rushing flood rises and the storm beats upon the citadel of our soul. For, against these contingencies we are obliged to strengthen ourselves in time of peace by frequent exercise, or *ascesis* as it is called, by the practice not merely

K

of restraint but of mortification, by cutting off not only all that is excessive or unlawful, but also much that is lawful and permissible. These are the peace-manœuvres and sham-fights of the spiritual life, or rather, of the moral life—for we are still in the realm of natural religion; *Nonne et ethnici hoc faciunt?* Did not the Pagan stoics teach us to do these things? Were they not truly ascetics, passing the same verdict upon life as St. Teresa : *Aut pati, aut mori*—life without suffering is impossible. If we are to be victorious in the conflict with self, if we are not to be castaways, we must suffer; we must chastise the body and bring it into subjection. If to stand is to live, if to fall is to perish—*Aut pati, aut mori*—we must either suffer or die.

Again, if we turn to the mystics, to the prophets, poets, and seers of all ages, to those who being lifted up from the earth have drawn all men unto themselves, whose eyes have been fixed beyond human wont on the intolerable brightness of the face of Truth, who have been caught up to the heavens and have heard words which it is not lawful for man to utter, save wrapped close in the shroud of symbolism; when we turn to these and ask them for the law of life, we get only the same sad answer: *Aut pati, aut mori*—you must either suffer or die. "If any man will come after Me," says the Truth, "let him take up his cross and follow Me;" "unless a man forsake all that he hath, he cannot be My disciple." If light and vision be life, if blindness and darkness be death—*Aut pati, aut mori* —we must either suffer or die.

For even the very body itself must be exalted, purified, and spiritualized by suffering, by fast and vigil and penance; it must be subdued, tranquillized, and, as it were, put to sleep before it is an apt medium for communication between this world and the other, before it is attuned to be a fit instrument of God's Holy Spirit. The spiritual man understands the deep things of the spirit because they are spiritually apprehended, but the animal man never rises beyond the laboured methods of reason; he knows nothing of the instincts of love, of that quick intuition which leaps to the truth, from crag to crag, and pinnacle to pinnacle, where others crawl and clamber and stumble. *Dilectus meus*, says Truth, *venit mihi saliens super montes*—" My beloved comes to Me leaping across the mountains." " What man can know the counsels of God, or who can divine His will? For the thoughts of men are timid, and their foresight is uncertain, because the corruptible body weighs upon the soul, and its earthen tenement drags down the mind with its many thoughts." As far as she can by suffering shake herself free from the embrace of this body of death, so far can the soul fly to the embrace of Truth, her Spouse, her Life: *Aut pati, aut mori*.

And if we inquire of religion in its various forms, with its doctrine of sin and expiation, we universally get the same response as from hedonism or stoicism or mysticism: *Aut pati, aut mori*—" Either suffer or die." Without the shedding of blood, without penance and sackcloth and ashes, there is no remission of guilt; the soul that sinneth it shall either suffer or die. For sin is more than the folly of self-hurt and self-destruction, more than a transgression of order. It is an offence against God the Ordainer; it is a rebellion of will against will, of person against person, of the creature against the Creator; it is the uprising of a wave that flings itself in vain pride against the solid rock, to be thrown back and dashed to pieces for its pains. Reason can ill-fathom the mystery, but the instinct of all races has taught them that sin is in some sense balanced and set right by suffering, and that without suffering the disease is irremediable and mortal. *Aut pati, aut mori;* if sin be death, if absolution be life, we must either suffer or die.

But in all this we have not yet touched the secret of St. Teresa's passion for suffering; for it is no other than the secret of the lover. Love must either suffer or die—*Aut pati, aut mori;* suffering is its very life and energy. As the ungrateful flame burns and destroys what it feeds and lives upon, so love seizes upon the heart and gnaws at it night and day, and wears and wastes the frail body, and consumes its strength with labours and sorrows. And this we see to the full in the Divine Lover, the Archetype of all lovers, the Man of Sorrows, acquainted with grief, poor and in labours from His youth, crushed and crucified and tormented by the tyranny of love, and brought down to the very dust of death. The Passion of Christ! Why Passion? The all-devouring passion of God's love for the soul! Was not suffering the very fuel and sustenance of that fire—a fire to be fed on the wood of the Cross, or else to die down and perish—*Aut pati, aut mori.* St. Paul knew well what love meant when he said to his little ones: "We would have plucked out our very eyes and given them to you." He had learnt in the school of the Good Shepherd, who gave His Body to be torn in pieces for His sheep, His Blood to be drained out to the last drop: "Take ye and eat, this is My Body; take ye and drink, this is My Blood; take all that I have, all that I am—*Aut pati, aut mori*—I must suffer for you or else die." *Nonne opportuit Christum pati?* If love must suffer, did it not behove Christ to suffer?

Can we clearly or fully explain this or justify it in the cold light of reason? Can chill philosophy tell us why love thirsts for suffering, why it is straitened till its baptism of blood be accomplished? Even if it cannot, what need we care? Far more things are true than can be explained, else, there were little truth to be had. The experience of mankind cannot only vouch for the fact, but can, so to say, *feel* the reasonableness of it, better than it can say it. *Expertus potest credere!* Which of the saints and lovers of Christ has not felt a craving that suffering alone can appease, or has not felt that he must simply die if he cannot suffer? And does not the history of every pure and noble human love tell us the same tale?

Love, then, was the secret of St. Teresa's passion for suffering; love ever seeking to express itself to the full; making difficulties, where it found none made to hand, that it might have occasion to embody itself in strenuous effort, and so relieve the pressure and tension of its unused energy and strengthen itself by strong acts oft-repeated. Suffering was the food and fuel for which it hungered: *Aut pati, aut mori,* without suffering it must have died down and perished.

And what was the secret of her love? For love is our life, the eternal life of our soul; and the secret of loving God is the one thing worth knowing. Alas! man can but speak the words of that secret, God alone can open the understanding; man can transmit the dead letter, God only can breathe into it the quickening spirit; man can plough and sow and water, God alone can give the increase. It cometh up we know not how. Let St. John, the Doctor of Divine Love, the guardian of the mysteries of the Sacred Heart, be our teacher. "We love Him," he says, "because He first loved us." It is when God first reveals Himself to the soul as her Lover, that she falls at His feet as one dead, pierced through, as St. Teresa saw herself in vision, with a fiery dart. *Vulnerasti cor meum uno oculorum tuorum* —"Thou hast wounded my heart with one glance of Thine eyes." One clear gaze upon that mystery, and the soul is for ever the slave of love. As long as our mind is filled with some distorted abstract, half-true notion of the complete self-sufficingness of God, as long as our puerile imaginings picture Him as merely benevolent and patronizing in our regard, as offering us the alms of His benefits, but caring little whether we accept or decline them; until we receive and believe without understanding or reconciling it with His self-sufficingness, the mystery of God's dependence and indigence, love will but slumber in our heart, as fire in the cold, hard flint till struck from it by the steel.

But let us once look upon the love-worn face of the Man of Sorrows, and read in its lines, its tear-stains and blood-stains, the record of the ravages of Divine love, pent up and compressed within the narrow walls of a finite heart; let us but see in Him the Spouse of man's thoughtless, thankless soul, coming to us in beggary, poor, naked, hungry, and thirsty, to be enriched, and clothed, and fed, and refreshed by our love; let us but hear Him as He knocks at our heart's portal and cries: "Open to Me, My sister, My spouse, for My hair is drenched with the dew, and My locks with the night rain;" let us but realize that in very deed our God wants us, pines for us, hungers and thirsts for us, and lo! we have passed from death unto life, from twilight to noonday, we have found a key to the seeming extravagances, the follies, the delirium, the reckless prodigalities of the saints and of the King of saints, to whom not to suffer was to die. Were that light to break upon us only for a moment we could understand, as now we cannot, the love that burned so fiercely in the heart of Teresa, a love stronger than death; bearing all things, believing all things, hoping all things, enduring all things; a love which swept aside every obstruction in its impetuous course; a love which for twenty dark years endured the searching sword of separation from the Beloved, the privation of all

consciousness of His presence, of all sensible conso·
lation and spiritual joy; a love whose insupportable
strength at last shattered the too straitened vessel
of her heart, and lending wings to her emancipated
soul, bore it up to its nest in the embrace of God;
towards the life of painless love matured and made
perfect by suffering.[1]

[1] A further elucidation of the doctrine of pain will be found in
the Appendix.

"QUID ERIT NOBIS?"

Ah! Christ, if there were no hereafter
It still were best to follow Thee;
Tears are a nobler gift than laughter;
Who wears Thy yoke, alone is free.—C.K.P.

It may not be altogether useless and unprofitable
for us to see in what sense, if in any, we can accept
the sentiment embodied in these lines, and recon-
cile it with the teaching of St. Paul, where he tells
us[1] that if our hope in Christ be only for this life,
then are we of all men most to be pitied, and
where he asks, what will it profit him (humanly
speaking) to have fought with wild beasts at
Ephesus if the dead rise not? "Let us eat and
drink, for to-morrow we die." Let us snatch the
fleeting day as it slips by, let us seize on each
precious "now" and make the most of it, let us
crown ourselves with the perishable roses of life
before they fade, let us, not work, but rejoice and
make merry "while it is yet day," ere the sombre
night of death wrap us in everlasting darkness and
forgetfulness.

St. Peter says to our Saviour: "Lo! we have
left all and followed Thee; we have forsaken all
that makes life valuable to the majority of man-

[1] 1 Cor. xv.

kind, and we have embraced the life of the Cross;
what therefore shall be our reward; what shall we
get by it?" And Jesus answers: "Amen, I say to
you that you who have followed Me, in the Resurrection, when the Son of Man shall sit upon the throne
of His majesty, shall sit on twelve thrones judging
the twelve tribes of Israel. And every one who
shall have left home, or brethren, or sisters, or
father, or mother, or wife, or children, or lands for
My Name shall receive a hundred-fold in the present
life, with persecutions, and shall possess everlasting
life."

At first hearing, this question of St. Peter's seems
to spring from a sentiment altogether opposite to
that which is expressed in the words:

Ah! Christ, if there were no hereafter,
It still were best to follow Thee;

and to that which taught Aquinas to answer the
question: "What reward wilt thou have?" with,
"None other than Thyself, Lord;" and which made
à Kempis cry out: "I had rather be a stranger
upon earth with Thee, than possess Heaven without
Thee. Where Thou art, there is Heaven;" and taught
St. Francis Xavier to sing: "My God, I love Thee,
not because I hope for Heaven thereby;" and even
which broke from the lips of Peter himself when he
cried, "Lord, though all men should forsake Thee,
yet not I. I will lay down my life for Thee; I am
ready to go with Thee to prison and to death"—as
though he would say: "Better to fail with Thee,
than to triumph without Thee; Truth is none the

less great even should it never prevail, and the gloom of Calvary no less glorious than the brightness of Thabor."

And so if we look closely into the matter we shall find that the very form in which he puts his seemingly ignoble question, exculpates him from all ignoble intent. " Lo, we have left all and followed Thee; what therefore shall be unto us?" Evidently then, when they left all and followed Him, they were moved by no definite prospect of other gain, and it is only some considerable time after the event that human prudence wakes for a moment from its dream, to seek reason for what has been done unreasoningly, in defiance of worldly wisdom, in a sudden burst of Divine enthusiasm. There was no reasoning or calculating, no *quid erit nobis?* when, at a word, or a glance, they left all and rose up and followed Him, lured away from home and kindred and possessions by the spell of His wondrous personality, by the irresistible magnetism which draws the soul back to the bosom of God, whence it came. He Himself was that hundred-fold beside whom all gain seemed but loss, whose possession secured an immutable peace in the midst of the bitterest persecution and temptation; He was that pearl of great price, cheaply purchased at the sacrifice of home and brethren and sisters and father and mother and wife and children and lands. Nor did they pause to think, as they let go everything to grasp at that treasure, whether it was to be the possession of a moment or of eternity. Love does not reason or reckon, but leaps up to follow

the Beloved blindfold "whithersoever He goeth,"
whether to prison and to death, or to victory and
life. "Where Thou goest," it seems to say, "I will
go; where Thou lodgest, I will lodge; where Thou
diest, I will die, and there also will I be buried."
Who has ever heard of any true human love which
tempered its sacrifices according to length of golden
days presumably in store for it; or which regulated
its fervour on the principles which govern life-
insurance; or who can believe that St. Peter's
enthusiasm would have been damped in any degree
had the cause of Christ been doomed to failure,
rather than to eternal victory? *Eamus et nos*, he
would have said, *et moriamur cum illo*—"Let us
also go and die with Him." Have not thousands
of heroes counted it gain to face death and defeat
beside a loved leader; and has any leader ever been
loved as Christ was?   •

It was for His own sake that they left all and
followed Him, and not for the sake of aught He
might give them. He Himself was the gift. But later,
when they heard our Saviour saying, "Go, sell what
thou hast and give to the poor, and thou shalt have
treasure in Heaven, and then come and follow Me,"
they wondered what this treasure in Heaven might
be which was promised to those who should do
what they had already done. And what, in effect,
was it, but to be with Christ in His triumph as they
were to be with Him in His defeat; what, but the
eternal prolongation of the bliss which they had
already entered upon? It was because they sought
nothing that they were to gain everything; because

in blind obedience to the call of love they left all,
that they were to find all—a hundred-fold in this
life, in spite of persecutions, and in the world to
come life everlasting; for in choosing Christ they
chose a treasure infinite and eternal, albeit they
knew it but indistinctly.

"One day in Thy courts," says David, "is better
than a thousand;" one instant of eternal life better
than a century of time; one kiss from the lips of
God better than unending ages of the tenderest
human affection. And this were true even were it
not equally true that the embrace of the Creator
locks the soul to God's bosom for ever and for ever.

If it is better to have been a man for a few brief
years, than a toad slumbering through a century or
more in the heart of a tree, it is also better to have
lived the highest life of the soul, to have breathed
the atmosphere of Heaven for even one day, than to
have passed a whole lifetime on a base or even on a
lower level,—

> One crowded hour of glorious life
> Is worth an age without a name.

How many lives have been ennobled, redeemed from
insignificance by the heroism or the inspiration of a
moment, or of a few moments, which has made
them immortal. How often have the stains of a
worldly or wicked career been wiped out by some
single purgatorial act of sacrificial unselfishness?
Have we not all moments of clear insight or high
aspiration which are more precious to us than
weeks and months of our normal mediocrity? Is

it not by the recognition of this that the Church is
rightly excused from the charge of prodigality and
extravagance when she crowns a momentary act of
pure love or Divine sorrow with the plenitude of
her absolution and indulgence?

Can we then doubt that if friendship with Christ,
the God-Man, be the highest life of which the soul
of man is capable, it must then be a good beyond
every other good, and one for which every other
should be sacrificed, since we should not attempt to
measure quantitatively, one against another, things
of a wholly different order. As a moment's thought
exceeds a life-time of sensation, so the briefest
experience of Divine friendship outweighs in solid
value all other possible experiences in a lower plane.
*Senectus enim venerabilis est non diuturna, nec annorum
numero computata. Cani enim sunt sensus hominis et
ætas senectutis vita immaculata*—"Life is measured
by experience, and not by years." One instant of
that immaculate life which the soul lives as it flits
like a moth through the bright, all-consuming,
all-purifying flame of the Divine presence, one
moment of close union with the Eternal, the
"Ancient of Days," and it has lived with a fulness
of life all but Divine,—"made perfect in a little
space, it has accomplished the labour of many
years."

We have spoken so far of conscious personal
friendship with Christ, as being the essence of this
higher life whose value were no less supreme, even
were it but of briefest duration; and of which it
may most truly be said,

'Tis better to have loved and lost
Than never to have loved at all.

But our concern here is rather with what we might call the unconscious friendship with Christ of those who walk with Him by the way, their hearts burning within them, though their eyes are holden so that they know Him not; those namely, who, not knowing Christ, yet to some greater or less extent live the life of Christ; who, not having the Gospel, are imbued with the principles and sentiments of the Gospel, being a Gospel unto themselves; who perhaps obscurely hear Him and feel Him guiding them through the voice of conscience—as the unseen Shepherd and Bishop of their souls, ever walking with them in the way; in a word, those *animæ naturaliter Christianæ* which the spirit of Christ fashions to His likeness in all ages and climes.

Can it then be said, speaking of the life and way of Christ, rather than of Christ Himself,

Ah ! Christ, if there were no hereafter,
It still were best to follow Thee,

it still were best, apart from all distinct recognition of that Heavenly Friend who *is* the Way, the Truth, and the Life, to walk in the narrow way of the Cross, to hold that truth, to live that life, for its own sake?

Needless to say, there have been many stoics and even professed Christians who have maintained that virtue is its own reward, apart from all its profitable consequences here or hereafter; so that if we assume, as well we may, that Christ gives us the very highest pattern of virtue, we can compel such thinkers at least to admit that to follow Christ were best even if there were no hereafter. Nevertheless, there are certain latent fallacies in their fundamental tenet which make us a little chary of such allies,—fallacies, however, rather in the analysis and expression of their sentiment, than in the sentiment itself, which, rightly apprehended, is the noblest we are capable of.

There is a certain proud, pharisaic self-sufficiency that may lead a man to seek virtue, not for virtue's sake, but for his own sake, in a spirit of acquisitiveness and self-culture. Virtue may be sought merely as an adornment of an idolized self, being subordinated to self as a means to an end; even as the same type of character seeks learning and artistic skill, not for love of their inherent excellence, nor even for their advantageous results, but simply because self must have the best of everything. As the pagan cultivated his body by gymnastics and made it obedient to his will, so by virtue he sought to secure a mastery over his spiritual faculties, enabling him to conduct himself skilfully and successfully through the warfare of life. If he was ashamed of a shambling gait, he was still more, but in much the same way, ashamed of intemperance or any other want of self-control. This was, in one sense, seeking virtue for its own sake, for its inherent excellence. Yet in that it made self the best-loved and ultimate end for whose sake virtue was loved, it was not really a pure love of virtue as of something greater than self, to which self should be submitted as a servant or slave. True, it was no small wisdom to reckon virtue as the best of acquisitions, the highest subjective perfection, to seek it, not as a means to any other less worthy acquisition, such as wealth or honour, and, so far, for its own sake; but it is only when truth and virtue are recognized in a more or less obscure way as having some strange, absolute claim over us, some objective right altogether irrespective of our private interest or subjective well-being, that they are strictly sought for their own sake, as ultimate ends to which self is wholly subordinated.

To the superficial this would seem to be a fallacy of the imagination, decreeing divine honours to personified abstractions writ large, leading the poet to an idolatrous worship of Beauty, the philosopher and moralist to the worship of Truth and Virtue. But on closer thinking, we have here but a confused recognition of the imperative authority of Conscience, which tells us that we are by nature but instruments for the working out of an end communicated to us in detail in our own reason, but conceived in its entirety only in the mind of that subsistent personal Reason whose creatures we are, and who guides and moves us through Conscience for the execution of His will—the will, namely, of the living and subsistent Truth and Goodness. Hence every good man, however dark or confused his theology may be, feels a conviction that the cause of Truth and Right has a claim upon him to which every private gain and pleasure must be sacrificed; that they are universal ends which he must prefer to all particular ends. He cannot resist the indistinct impression that in trespassing against Truth and Right, he is violating not merely a possible harmony and order, but a harmony and order actually willed by a will other than his own, a will with which he therefore comes into a relation of hostility and conflict.

Wheresoever conscience is awakened even to this extent, it is universally confessed that Truth and Right are to be followed for their own sakes, and apart from all other considerations of advantage; although when once we recognize that they are personal and not mere personifications, then "Truth for its own sake," means "God for His own sake."

It is sometimes contended that the joy which springs from the sense of having done right (that is, interpretatively, from a sense of union with God), and which is after all a subjective pleasure, however spiritual and exquisite, is the true and only motive of such conduct; and that it is because this pleasure outbalances all the pleasures of wrong-doing that some refined natures find virtue the best investment for yielding good interest in the way of enjoyment.

But, in the first place, it is those who act conscientiously as a matter of course and habitually, who are least sensitive to any particular glow of self-satisfaction when they do well; as, on the other hand, it is the oldest and hardest sinners who are most utterly dead to all sense of uneasiness and remorse. An act of virtue is one by which we chose to do what is right because it is right, and not because it is pleasant; virtue sought for the sake of the afterglow is not virtue at all, but the subtlest self-love. That same sweetness may be foreseen as a side issue, and may even be desired secondarily; but as soon as it diverts the soul's eye from its direct intuition of right for right's sake, and becomes itself the direct end to which virtue is but a means, then virtue is dishonoured and its supreme claims are disallowed.

Besides, human nature is, after all, calumniated by this quasi-hedomist view of the matter; and every really good and virtuous man, and every man in his really good and virtuous acts, implicitly confesses the truth:

> Ah! Christ, if there were no hereafter,
> It still were best to follow Thee.

It may even be said that in this, the verdict of the purer and nobler refinements on Epicureanism is not different from that of the higher stoicism. It is possible to take the grosser sense of the maxim, "Let us eat and drink, for to-morrow we die," as a summary of historical Epicureanism; but in the abstract this grossness is no essential part or product of the theory, and is indignantly repudiated by its most authoritative exponents. "*Carpe diem,* live each moment in the best way possible, get all you can out of it, as though it were your first and last, make the very most of every atom of time, so as to live as fully as possible, to taste and experience all that is really best while it is within your reach." This is the cardinal principle, rather than any final view as to the precise nature of the "best" in question. To regard sensual pleasure, or any lower sort of enjoyment, as the best and ideal form of experience, is, theoretically at least, no necessary part of this philosophy. So far, at all events, there is an accord between Epicurean and Christian teachers as to the supreme and in some sense independent value of each present moment of experience viewed in its isolation. If there be a duty of looking back to the past and forward to the future, in order that we may make the very most of the present, there is also a dreamy, profitless retrospection, full of vain regrets over what is sealed up and irremediable, and an impossible or excessive straining into the future with anxious eyes and doubting heart, which is altogether contrary to the virtue of Christian hope. Each little act of the saint is idealized, at least by the end to which it is directed; at every point of his conscious existence he can, if he will, touch the highest, living the soul's fullest life, an eternal life, each instant as it passes. This is the lesson of three lives lived at Nazareth, and of thousands fashioned to the same type.

The very sorrows and crosses of life, borne rightly, have a sweetness of their own known to the elect few; even as what is biting and severe to ordinary taste, pleases the discriminating palate, or as seeming discords are harmonious to the trained ear. Surely none ever tasted life so deeply, so fully, as the Man of sorrow and tears; and if there never was sorrow like unto His sorrow, neither was there ever a secret joy like unto His joy—the joy of a soul that loves widely, deeply, and utters its love in suffering. Take the world as it is, with its sorrowing and afflicted millions—what life were so full, so glorious, so joyful in the midst of sorrow, as the life of one who should love all with a passionate devotion, who should seek and find relief in suffering for all.

Thus, following in His wake whose meat was to do the Father's will and to perfect His work while it was yet day ere the night came on, the saints have made the maxim of carnal prudence their own in a mystic and spiritual sense: " Let us eat and drink, for to-morrow we die." Christ is that food and Christ is that drink. In expressing Christ, or the Christian ideal, in every moment of its activity, the soul lives its highest and most blessed life; it snatches the passing "now," that acceptable time, that day of salvation, doing with its might, in the highest and noblest way, all that its hand finds to do, working while it is yet day, ere the night cometh wherein no man can work.[1]

The real fault of even the most refined form of Epicureanism seems to be the tendency to luxuriate in the sensation of satisfaction which accompanies the highest life, and to pervert this side issue into an end; to practise self-sacrifice, not for its own sake, but for the exquisite pleasure consequent on the thought that we have acted nobly or beautifully.

[1] Cf.   " ' Live while you live,' the Epicure would say,
     And taste the pleasures of the passing day;
   ' Live while you live,' the sacred preacher cries,
     And give to God each moment as it flies;
   Lord, in my life let both united be,
   I live to pleasure if I live to Thee."

As for the modern school of positivism, which claims Comte as its founder and exponent, it is avowedly in agreement with the principle for which we are contending. For all to whom kindness is the noblest and sweetest use of life, to whom it is its own reward, are agreed that even if there were no hereafter, yet of all lives the life of altruism is the best. Mill and others have hopelessly failed in their attempt to show that altruism and real unselfishness are mere refinements of self-seeking; for in truth the "other-regarding" instinct of our soul is as irreducible and as primitive as the "self-regarding," nay, more so. Nature's first care and deepest implanted impulse is for the specific and common good, to which the good of the individual but ministers. That apart from Divine sanctions, but few would embrace the life of altruistic self-sacrifice, does not make it less true that it were the best life to embrace. Few know where true happiness is to be found. In philosophy, as in faith, strait is the gate and narrow the way that leads to life, and few there be that find it for themselves, if they are not taught and guided. Our chief quarrel with positivism is that, while rightly insisting on the promotion of human happiness, it evades the difficulty of defining that happiness; or still worse, it places it in conditions that can never possibly be realized on earth for the great majority of mankind. It deludes us with the hopes of some distant terrestrial paradise as unsubstantial as fairy-land. Christ, on the other hand, tells us with terrible frankness that there is no escape from the

Cross, and that all we can do is to learn to love it, and to utilize its hidden healing power. He does not beguile us with the fond fancy that this earth will one day cease to bring forth thorns and briers, but teaches us to plait them into garlands. *Ecce Homo!* Behold the perfect man, the perfect human life, the life of mighty love uttering itself in the endurance of pain and sorrow and humiliation!

For we cannot, as Catholics, agree with those who would commend the Way of the Cross as the best, simply because it leads to Heaven in a life after this; or even because, being the way chosen by Christ, it derives an extrinsic honourableness from Him. We hold rather that, taking this finite world *as it is*, the Way of the Cross is, *in the nature of things*, the most perfect way, the best way, the way most befitting the highest capacities of the human mind and heart. It is not the best because it leads to Heaven, or because Christ chose it; but contrariwise, Christ chose it, and God rewards it, because it is the best. It is *par excellence* the way and the truth and the life, by which alone man comes to the Father and puts on divinity and immortality. So far as the rewards attached to the following of Christ are in any sense additional to its natural consequences, it is because, that life being the best, God wills to crown it and make it still better—*Habenti dabitur.*

To return, then, to St. Paul. Truth, however seemingly many-membered, as apprehended piecemeal by us, in itself is one and simple. Let a single article of the Catholic creed be tampered with, and

the whole fabric crumbles to ruin. The glorious
Resurrection of Christ and His saints from the
dead, is the seal of Divine approval set on the
eternal worthfulness of the Way which He walked,
the Truth which He taught, the Life which He
lived. It is the sign, not the cause, of that worthfulness, which, moreover, needs this Divine affirma-
tion and sanction for the sake of the many whose
eyes are too weak to discern the secret beauty
revealed to the chosen disciples of the Cross. Nay,
even the faith of these is ever apt to fail, is ever
failing, in a world to which Christ is a fool and
His Cross folly; and in hours of darkness and
weakness—

> When our light is low,
> When the blood creeps and the nerves prick
> And tingle; and the heart is sick
> And all the wheels of being slow—

in such hours we need a Divine assurance that our
faith is not vain; that we are not mere dreamers,
in love with the fictions of our own fancy, as we
might be tempted to think were it not that our
trembling soul is steadied by the solid fact of the
resurrection, which assures us that God judges as
we judge, and that our reason is true to the Divine
Reason when we say:

> Ah! Christ, if there were no hereafter,
> It still were best to follow Thee.
> Tears are a nobler gift than laughter;
> Who wears Thy yoke alone were free.

THE LIFE EVERLASTING.

Locum refrigerii, lucis, et pacis.
"A place of refreshment, of light, and of peace."

Canon of the Mass.

I.

AMONGST the other outworks and safeguards of Divine charity, we must number a longing and desire for Heaven. Heaven is counted among those four "last things" which are to be the theme of deep and continual meditation. As we should pray for an abiding fear of Hell, so also should we pray for an ardent desire of Heaven, lest at any time our love of God having grown cold and feeble, we should need the assistance of a motive appealing directly to our rational self-regard. For though Heaven consists substantially and principally in the love of God, wherein our soul reaches its highest perfection and happiness, yet this desire for our own happiness remains strong and intact even when we have ceased to identify our happiness with the possession of God. Charity is a purely unselfish, "unselfing" virtue, whose object is God and God's glory, whose motive is God's inherent goodness and beauty; but holy hope is self-regarding—wisely, rightly, supernaturally—it looks to our own perfection and happiness, which, as we have said, is rightly to be found in Divine charity. Charity then is the object of Christian hope; or, as we say, "grace here and glory hereafter"—grace being the seed, and glory the full-blown flower of Divine love. Our happiness lies in unselfish love, in forgetting ourselves and living in God, and in our fellow-man. Hence, true, wise self-regard bids us cease to regard ourselves, or rather to take a truer and wiser view of ourselves, to recognize that we are made, not for ourselves, but to be members of God and of one another; for a collective life, love, praise, and joy.

Thus when our love of God is growing cold, it is well for us to appeal to our rational self-love; to remind ourselves that His ways are ways of pleasantness and all His paths are peace; that, eventually, the yoke of the Cross is easy and the burden light compared with the galling yoke of sin; that the steep and narrow way of unselfishness leads to fuller life and joy; while the broad, easy, down-hill, selfish road ends in destruction, death, and misery. For when we have ceased to love, we can still remember the joy that we found in loving, and long to be able to love once more.

And if even on earth we find our substantial peace and joy in the love and friendship of God, in unselfish service and devotion to His mystical members, we may well find a strong motive for perseverance in the prospect of the marvellous amplification which that charity will receive when it breaks through the sod into the light and sunshine of eternity and unfolds its latent treasure of leaf and flower, of colour, form, and fragrance.

We assume as a first principle that man was made to praise God, and that this life of praise is here but rudimentary or germinal; that our present mortal state is essentially embryonic,—a time of development and growth; a time of trial and combat. Man's life on earth is a warfare. Warfare is essentially a transitional state, being eventually a means to secure a fuller peace. All evolution and growth is attended with great pain and suffering. Nature herself is said to be groaning and travailing, expecting her deliverance. This is the Christian view of the present life—a view abundantly denied by the world and by the worldly. Man was created, not for this world, but for the next; just as the grub does not exist for its present larval condition of life, but for its final life of winged liberty.

This in no way countenances the heresy which denies all value to our natural and temporal existence, as though it had no reference to the next world or were not altogether subordinated and directed to it. At the other extreme, we have the base view of utilitarian Christianity, which believes, indeed, in the life to come, yet subordinates it to the present life, as though it were merely a sanction, a bribe, or a threat to secure such conduct as conduces to social and individual welfare and prosperity in the present world; thus making, so to say, eternity a useful appendix to time, instead of regarding time as but the preface or prelude to eternity. This is a view well according with the Erastian form of Christianity fairly prevalent in this

Protestant country, where the Church is regarded as a function of the State, subservient to social and political ends, its work being to secure those public virtues indispensable to commercial success and to civic tranquillity and health. This it is to effect by godly doctrine, and by an insistence on that almost pagan aspect of the Deity which views Him as a "State-God," as a God concerned, not principally with the sanctification of individuals, but with the national greatness and prosperity. Such is, of course, the teaching of Hobbes and the British philosophers of the Protestant era, who subordinate the individual to the State, as though the State could have any other *raison d'être* but the perfection of its members distributively and individually. It is altogether in harmony with such a thought to regard Heaven and Hell and the life to come, as mere sanctions to secure good conduct in the present life, as means to that end; in a word, to invert the true order of things.

It is because we live in such an atmosphere of unbelief and misbelief that we ourselves come to be so listless about Heaven; or even to think it something spiritually imperfect to dwell much upon the theme, lest we should be reproached with holding a "reward-and-punishment" Christianity; a reproach which Erastianism has, not unreasonably, earned, and which unfortunately is extended to Catholic Christianity by those who are as ignorant of that religion as South Sea islanders.

We are also to some extent affected by the purist or quietist fallacies of certain Catholic

writers, or by our false understanding of the sentiments of others who have written and spoken truly
enough of the self-forgetful nature of perfect love.
We think that, because hope and fear are in some
sense cast out by perfect love, that we should not
concern ourselves much about them, but should
regard them as transient phases of our spiritual
evolution, as "the things of a child," to be put
away by those who have reached manhood's
maturity.

Yet, in very truth, both hope and fear are so
indissolubly connected with love that they all grow
pari passu. Fear, as we have elsewhere said, is the
very fibre and backbone of reverential love, being
begotten of a sense of God's greatness, justice,
power, indignation, and other "masculine" attributes, which very attributes are components of His
lovableness, since what wins our love is the thought
that one so great should love one so little, that
one so high should stoop so low, that one so
great should be so merciful, that so strong and
invincible an indignation should be chained down in
the bonds of a love yet stronger and more invincible.
And thus in the saints the measure of love has
always been the measure of fear,—albeit their fear is
no longer servile when it has given birth to love and
when love is matured so as no longer to need the
aid of servile fear, but to be itself an all-sufficient
spring of action. It is not fear but, as Aquinas·
says, the servility of fear which is cast out by
perfect love.

And so with holy hope, as far as it too is in·

some sense servile and self-regarding; bound and not free; narrow and not universal. This servility of hope is cast out by perfect love; though hope itself grows pace for pace with love. It is the rational desire of our own highest happiness and of our spiritual development that makes us seek to become unselfish and full of self-forgetting charity. We come to recognize that our own happiness must never be the direct object of our quest; that it is by resigning it, by ceasing to seek for it, nay, by sacrificing it, that we best secure it. "He that seeketh his life shall lose it; he that loseth his life shall save it." Happiness comes to us as a side issue of a nobler end, and surprises us by its presence just when we have at last succeeded in putting it out of our heads as an object of consideration. Even then, if we dwell on it, caress it, foster it, and try to retain it, it eludes us like our own shadow; so coy is happiness, the child of self-forgetting love.

Their hope is undoubtedly the keenest and strongest who have tasted the peace of God which passes all understanding, who have known the happiness of unselfish love,—if by hope we mean placing our whole happiness, our heart's supreme treasure, in God. Hope and fear alike are strongest when love is strongest. The more we realize the loveliness of God the more must we long for Him, that is, long to love Him more.

The quietist view falsely supposes that all self-regard is selfishness in the bad sense. But, in truth, these two fundamental, self-regarding impulses of hope and fear, even in their imperfect or servile form, are not only blameless but laudable. The tendency towards self-good, self-evolution, and private interest is a force which, unlimited and unrestrained, would tend to lawlessness and evil; but governed by a higher law and love to which it subserves, it is altogether right and helpful. Nature never intended it to be a free force; but one essentially destined to subjection and bondage to a higher force. Under the guidance of God the self-seeking instinct of the individual brute-animal is subservient and conducive to a wider interest, namely, the good of the species, which is God's more principal care. And this is no less true of man's spiritual self-seeking instinct. Thus, for example, there is no positive selfishness in the conduct of one who is occupied wholly with fitting himself and his family to fill creditably their due station in society, albeit he does not explicitly think of or intend the general social good thence resulting. But if, in the pursuit of wealth and culture he implicitly or explicitly excludes the desire to benefit society, if he injures others by injustice or cruelty, or if he otherwise impedes their due prosperity, he is positively selfish and formally hurtful to the common welfare. If, on the other hand, he explicitly adverts to the bearing of his own on the public advantage, if he intends the latter so principally that he would freely forego his private gain for the sake of the general welfare, then he is positively unselfish, and uses his natural self-regarding impulse for that very end for which it was given him, and in the way in which it was intended to be used, that is, to facilitate the fulfilment of his first and highest duty—his duty to God and to God's interest in human society. Thus, too, we say that all the virtues subordinate to charity, such as mercifulness, temperance, purity, and the rest, are not useless because charity includes the aim of all others; but their work is to facilitate the designs of charity, who governs them all as her ministers.

Hope and fear, therefore, are the ministers of Divine love, governing us in its absence or during its minority; serving it when it is present.

There is another form of self-regard which, far from being selfish, is pure unselfishness, namely, the self-regard of him who has died to himself, who has put on a wider self, who has merged his being and life, his sorrow and joy, his interests, his hopes, his fears in those of Christ and of the children of Christ, his fellow-members in Christ's Mystical Body. For it is the self-regard of one who really and adequately knows himself—what he is by nature and by God's intention; who knows that he is not for himself but for others; that he is God's instrument before all else—intended primarily for God and God's Kingdom, and that he is to secure his own happiness in the universal happiness which he shares. But plainly it is only by a violent non-natural use of language that we can call this, "self-regard," while to call it selfishness were absurd. This deepest appetite of our spirit which demands a Divine and universal happiness for its food, is indeed within us. It is ours, and yet it is ours precisely in virtue of our essential subordination to God as instruments of

His universal purpose, and as moved by His will, even as the members are guided by the head to an end of which they have no consciousness. Man, indeed, being intelligent, comes gradually to understand the *whence* and *whither* of his extra-regarding instincts; he comes to recognize them as the will of God working in him, and to throw himself freely into sympathy with them and to obey them as Divine behests conveyed to him by the voice of conscience. It is then only that man knows himself, recognizes his true self, and no longer lives for that false, separate self, but for the self which is merged into God.

II.

St. Paul tells us that the saints of God when on earth were as strangers and pilgrims, having here no abiding city, looking for "the City that hath foundations," no mere encampment in the desert, but Jerusalem, the city of peace, founded on the everlasting hills, immovable as the Eternal Rock, "whose builder and maker is God." They were as one in a foreign country on some brief business, where the faces, the language, the ways are strange, uncongenial, repugnant; whose heart is elsewhere, who impatiently counts the days and hours which must pass before he can gather his effects together and hurry to that goal of his desires called *home.* "Strangers and pilgrims;" strangers to all around them, awkward and out of place, as one of noble and refined nature whose lot has cast him with the vulgar and semi-barbarous, who,

M

notwithstanding, have their own curious code of honour and etiquette, or what corresponds to such. " Pilgrims," moreover, for they never stay their homeward march for a moment, seeing in this life the ladder that leads them upward step by step to the face of God, to their *Patria*—the dwelling of their Father who is in Heaven.

And if we speak of this *Patria* in terms of place, as a pilgrimage from earth to Heaven ; or in terms of time, as a passing from the present to the future life, we but figure forth the process by which the soul is transformed from the death of nothingness whence it was drawn, into the fulness of life in the bosom of the Father whither it is drawn. For if our Father is in Heaven, our Heaven is also in the Father ; nay, our Father is Heaven. We speak indifferently of our entry into God's Kingdom,[1] or of the advent of God's Kingdom into us ; for in substance Heaven is the absolute domination of Divine love over the soul whose eyes, first opened in this dim cavern of time, have been taught to bear the growing brightness until at last they have dared to fix their steadfast gaze upon the very source of all light—the True Light which enlighteneth every man that cometh into the world.

In each of its free acts the soul tries, then and there, to realize itself, to enter into that beatitude

---

[1] Cf. " Licet gaudium æternæ beatitudinis in cor hominis intret, maluit tamen Dominus ei dicere : Intra in gaudium ; ut mystice innuatur, quod gaudium illud non solum in eo sit intra, sed undique illum circumdans et absorbens et ipsum velut abyssus infinita submergens." (St. Bernardine of Siena, *Serm. de St. Joseph.*)

which it dimly conceives, and by the desire of which it is moved and governed continually. It is as a caged bird whose every fruitless struggle and effort aims at perfect liberty, and cries out: "Who will give me the wings of a dove? then would I fly away and be at rest;" for it is this dream of rest which is the motive of all our action, and labour, and strife. No two conceive quite the same notion of rest for their souls. Many conceive it altogether amiss; others, with Augustine, look only to God, and cry: "Our heart is restless, Lord, till it rest in Thee;" but all alike are dominated in every free act by some such End or Ideal or Final Rest struggling to be born in them—be it true rest or false: be it Heaven or Hell. All are striving to pass from time to eternity; from restlessness to repose; from a state of change to an unchanging state; from their pilgrimage to their home; from the tent-city of nomads to the "city that hath foundations." Our free actions may be likened to the blows of some engine of war which beat and beat against a fortress gate till one of them at last realizes what all the rest, of their very nature and purpose, tended to realize, or which any of them might have realized. So each free act by itself is governed and informed or at least checked by the latent presence in the soul of an ideal of rest, of happiness, of home, which it abortively tries to realize, but which some last act will alone succeed in realizing. On the direction of that last act after which we pass into our timeless, changeless state, all depends.

The saints, then, on earth have ever echoed the

aspiration of St. Paul: *Cupio dissolvi*—" I long to be dissolved and to be with Christ," to be uncaged and fly away and be at rest. The first instinct of love is to seek the closer company of the Beloved, to enjoy His sweet converse, to lean on His breast at supper, to sit at His feet and hear His words. And as love grows, this instinct becomes more urgent and imperious, more painful and galling when thwarted; and yet the very strength of unselfish love nerves the soul to endure the bitterness of separation in the interests of the Beloved. If for his own sake Paul longed to be released and to be with Christ, yet for the sake of Christ and Christ's little ones he was content to remain, and to remain for ever, were it needful for their confirmation and consolation.[1]   And this was the love of the glorious St. Martin when he prayed, " Lord, if I am needed for Thy people, I do not begrudge the labour; " and of the Blessed Mother herself, who willingly lingered in exile after her Son's ascension that she might be to the infant Church all that she had been to Him. *Coarctor e duobus*—St. Paul is on the rack between these two desires which are born and grow and strengthen together; between the claims of the individual member and those of the whole body; between supernatural self-regarding tendencies, and the demands of charity and unselfish love which in certain adjuncts require the repression and mortification of the former.   Thus in our time of pilgrimage—*dum peregrinamur a Domino*—the tension and the pain is, or should be, ever on the increase,

[1] Philipp. i. 23—25.

according as the conflicting desires—the desire to stay and the desire to go—grow stronger. "But when that which is perfect is come, then that which is in part shall be done away," the interests of both tendencies shall coincide, "and there shall be no more sorrow," no more *coarctatio e duobus.*

Further, this very "longing to depart and be with Christ" is of itself blind and self-defeating, and a more clear-sighted self-regard will be prudent to see that the interests of hope and charity are in truth identical, and that the self-restraint and self-denial involved in the submission of the single member to the whole Body, is really for its eventual and more lasting well-being. He whose love leads him to mortify the present "longing to depart" strengthens and deepens that longing with every new exercise of love, and strains more tightly the tension of that bond which at the instant of release will draw him to the bosom of God, to the embrace of Christ:

> O days and hours your work is this,
> To hold me from my proper place,
> A little while from his embrace,
> For fuller gain of after-bliss.

No will or appetite, however high or holy, can be obeyed blindly and without limit, save only the will and love of God. Every other wish and interest must be stayed, and questioned, and examined by that sovereign rule and law in subjection to which it eventually finds its most solid gain. Else its rebellious impetuosity is self-defeating, and a series of ever-weakening present ecstasies ends in a total enfeeblement and degradation of the impulse.

Never, therefore, may the desire to be with Christ, viewed as our own personal rest and separate gain, be supreme and unqualified. It must always be subordinate to love, whose minister and child it is: "Father, if it be possible—yet not my will but Thy will be done." But as an accelerating and secondary motive it can never be too strong. Thus it is in all true, pure, reverential human love, which is ever willing to bear pain, even the pain of separation— the greatest of all pains, the last and hardest sacrifice. It is no pure or unselfish love which basks in the presence of a spouse or child, in the warm glow of domestic affection, when their true interest, as well as the will of God, demands that heart-strings should be rent on both sides and the keen sword of separation endured unflinchingly. It is the stronger and nobler love which both nerves to the sacrifice, and sacrifices most; which suffers most acutely, and yet most readily.

It is in conformity with all that has been said that we read how our Divine Saviour, "for the joy that was set before Him, endured the Cross and despised the shame." Not as though this personal, and in some sense private joy and glory, were the leading or principal motive of His endurance. That motive was the love of the Father, of the Father's will and the Father's Kingdom. Yet so far as the Cross and the shame were grievous to the weakness of the flesh, their burden was lightened or counter-poised by the prospect of a more than compensating joy and glory. So it is St. Paul balances the light and momentary afflictions of this life against the great weight of eternal glory in the future, and finds the former in comparison not worthy of consideration. It is the "What doth it profit?" motive in another form—not the highest motive, but subsidiary to the highest; not love, but the prop and fence of love. And he tells us how this saint and that suffered various torments and privations "looking to the reward"—*Adspiciebat enim in remunerationem; i.e.*, not disdaining to enlist the services of prudent and supernatural self-regard in the cause of love—thus counteracting the weakness of the shrinking flesh.

And, after all, what is this reward that Christ and His saints looked forward to? Surely no selfish or isolated joy; but the joy of one who lives for others, and in others, and makes their happiness his own; who finds—though he does not seek—his own reward in the attainment of his unselfish ends. It is not his own paltry share in the booty, but the glory and triumph of his country that animates the loyal soldier to bravery. That is the joy that he sets before him. He knows that even his own personal share in the general triumph, the mere gratification of his passionate patriotism, will more than repay the toils and wounds and perils of the present moment. Similarly, he who is wise enough to see that in unselfishness and self-forgetfulness lies the shortest road to private happiness, knows well that in losing his life he is saving it; and though private happiness is not his direct aim, yet with the assured expectation of it he can quiet the rebellious clamours of short-sighted self-love.

Such was the joy that Christ set before Himself;

the joy of the Father, the joy of the whole body of the redeemed, of His Blessed Mother, of all the angels and saints; that common joy whereof He was the cause, and wherein, as Head of the Mystic Body, He was to be chief participant; that *Gaudium Domini* into which the saints enter, as members enter into the life of the head.

How impossible, then, for them not to long and cry out for that consummation of all their desires; for that full and perfect possession of God, or rather possession by God, which is the very substance of Heaven—all accessory and accidental joy being but the setting of that "Pearl of great price," the Kingdom of God in the heart. "Oh, how lovable are Thy dwellings, Thou Lord of hosts," cries David; "my soul hath a desire and longing to enter into the courts of the Lord; my heart and my flesh rejoice in the living God. . . . Blessed are they that dwell in Thy house." And why blessed? "They will be always praising Thee," always entering into the life and joy and praise of their Lord; always fulfilling the end for which their soul was created and designed by Love. And again: "One day in Thy courts is better than a thousand;" the *now* of eternal "being," better than ages of imperfection and "becoming;" the joy of a single instant of that rest, than the accumulated joys of an endless pilgrimage. And, "As the hart longs for the water-springs, so longs my soul after Thee, O God. My soul is athirst for God the strong, the mighty; when shall I come and appear before the face of my God?"

We, on the other hand, know little of these longings. Far from feeling ourselves strangers and pilgrims on earth, we find ourselves only too much at home in this world; our surroundings are by no means very uncongenial; and if at times death seems welcome, it is rather in its negative aspect as an end of ills we know, than as an entrance into a life which has but feeble attraction for us.

This may be partly due to the dimness of our faith, which must almost necessarily languish in an age and country where it has lost the support of public acknowledgment and profession, where we feel that perhaps the majority of the cultured and educated question the very existence of a future life, or at most regard it as a tenable hypothesis, but in no way to be used as the governing principle of individual and social conduct. Partly it is to be ascribed to our own spiritual state and to the neglect of meditation on the mysteries of our holy religion. While in every other department of knowledge our interest leads us from stage to stage, from the puerilities of our first conceptions to a greater maturity of comprehension; here we remain content with the notions gathered in our childhood, which are no more suitable for our adult mind than is milk diet for strong men. We go through life with some child's dream of Heaven, as of a cloud-built city radiant with gold and colour and gleaming jewels, peopled with bright-winged beings, and with those whom we have loved here on earth; where God, too, has His throne of state and receives a service of sweet song, of fragrant incense, of ceremonious adoration. Nor do I say that our sensile imagination can ever rise beyond such gaudy symbolism when it endeavours to picture the unpicturable, and to make visible the invisible. Nor yet are we free to deny that with the risen and glorified body, there will be also a "new heaven and a new earth," in which this sensible and physical order of existence will endure in some spiritualized and transfigured condition as an instrument of Divine praise. But riper thought should teach us to see in these things only the outward symbols and accessories of the substantial joy of Heaven, which consists in the possession of God, in the Communion of the Saints; a joy which we begin to taste even here when the charity of God is diffused in our hearts by the Holy Ghost. Our reason working on our gathering self-experience should convince us that it is only in personal love, self-annihilating, adoring, unchanging, eternal, that our heart can find rest and happiness; and that Heaven is Heaven just because it offers us this. For what is Heaven but Eternal Life, an entering into the Life of the Eternal, through the unitive virtue of love. It is to see face to face that Beauty, the very hint of which, known as we here know it, by the rumour of faith or by the fringes of its garment, can kindle a love which devours the heart of the saints. If to hear of it can so dominate and subdue the soul, what must it be to behold it?

Nor let us forget what our faith teaches us as to our supernatural elevation to a destiny such as no introspection would ever remotely suggest. Reason alone might possibly verify the assertion that we were made to find happiness in some very close knowledge and love of God, shared in common with all the souls of the just made perfect. But faith tells us that by grace we are re-created for a more intimate union with the Divinity; not merely to know and love and rejoice in the same Divine Good wherein God rejoices, but in some sort to apprehend it with the same kind of act wherewith He apprehends it— an act which we call *knowledge* for want of a better name, just as at times we speak of understanding as *seeing*. It is principally by reason of this conformity to God in the *mode* of our knowledge and love and joy that we are said to enter into that life of the Eternal, "which eye hath not seen nor ear heard nor heart conceived."

And though in itself the Godhead is the same, whether it be viewed with the eye of the natural intellect or with the grace-anointed vision of the saints, yet the aspect it presents to the beholder, the impress it creates in him, the love it enkindles, is all other. Indeed, even in the order of natural vision, no two see quite the same beauty or are incited by it to a precisely similar affection. Still less can we compare the supernatural love and joy of the blessed with that of nature "unelevated."

And if we turn to the object of this vision and love, it is that same object of Divine self-praise wherein God rejoices and wherein all His saints rejoice, their joy and praise being, so to say, a created and finite reverberation of the uncreated and Infinite. It is found principally in the intrinsic glory and beauty of the Divinity Itself, and secondarily, in such communications of His glory as He has imparted to His saints, whom He has gathered round Him as a not unworthy crown of love's triumph—even as the Sun rays itself round with a halo of brightness. In all this He rejoices as the Sun in its own splendour. And each of the blessed rejoices with Him in this collective glory—self-forgetful, save so far as the glory of each is an element in the glory of all. And if to none of those blessed souls that glory is manifest as it can be only to the mind of the Infinite, and if to no two of them under the same aspect, yet there is a certain harmony in their knowledge and love and praise; each filling and complementing what is wanting to the other; each an essential part in a perfect mosaic; each necessary to the effect of the whole; all collectively making one mirror wherein God sees and loves Himself anew, one complex chord of everlasting praise; many eyes, yet but one vision; many hearts, yet but one love; many voices and tongues, yet but one song.

III.

If, however, our feeble mind soon wearies of the strain, when it would try to form some conception of that Eternal joy, that joy of the Eternal, which eye hath not seen nor ear heard nor heart conceived; if we can never form any real image to ourselves of what Heaven is, we can at least find rest and repose in the thought of what it is not. "God shall wipe away all tears from their eyes, and there shall be no more death, neither sorrow nor crying nor any more pain, . . . for the former things are passed away." And again : " They shall not hunger nor thirst any more ; nor shall the sun nor the heat beat upon them ; for the Lamb in their midst shall be their Shepherd, and shall lead them to the living water-springs." And once more : " Blessed are the dead who die in the Lord, for they shall rest from their labours."

When we look upon this ruin of a world, such as sin and its consequences have left it, we are still able to figure some image to ourselves of that Paradise which God intended to be the vestibule of Heaven, the place of man's light exile and easy probation. We can in some way conjecture what this earthly life would be were there no sin or selfishness, " no more death, nor crying, nor grief, nor pain," no fruitless spiritual longings, no darkness of ignorance and error, no wearisome toiling with sweat of the brow for the bare necessities of life. Even the poor relics of this ruin, how fair they are ! how we treasure them up as the art-lover does the stray fragments of some noble sculpture whose lines tell the tale of the beauty that belonged to the whole ! How lovely still is the face of nature; how sweet her myriad voices ! And man, with all his vileness and weakness, how lovable in spite of it, nay, because of it ! If God Himself delights to be with the children of men, if " our Maker is our husband " and lover, is it wonderful that we should be tempted to cling to one another—

As if our heaven and home were here.

And chief among the factors of our earthly happiness, that which binds together, preserves, purifies, strengthens the rest, is God Himself dwelling in us and in all around us, revealed to us in His works, communing with us in our inmost heart and conscience, imparting His light to our mind, His warmth to our heart, filling with peace and gladness those souls who willingly seek for Him with open ear and eye, and who most surely find Him far nearer than they ever dreamt. Take sin and its consequences away, and earth were indeed such a Paradise as might make us to cry out: "It is good for us to be here!" Yet it would be but the vestibule of Heaven; the shadow of the substance.

At times it may seem to us that we desire nothing but rest, the mere cessation of toil and pain, of sorrow and temptation, the mere "not-being" of annihilation. Millions profess with their lips that to desire is to suffer; that to be, is to desire; that it is alone by not-being that we can escape from suffering; that our wisest desire is to cease to desire and to cease to be; to be merged once more into the calm bosom of that nothingness whose surface is by some malign cause rippled for a moment and disturbed by our individuality and existence.

They do not discern that desire is woven of a double strand, namely, the love of an absent object, together with a sense of need,—the former pleasurable, the latter painful; or that desire makes not only for the cessation of the sense of pain, but principally for the fulfilment of love in the joy of possession and attainment.

If we desire the absence of pain, it is not this mere negation which attracts us. We cannot be attracted by nothing. The full object of our hope is our conscious, existing self in a state of freedom from pain. Even the unbelieving suicide is deluded by the imagination that he will be *conscious* of his deliverance from suffering, though his intellect may reject the doctrine of immortality. We cannot then arouse in ourselves a longing for Heaven by the mere prospect of negative rest, of no more death nor sorrow nor pain, but only by the prospect of a life immeasurably fuller and more lovable than this life would be were it once more transfigured into Paradise, and every weed and bramble of sin plucked up and destroyed. Even our present narrow, humble mode of existence is at times very sweet to us, when the removal of some passing bitterness has made us realize the blessing which before we unconsciously enjoyed. If, then, in its lower phases, a painless life can be so longed for, how much more the highest plenitude of being of which we are capable?

Lastly, Heaven is described in our liturgy as "a place of refreshment and of light and of peace;" which again must be understood as telling us both what it is not, and what it is. In this world God tries His saints in the fire of tribulation, temptation, persecution, even as gold is tried in the furnace. The noon-day sun scorches them, and the heat stifles and oppresses them. They are athirst with their battles and labours, with loss of blood. But there "the Lamb that is in their midst shall shepherd them, and lead them by the living water-springs," by that "pure river of the water of life, clear as crystal, proceeding from the throne of God and of the Lamb."

Here they are led blindfold by the hand of faith, or if they see aught, it is by the flickering, uncertain light of reason; their eyes are wearied and dim, straining through the gloom, and watching for the morning which seems so long in coming. God's ways are so puzzling, so mysterious, so incalculable, fooling our presumption the moment we pretend to have discovered their law. Here we can but cry out in our humility: "How incomprehensible are His judgments and His ways past finding out." But there the weary mind will at last repose in the full clear light of truth, and the doubts and difficulties will be forgotten, as the cloudlets that flecked the sky of a day long past. And if there is laughter in Heaven, it will be at the guesses and conjectures and vain theorizings of our child-life on earth, as now we laugh at the fancies of our early years. There "the city shall need no sun nor moon to enlighten it," no created or reflected light; "for the brightness of God hath illumined it and the Lamb is the Light thereof."

Here there is unending war: war with oneself, with the world, with the powers of darkness: *Militia vita hominis super terram.* "Never art thou secure in this life," says à Kempis, "but while thou livest thou wilt need thy spiritual armour; for thou art in the midst of enemies, and art assailed on the right hand and on the left." But there, there shall be peace at last: *Pax solida; pax imperturbabilis et*

secura; pax intus et foris; pax ex omnis parti firma—
"Solid peace, unshaken and unshakable, firm on every side, within and without."

"A place of refreshment, of light, and of peace"
—and why? Because it is the place of God, who is at once our Rest and Refreshment, our Light, our Peace; because it is the home of our Father who is in Heaven, and who is Himself our Heaven: *Ubi tu, ibi cœlum, atque ibi mors et infernus ubi tu non es*—
"Where God is, there is Heaven. Where God is not, there is Death and Hell."

And so we return to the starting-point, to the First Principle and Foundation, to the truth that man is created, not for earth, but for Heaven; not for time, but for Eternity; not for himself, but for Another; not for the creature, but for the Creator. "Thou hast made us for Thyself," says Augustine. "Thou hast made us"—God, our first Beginning. "For Thyself"—God, our last End.

"And our heart can find no rest till it rest in Thee."

N

THE ANGELIC VIRTUE.

Erunt sicut angeli Dei in cœlo.
"They shall be as the angels of God in Heaven."—
St. Matt. xxii. 30.

IT may be safely asserted that Catholic Christianity
has developed the idea of the virtue of purity and
emphasized its importance, to a degree previously
unknown to the world, and hardly now known
outside the limit of the Church's influence. Within
those limits, no doubt, are included many non-
Catholic Christians, and perhaps many whose
Christianity has been puzzled out of them, but
who still retain a practical veneration for its
moral ideas and are unconsciously imbued with
its instincts.

No doubt the intensity of the stress which the
Church lays upon this virtue finds its justification
in some of the deepest mysteries of faith. For
granted that impurity is a violation of the natural
dignity of man, it follows that every addition to
man's spiritual elevation increases the malice of
any act of defilement or profanation. Thus when
St. Paul says: "Lie not one to another, for ye are
members one of another," he does not mean to
give the ethical reason against lying, but he supposes

the malice of falsehood to be admitted on all hands, and adds a supernatural reason which makes it more odious among those who are united by special ties of fidelity as members of one mystical body. In like manner, Christian doctrine takes for granted that the law of reason condemns all.impurity, and then adds to the prohibition of reason other motives and sanctions drawn from revelation alone.

Still it must be confessed that, as in other matters of natural religion and morals, so more especially in this, revelation has helped reason by way of suggestion. A passage in some foreign language may be utterly beyond our comprehension and seem to us hopelessly tangled and faulty, and yet a glance at a translation puts everything in its right place and proves the confusion to have been purely subjective. So the revelation of natural truths enables us to see them by the light of reason —paradoxical as it may sound; or, if we saw them at all before, to see them now more clearly, to hold to them more firmly, and to penetrate to their further consequences. Besides, what would with difficulty have been within the grasp of the talented, leisured, industrious few, is now by revelation made " current coin " and the abiding heritage of all.

If then, remaining within the purely ethical order, we seem in some points to find but a frail support for the bold teaching and instincts of the Catholic Church in this matter of purity, it need not surprise us, since we find a like difficulty in justifying many of our other natural moral instincts and beliefs which we hold to none the less firmly, knowing well that more things are reasonable than reason can analyze or set out in form.

Yet there is hardly any point of the Catholic doctrine of purity, which mere reason does not to some extent bear out, while in no point can it be shown to be contrary to reason.

Before, however, examining the rational foundations upon which this body of teaching rests, we may give a brief glance at the buttresses and supports it receives from faith and revelation.

If the very inclinations of sensuality, which are natural to man regarded physiologically, are in the present order a fruit of original sin, then whatever natural unseemliness or disorder there may be in them is augmented and aggravated in so far as they are doubly against the Divine will. We suppose, for the present, that man advances from imperfection to perfection, and that since he rightly strives to obtain complete control over his passions, he cannot fail to regard their insubordination as a misfortune, as a moral disorder or disease—something to be eradicated and overcome, something which lowers him to the " ape and tiger " level.

Remaining merely in the natural order, our lack of perfect self-control in this matter is against our *final* dignity, *i.e.*, against the *ideal* which reason bids us strive to realize. But according to Catholic doctrine, Adam was created with perfect and preternatural self-control in this matter—starting, so to say, at the goal of nature's utmost endeavour. This was, of course, an altogether preternatural endowment, as much so as was the infusion of that knowledge and culture towards which he would otherwise have climbed laboriously and never so effectually. That the race in its representative and head forfeited this preternatural gift by sin, makes that a penal privation which otherwise had been only a natural negation. Sensuality is, therefore, not only contrary to man's natural "final" perfection, but also to what God intended him to be in the present order. He raised us to better things, above our nature, and our present humiliation is culpable, not indeed through the fault of the individual, but through the fault of the race. This makes all insubordination of the passions irregular by a new title, that is, as a disturbance, not only of the natural, but of the supernatural order.

The passions being at least indirectly under our free control, their irregularity is not merely a physical, but a moral infirmity. The cardinal virtues of Temperance and Fortitude are in some way defective until they have extended from the higher will into the emotional faculties which it is their office to control. However inculpable, the insubordination of the lower to the higher will partakes of the nature of vice, and is a disposition towards evil. As far (and no further) as the behaviour of our passions is not determined by necessary causes, but is determinable by our free choice, just so far is their rebellion a vice, whether culpable or inculpable, whether resulting from negligence or preceding it. Sensuality is, in the present order, not merely a penalty, like sickness or death, but an ethical blemish which cannot be acquiesced in without fault.

Again, the Catholic doctrine of grace, which is

declared either to be or to involve a real mystical indwelling of the Holy Spirit in the soul, and thereby in the body of the unfallen Christian, makes every defilement of that temple in some sense sacrilegious. "Know you not," says St. Paul, "that your members are the temple of the Holy Ghost who is in you?" "Whoso defileth God's temple, him will God destroy." As in the building of Solomon's temple, reverence for the sanctuary that was to be, forbade the noise of axe or hammer, and required the stones to be cut elsewhere, and thence taken and set silently in their destined places, so the tumult of unruly passions, even where blameless, is unfitting in the sanctuary of a far higher indwelling, in the soul which is a consort of the Divine Nature; which lives and breathes with a Divine Life. It was this sense of fitness which secured for Adam the gift of perfect self-control or "integrity" (as it is called); and if it has not been restored to us by redemption, it is only because our redemption is as yet but imperfect, and remains to be perfected at the resurrection in the glorification of the "body of our humiliation." "Behold, now are we the sons of God," *i.e.*, in some true but inchoative sense, "but it doth not yet appear what we shall be; but we know that when He shall appear we shall be like Him."[1]

If the sanctity of this spiritual temple is in some sense marred by even involuntary irregularity in the passions, much more real is its violation when the will approves and rests in such an unbefitting state of things, or encourages it, or brings it about.

---

[1] 1 St. John iii. 2.

Another aspect of the sacredness of the Christian's body is presented in the doctrine of Christ's Mystical Body, of which we are members. Our union with Him, and with one another, is not merely the moral union of any body-corporate, but a real though mystical union: "One Body and One Spirit." As the act of the member is ascribed to the whole body, so the sinful actions of Christians bring a sort of extrinsic disgrace upon Christ and His Saints, upon the family to which they belong by a tie far closer than blood. Further, as subject to the Head, the member is not *sui juris*, is not its own, but Christ's. Hence St. Paul argues, "Shall I take the members of Christ and make them members of an harlot? God forbid!"

Closely allied with the same mystery is the dogma concerning Christ's Eucharistic or Sacramental Body, by every participation whereof, the body and soul of the Christian are mystically transmuted and in some sense made conspecific with the glorified Body and Soul of God Incarnate. So much so that by each sacramental Communion our body acquires, if not a physical, at least a moral exigency of deliverance from perpetual corruption. For it shares in some degree His sanctity of whom it is written: "Thou wilt not leave My Soul in Hell, nor wilt Thou suffer Thy Holy One to see corruption."

This belief in the future destiny of matter in general, and of the Christian's body in particular, to a share in the final glory of creation to which it has ministered, both in the order of nature and of grace, is at the root of Catholic reverence for the remains of the dead, for the relics of the saints, and for bodily purity and integrity.

Finally, the union of the Divinity, as it were by intermarriage, to the human family has raised our race, as a whole, above the dignity of the highest angelic orders,—even as the low-born can be lifted above their social superiors by union with a prince of the blood-royal. "He never took to Himself the angels, but He took the seed of Abraham." Although this union is not so close as that which binds together the members of His Mystical Body, still it is a moral tie such as holds one tribe or people together by community of blood. The Son of God is reckoned in the census of humanity, but not in that of the angels, who count it an honour to minister to the fellow-mortals of the Incarnate God. Hence the King of men is *à fortiori* the King of the angels, and Mary is the angels' queen, and Gabriel her minister and messenger. All this imparts a new dignity to every man as such, and adds a new indignity to every impurity, voluntary or even involuntary.

All these motives, which are at the root of the intense stress which the Church lays upon the virtue of purity, rest on revealed dogma. They are non-existent for those who do not accept these dogmas, *i.e.*, not only for non-Christians, but to a great extent for non-Catholic Christians, amongst whom as much of Catholic feeling as survives is to be ascribed to sentiments which linger on after their reasonable basis is gone.

Yet throughout we have been supposing that, viewed merely in the light of reason, impurity is an indignity, a violation of man's spiritual nature. This given, then whatever adds to man's dignity, aggravates the offence. Let us, then, see what sound reason tells us on the point.

By a certain world-old philosophy which has gone under various names in various times and places, purity has been assailed on ostensibly speculative grounds. The difficulty of the virtue has at all times driven men to invent and to embrace a theory which will square with their inclination and practice; for no man likes to admit openly to others that he lives in defiance of reason, nor will he care, as a rule, to admit it to himself.

Sometimes this philosophy strives to show that purity is at most a social virtue, a matter of convention and custom; and this doctrine is more dangerous when with it is held that other which regards society itself as in no sense natural or demanded by reason, but the artificial creation of formal compact or tolerated custom. At other times it proclaims more boldly that purity is a moral impossibility, that it is a violation of nature, against our first instincts, and in no way obligatory. We have a growing school of modern "after-Christians," as they have been called, which raves against all restraint of concupiscence as a superstition of priestcraft.

"Modesty was only made for those who have no beauty. It is an invention of the modern world; the child of the Christian contempt for form and matter. . . . O purity, plant of bitterness, born on a blood-soaked soil, and whose degenerate and sickly blossom expands with difficulty in the dank shade of cloisters, under a chill baptismal rain; rose without scent, and spiked all round with thorns! . . . The ancient world knew thee not, O sterile flower! . . . In that vigorous and healthy society they would have spurned thee under foot disdainfully!"

The writer is modern,[1] but his sentiment is as ancient as the Fall. It is but the utterance of that paganism which is latent, like a seed of death, in every human heart, and only awaits favourable climate and environment to germinate and fructify. From the very first the appeal is couched in the same specious form. The fruit is fair to the eye, pleasant to taste, gratifying to curiosity, evidently devised by nature for our enjoyment; and the doubt arises, " Hath God said ye shall surely die?" And then comes the conclusion, " Ye shall not surely die."

" The voice of Nature," we are told, " is the voice of God. In other animals we see how promiscuous obedience to their impulses leads to no disastrous results. Society and the family are violent and artificial institutions, and can bind our conduct only so far as they can force it. Outside that limit there is complete moral liberty. Further, is it not more evident daily that the distance between man and brute is one of degree, not of kind—a tenet which justifies to some extent his claim for equal

[1] Théophile Gautier.

liberty." No doubt evolutionary Utilitarianism would prohibit any excesses that might lead to the deterioration of the human type in future ages; but such a sanction would avail little, under pressure of temptation, with the majority, who care nothing for the state of posterity at so remotely distant a period, especially when the effect of a single excess is so infinitesimally insignificant in the result.

That all grosser hedonistic reasoning is based on a low and inadequate view of human nature, is abundantly plain. If man differs from the brute only in the higher and more effectual development of his senses, we must allow that the final happiness to which those senses minister is of a like *kind* with theirs. If, on the other hand, we hold that evolutionist philosophy has not lessened human dignity, but has only raised that of non-human animals, conceding to them a germinal intellect, reason, conscience, then the same reasons which will presently force us to condemn sensuality in man, will equally compel us to condemn it in them,—unless we agree with a speaker at the Anglican Church Congress in 1896, who explains that sin in its essence is simply an anachronism, *i.e.*, the abnormal survival of a habit which was laudable in our savage or brutal ancestors, but which is old-fashioned and out of date in modern man. Evolutionists and zoophilists cannot play fast and loose with common sense in these matters. If we credit brutes with moral virtues, we must blame them for their vices, or else frankly come forward as determinists, and deny imputability all round. This latter would be to

deny virtue and vice in any sense hitherto accepted
by the world; for who would call strength, health,
beauty, or temperament, virtues, or their contraries
vices?

We can accept only that anthropology according
to which man is of two distinct elements; one,
higher and spiritual, the other, lower and animal—
the lower being obviously ministerial and organic to
the higher; not, however, merely an instrument, but
also a secondary partner in a common interest.

Against the view, favoured by dualist religions,
which regards the body as the prison-house of a
fallen spirit, or as the creation of some malign
power hostile to light and truth, something to be
detested and destroyed, the simple philosophy of
the Church (which is that of common sense and
common language) shows us that the senses feed the
intellect and supply it with the raw fabric of its
ideas; that through them alone is the soul put *en
rapport* with that revelation of truth which God's
finger has traced on the face of nature; that man's
passions and emotions are, as it were, so much rough
material to be hewn and shaped into conformity
with the pattern of reason, with the ideal that nature
hints at and strives with trembling hand to realize.
Of themselves, these impulses are blind erratic forces
in some ways, but they can be trained to run in
harness, and to bear man onward to his self-chosen
mark, instead of running off with him.

But man has his period of unreasoning infancy,
and throughout life there are innumerable daily
crises and intervals where reason is either in

abeyance, or only free to attend to one of a crowd of simultaneous urgencies. Then it is that instincts and habits, natural or acquired, play an important part in his life, even as they play the entire part in the life of unreasoning animals.

Still instincts and habits, like all general legislation, fail in particulars, though their average result is good. These failures man can supplement by the adapting power of reason and by the free modification of his tastes and habits. And this more especially when such impulses urge him towards his animal and bodily interests, to the disregard of his higher and adequately conceived good. Man, alone of animals, knows himself reflexly, knows his own double nature, his final perfection, his Creator and Owner. He alone can enter into conscious sympathy with the plans of his Maker. Other creatures are evolved; man is self-evolving, free to co-operate or to resist. It is the very nature of his probation to see whether he will choose to act as man, bringing out fully all that specifies him and distances him from the brute. His final perfection is intellectual and moral before all things. Animal nature is fully evolved on the completion of adolescence, but man's spiritual nature is undeveloped for years, and at best only partially advanced towards an ever-receding goal of possible perfection.

In a certain wide sense of the word we might say that the distinctive perfection or virtue of a human being, man or woman, is courage: that it is in a man what physical strength or brute force is in a horse or a lion. Courage is moral strength or will-force, a power of resisting the continual straining of pleasure and pain against the law of the Divine will, and against the claims of conscience. Those who lack this power are quickly dehumanized and degraded, being enslaved to sensuality or to vainglory, or to some other tyranny. Many counterfeits pass for courage, as, for example, a certain insensibility to bodily pains and pleasures on the part of those whose nerves are coarse-fibred and whose imagination is dull and sluggish; or a natural indifference to the praise and censure of others on the part of those who are solitary and self-centered and deficient in that desire for the esteem and affection of others which, however hurtful when abused, is one of the noblest and most helpful of the instincts God has planted in our hearts. Again, there are some whose affections are feeble by nature, and still more enfeebled by habitual selfishness, and who are consequently free from the temptation of any violent love or hatred or grief or fear. If, through mere insensibility of these kinds, men seem to endure great pains or humiliations or sorrows or else to forego great pleasures and honours and joys, this is but a counterfeit courage. Nor again is it courage when one goes out to meet danger full of self-confidence and with a moral certainty of victory and escape, as when Goliath came forth against David; nor when through thoughtlessness or excitement or inexperience, one under-estimates the risk to be encountered. There is but little courage in hot blood, unless we are to credit wild bulls with courage, nor does all that passes for bravery on the battlefield deserve to be confounded with that rare moral force which it would be a miracle to find widely distributed in such a chance assortment of men. "To fear nothing," says a recent writer, "and face danger, is the courage of a noble animal; to be afraid yet to go through to the end, is the courage of a man."[1]

At times men will face present pain simply in order to escape far greater pain of the same kind; they will allow a tooth to be drawn or a limb to be cut off, counting it good economy of suffering in the long run. This may be excellent good sense, and akin to courage, but it is not true courage. A poor timid bird will often turn desperate and fight for its life with what might seem to be courage, but is only the very pressure of extreme fright. The miser will go far beyond many a saint in his austerities and self-denials, not because he is master of himself, but because he is the slave of avarice; and the courtier will brook many an indignity and bitter humiliation, not because he is master of his resentment, but because he is the slave of ambition. And so in a thousand ways men who are by no means insensible to suffering will deliberately endure pain and contempt and annoyance in order to avoid what they consider greater evils, or to secure greater advantages. Their action in so doing is usually prudent and justifiable, and has certain elements of true courage in it, since it is governed by foresight and reason, and not merely by the pressure of present feeling. But courage in the true sense requires that we should endure or abstain, not for any kind of

[1] *Man.* By Lilian Quiller Couch.

motive whatever, but for the sake of that highest spiritual good to which alone our subjection as reasonable beings is due or permissible; for the sake, that is, of principle, of truth and right and justice, of God's cause; or still better, for the sake of God Himself, explicitly known and loved and reverenced. *Non passio*, says Augustine, *sed causa facit martyrem*— "It is not suffering, but suffering for a good cause, that makes a martyr."

It is in such suffering that man fully realizes himself and attains the summit of his glory; as indeed we see in the great Archetype of humanity to whom Pilate, unconsciously prophetic, pointed as He stood before the multitude, scourged, mocked, and rejected for the cause of God, and said *Ecce Homo*—"Behold the Man!" He truly was not insensible to pain, contempt, or grief, whose body and soul were framed and devised by Divine Wisdom to be the instruments of that suffering which was to redeem the world, and who went forth to His Passion "knowing all things that were to come upon Him," and yet was silent as a sheep before its shearers— calm with seeming apathy, as if He were deaf, hard, and senseless—"so that the governor wondered exceedingly."

As it behoved Him to suffer and so to enter into His glory, so it is in the act of suffering for God, or for God's cause, that every man reachest his best and enters into his glory as man. Because Christ was strong to suffer and to die, therefore were all things put under His feet; and so far as we are filled with a like strength are we invincible against those who shrink from pain as the worst of evils. Hence it is said that the blood of the martyrs is the seed of the Church, and she, who knows the secret of the Crucifix, will ever have among her children those whose faith in the unseen good, will "overcome the world" by suffering.

The Church, taught by Christ, bids us acquiesce in the truth that this world is not our home, but our school; that it is designed to school us in that which is best among our capacities, namely, in courage, in an heroic endurance of suffering for the sake of God and God's cause. For in this our very highest capability is exerted and strengthened and perfected.

Hence it follows that manhood is most properly manifested in the mastery of impulse. We stigmatize one who is deficient in self-mastery as weak, or wanting in that moral strength which is to man what bone and sinew are to the mere animal. The vituperatives " effeminate," " childish," " savage," " brutal," all confess the same conception of man's nature, and of God's intention. God is therefore at once the author and moving force of our animal impulses, and of the dictate of reason which bids us control them. He supplies us with the task, and with the instruments by which it is to be accomplished. It would be indeed a difficulty were He the author of two contrary tendencies, unless, as is the case, He willed one to prevail, and made provision for its prevalence. Nor is He strictly the author, but rather the permitter, of the contrariety; nor does He will the useful force of

o

passion to be wasted and extinguished, but to be used and applied in due place and season.

It is, then, precisely as being unworthy of true manhood, and of our nature adequately regarded, that we feel moral shame over any exhibition of imperfect self-control *where such control is due and possible.* We blush to be detected in cowardice, greediness, meanness, selfishness, curiosity. Profligates who brag most shamelessly of their vices, always represent them as proofs of their bravery, manliness, independence of superstition, of religious fear, of human respect, but never like to allow their sheer weakness and inability to conquer them.

The shame that we feel at our subjection to purely involuntary animal needs and infirmities, which neither are, nor can be under our control, is in no sense "moral" shame as of something whose deformity is imputable. And the same is to be said of our shame about merely conventional disgraces, like poverty, ill-birth, breaches of etiquette. Unruly passions, on the other hand, even if not a self-chosen or a self-permitted deformity, are a remediable defect which may not be complacently tolerated.

Now, what is true of all controllable impulses is more emphatically true of that which is chief among them, in so far as it concerns that animal function whose results are of the greatest moment both to individual and to social life—namely, the multiplying of human beings, the bringing of new personalities on to the stage of human life. If it is a momentous thing for any man to usurp the authority of God, and by the crime of murder to cut short the allotted space of a human life, surely the "to be or not to be" of unborn personalities is a question of great consequence, where it behoves man, with whom its decision rests, to be fully master of himself. If it is bestial that he should be so enslaved by greediness as to endanger his own health, what can be said of his slavery to an appetite fraught with so much more consequence to others ? In this matter to be determined, like a brute, by pleasure alone, is surely the most extreme irregularity, and to approve and consent to such irregularity is, in the light of mere reason, the gravest immorality. Proportional, then, to the gravity of the end is man's obligation of holding this instinct well in hand.

Still, according to the insistence she places on the preservation of the species, Nature (*i.e.*, God in nature) has made this instinct the strongest of all. Hence, while the mastery of it is most necessary, it is also most difficult, and this it is that makes chastity the very crown and seal of perfected manhood.

The usual effects, physical and moral, of sensual indulgence on individuals and on society at large, are sufficient indication of the sentence which outraged nature passes on such vice, nor need we amplify so disagreeable a topic. When man once makes carnal pleasure an end in itself, reason enables him to devise and organize a thousand ways of procuring and multiplying it which are inaccessible to unreasoning animals. He sinks not merely to their level, but indefinitely lower.

The physical and moral degradation which

results, not indeed from any one act, but from single acts multiplied like plague-spots, is enough of itself to warrant a precept of nature against any exception to their universal prohibition; thus adding a grave extrinsic malice to the already grave intrinsic malice of any single act.

In fine, the root-malice of impurity, viewed in the mere light of reason, lies in the fact that God has given us a certain very imperative instinct, for a certain clear purpose of the most vitally momentous consequence. He intends to prove and perfect us as reasonable beings in this matter, as in many others, that we may freely choose to resist this impulse where it is contrary to His declared purpose, and use it where He wills us to use it, and in the same way as He wills it. That He wills no use of it outside wedlock is a further question, and does not belong to the present discussion, which is general.

Any impulse to do what is irregular is itself irregular, and cannot be approved or encouraged by reason. If murder is wrong, I may not encourage a tendency to murder. If I may not take my neighbour's property, I may not wilfully long for it. So every impulse towards sensual satisfaction which would be unlawful, is itself naturally unlawful. Man is under a natural obligation of tending towards the perfect control of every controllable impulse; hence even inculpable rebellions should displease him as being opposed to his *final* perfection, *i.e.*, to that ideal which he should aim it. They are not matter for blame, but for regret; but to approve them or not to regret them would be blameworthy. My temper may be quite beyond my present control, so that I am free of all self-reproach; but I may not acquiesce in this state of things as long as there is room for further self-mastery. Thus, reason is in sympathy with the Church's high esteem of what we might call *effectual* purity, as opposed to that which merely exists in firm will and purpose; as well as with her more adequate view of human nature and human virtue,— each composed of two elements, internal and external, soul and body, neither perfect without the other, yet the soul absolutely self-standing, self-sufficing, while the body apart from it is wholly valueless.

Temperance in will and purpose is compatible with dipsomania; fortitude with physical nervousness and timidity—although they lack their proper embodiment and expression, since they have not realized that effect which of their own nature they tend to realize in normal circumstances. Again, there is a mere placidity of physical temperament that simulates peacefulness, an insensibility which passes as continence, a general negation of passion which looks like self-conquest; but these are nothing worth: virtues in no sense of the word. The full and perfect virtue is that which is measured and duly conceived by reason, enforced by the will, and gradually conformed to by the passions. It is normally the result of industry.

The efforts of the will may be partly or wholly ineffectual, owing to obstinacy of the natural temperament; and in this case the defect is not morally imputable or blamable, but only regrettable; one may not be glad of it, for it is an infirmity dis-honouring our human dignity, a matter of humili-ation, a defacing of God's image. Given, in two cases, equal internal virtue, the addition of the external virtue in one adds a certain moral dignity or ornament which the other has not. To have it in the one case, to lack it in the other, may not be imputable, either as merit nor as demerit; although to have it may be a means of merit, and to lack it, a safeguard of humility and therefore indirectly a means of greater merit.

So with regard to that perfect immunity, not merely from voluntary faults against chastity, but even from all natural irregularities which the Church bids us pray for. It is not a matter of merit so much as of spiritual dignity. We should regret (not blame ourselves for) every want of that perfect self-control which is the final dignity after which reason should strive, and the want of which is contrary to God's first intention with respect to the children of Adam and the brethren of Christ. We should regret it out of reverence to God's image which it is our duty to educe and perfect in ourselves; out of reverence to this nature which the Eternal was wedded to Himself in unity of Person; out of reverence to that Eucharistic Flesh and Blood which we feed on; out of reverence to our own flesh and blood rendered conspecific with it by reiterated Communions and destined to a like glorification; out of reverence to the indwelling Spirit whose temples we are; out of reverence to the Mystical Body of

which we are members, and to Christ its Head, and
to Mary and to all the saints our fellow-members,
who share our honour or dishonour.

Hence, *cæteris paribus*, the Church prefers, not
as more meritorious, but as spiritually more exalted,
the condition of those who are thus exempt. Not
that she prizes physical impotence or defect of
passion, as possessing any beauty in the spiritual
or moral order, but rather full passions and warm
affections controlled and conquered by an overmastering passion of Divine love. This mastery of
the strong man by the stronger is in the case of
some saints the result of a suddenly infused strength
of charity; in most, it is of slower growth. We
should indeed do ill to conceive it as a privation
of any strength or fulness of vitality, an emascu-
lation of character in any sense. Mere immunity,
without a will firm enough to resist all rebellion,
would be only material purity; but where the
immunity is due to a continual overmastering of
the lower impulses by the higher, too firm and
strong to be sensible of any difficulty or resistance,
we are in the presence of heroic and almost super-
human virtue.

Closely connected with this high estimate of
effectual purity is the value the Church sets on
celibacy and virginity. It is no mere economical
or prudential motive that binds her priesthood to
chastity, but a sense of the spiritual dignity befitting
those who minister at the altar of the Virgin-born
and dispense the Bread of Angels to others. It is
strange how any school of Christianity can fail

to see the high esteem set upon bodily virginity by our Saviour, and how those who were closest to Him were graced by this ornament: His Mother, His precursor, His foster-father, His bosom friend, His heavenly bodyguard. Apart from this mystical reason, there is also a reason which is eminently practical, namely, the unfitness of a married clergy to preach to others a continence and self-restraint which they have little or no occasion to practise themselves. "Keep up! Don't give in!" they seem to cry to the many who are struggling in billows, while they themselves are enjoying the comparative security of a life-boat. With her eyes wide open to all the sin and sacrilege that celibacy has occasioned and may yet occasion, the Church insists upon it for the sake of a greater good which immeasurably outbalances all that evil, for the sake of the encouragement of those millions upon whom restraint is for one reason or another incumbent, whether for a time or continually,—and that, often in the very years when it is most difficult. Again, she knows well that the man who fights, even though he fall from time to time, gives more glory to God than he who sits at home. She knows that marriage does not create purity or the power of restraint where it did not exist before, and that to the impure and incontinent its liberty is rarely sufficient, while the transgression of its restraints is a far deadlier sin than a celibate is capable of.

Reason tells us that if the unruliness of any controllable appetite is a grave disorder, far more is the unruliness of sensual desire, so momentous in its consequences. Even the first impulse to so grave a disorder cannot be regarded as a slight irregularity. This, again, bears out Catholic teaching to the effect that, given full advertence and self-control, no fault in this matter is light, although there are various degrees of gravity. Here the severity of the Church's teaching seems at first sight excessive; for indeed it comes to this, that any deliberate and direct concession to sensual inclination, however slight, whether in thought or deed, is grievously sinful. It must, however, be fully deliberate, a condition which supposes perfect advertence both to what is being done or thought about, and to the gravely sinful character of such thoughts or actions; and also, perfect self-control, so that the thought or act is in no way automatic or involuntary. These conditions are, of course, very frequently absent in the first beginnings of sensual rebellion. Again, the concession must be direct, that is, it must have sensual gratification for its motive, and not some other necessary end which would perhaps justify the toleration under protest of an involuntary gratification.

But the practical wisdom of the Church's severity in regarding the slightest direct and deliberate concession as grievous, is evident when we reflect that here, as in some other matters, a slight concession, far from mitigating irregular desire, increases it; and if the first impulse is not resisted, it is indefinitely less likely that the second will be. In fact it is like starting a boulder rolling down a hill, which becomes more hopelessly unmanageable at

every bound. It is the failure to realize this law,
or to accept it in faith from the experience and
wisdom of the Church, that lies at the root of so
much difficulty in this matter.

Here indeed the rule is the same for all, for
those who walk by the commandments or by the
counsels. But when it is a question of justifiable
occasions of involuntary gratification, there is a
wide range between the maximum and the minimum
of liberty, which leaves room for many refinements
of purity that are of counsel and not of command.
There is on the one side a point after which the
pretended justification is quite inadequate to the
resulting irregularity of which it is the occasion
or indirect cause; on the other, a point beyond
which abstinence from lawful occasions would inter-
fere with plain duties or with greater good. As
the counsel of evangelical poverty is: "If thou
wilt be perfect, sell all;" that is: Do not ask
how much, but how little may you keep; so the
counsel of purity is, that we should inquire rather
how far we may reasonably avoid lawful occasions,
than how far we are free to encounter them.
Both these limits, maximum and minimum, are
relative and not absolute; that is, the temperament, circumstances, antecedents, state of life, of
each individual determine for him to what length
he can go one way or the other without a violation
of conscience or an infringement of duty. In
practice there can be little doubt as to which is
the easier, the safer and more generous course to
adopt; or which the Church everywhere encourages

and approves, so long as counsel is not confounded with precept to the hurt of conscience and the eventual injury of simple purity.

Last of all, reason goes further, and tells us that if we have any strong vicious propensity whose satisfaction is unavoidably occasioned in the fulfilment of some imperative duty, we should regard the circumstance with a certain regret, on account of the gratification of a mortal enemy. For example, as a magistrate one may have to condemn his mortal foe, and thus to gratify his natural vindictiveness; or one prone to drunkenness may be ordered spirits by his doctor. If there is sincere good-will in either case, the purely involuntary gratification of these lower propensities will be a matter of regret to the higher part of our nature. These evil tendencies are our spiritual foes whom we desire to starve out; and therefore if, in spite of ourselves, we are constrained to feed them in any way and so put off the date of their extermination, we shall hardly be pleased.

Thus even in the subtlest points we find reason running parallel with the instincts and intuitions of the Catholic religion touching the angelic virtue, and confessing that God is just, and His judgments are right: *Justus es, Domine, et rectum judicium tuum.*

A GREAT MYSTERY.

..

" A help, meet for him."

WE are told in the Book of Genesis that God
created man and fashioned him to His own image
and likeness, and breathed into his nostrils the
breath of life; that He created him to have dominion
over all the other creatures on the face of the earth,
to use them in the carrying out of his own work
and end; that in this especially man differed from
the brute animals, that by reason of his power of
thinking and choosing, he had dominion not only
over them, but over himself, over his feelings, his
passions, his instincts; he was not to be swayed
by them, or carried along helplessly and thrown,
as an unskilled rider by a spirited horse, but
to make them serve him and carry him wherever
and however, as long, and as far as he should judge
right. And if in respect to his passions and appetites
he is in authority, with respect to God he is
under authority, God saying to him, as he to
his passions, "'Go,' and he goeth; 'come,' and he
cometh; 'do this,' and he doth it." Man was
created to be God's absolute slave and servant, to
do God's will and God's work and nothing else, and

therein to find his perfection; while every other creature then created, was created to be man's absolute slave and servant, to help him in the performance of this work. What, then, was this work? To prepare himself here in order to live hereafter with God for ever, to see Him face to face; to know as God knows, to love as God loves; to be happy with God's own happiness.

Fresh from God's moulding hand, man looked round upon creation, upon the innumerable helps that God's bounty had provided for him, sun and moon and stars, earth and ocean, mountains and valleys, springs and streams, glades, meadows and forests, trees and flowers, beasts, birds and fishes, all praising God in chorus, "telling His glory, showing His handiwork," speaking of His goodness, wisdom, and power; helping man to know Him, and, knowing, to love Him with his whole heart, and whole mind, and whole soul, and whole strength. And yet, gazing round upon all these helps, man felt helpless, for there was no help found meet for him; there were dumb slaves in abundance, but no companion; servants by necessity, and not by choice. "All things were put under his feet," but he had no partner to share his dominion and sovereignty. He had the power of speech, but none to speak to; the power of thought, but none to think with; a human heart, but no human object for its affections; helps, therefore, in abundance, but no help meet for him. Surely it was not good for him to be alone, neither for body nor for spirit. As his body, so neither could his soul increase or fructify in his helpless and solitary state. And yet God created him alone that he might, as it were, feel and experience his neediness, that he might value and reverence the crowning gift of creation, the highest and noblest that God had yet in store for him, the only help that was meet for him, that could deliver him from solitude midst the teeming life and endless stir of the natural world.

Yes, God had withheld the good wine till the last. And whence is He to fashion this help for man? Not as Adam was fashioned from the rude dust of the earth, but from man himself, "bone of his bone and flesh of his flesh," taken from his very substance, in a sense his child, his offspring; bound to him with all the ties that bind child to parent, and with others not less close and tender. And so, when Adam had sought in vain a help meet for him, God created woman and brought her to him; and man said, "'This is now bone of my bone, flesh of my flesh; she shall be called woman, for that she is taken out of man:' for this cause shall a man leave his father and mother and cleave to his wife, and they shall be two in one." Two in one: one perfect being made of two parts. Neither complete without the other, bodily or spiritually. If, as the religion of Mahomet teaches, woman's end were but to help man in the work of perpetuating the race, then indeed she need not have been spiritually man's equal; God need not, as the Mahometans suppose He did not, have endowed her with an immortal soul. He might have created her to be man's abject slave, in no sense his human equal.

But man's work, man's end, is not merely animal, is not merely to live and multiply. Our mind refuses to rest in the thought that one generation exists principally for the sake of the next; and not primarily for its own sake. Man's chief and only essential duty, end, and work is to praise, reverence, and serve the Lord his God, and thereby to save his soul; and it is principally to help him in this *spiritual* work that woman was created, and matrimony instituted. In this she could not help him, were she not destined with him for a like end; were she not capable herself of praising, reverencing, and serving God, and had she not a soul to save.

How, then, does she help him in this work? As a wife principally, and then as a mother.

It is needless to point out how imperfect a man's spiritual education must be, if he lives a life of complete solitude; how many possible virtues must lie dormant and inactive, or simply wither away for want of exercise. There are recorded cases of children who have been lost in woods and forests, and have grown up in the company of wild beasts, far removed from all human intercourse. And when they were discovered, they were found to be dumb, savage, and unreasoning, like the animals among which they had lived. Now the marriage-bond is the elementary bond with respect to human society, and community of life. It is the first, the natural, the universal and most absolute of all partnerships, by which two become one. All other bonds and ties shadow some aspect of this, more or less imperfectly. The husband and wife are constant companions, life-long friends. They have not one or two common interests only, but a thousand; and there is hardly a single virtue which is not needed, which must not be practised and strengthened, if they are to fulfil their duty by one another —patience, meekness, justice, prudence, fortitude, self-restraint, generosity, in a word, all manner of unselfishness.

Nor is it only as the closest and most intimate of his companions and friends of his heart that the wife helps towards the husband's spiritual development; but as being in some sense his moral complement, even as she is his physical complement— the two dividing the one perfect human character between them, one abounding where the other is deficient; one strong where the other is weak; each soul fitting into the other, supplying its defects, filling its emptinesses, making with it one perfect image and likeness of the ideal humanity as conceived in the mind of God. Only in the one perfect Exemplar, only in the soul of Christ were all virtues, graces, and perfections, fully developed, perfectly balanced and adjusted, justice and mercy, strength and gentleness, truth and caution, courage and discretion, energy and patience, generosity and prudence, liberty and restraint. He alone was "beautiful above the children of men," for all beauty lies in justness of proportion and delicacy of temper.

But other men, if they are strong, they are often rough; if they are just, they are harsh; if they are courageous, they are rash; if energetic, impatient; if generous, extravagant. Women, on the other hand, if they are gentle, merciful, prudent, patient, if they abound in tact, delicacy, spiritual-mindedness; they fail more easily in the rougher, sterner, and more primitive virtues. It is only in man and woman, taken together, that we have the fulness and perfection of human graces and virtues; not merely the diamond in the rough, but set and cut and polished till all its brightness gleams out to perfection. We all recognize this when we speak disapprovingly of a man as womanish or effeminate, not because he possesses the special virtues of womanhood — chastity, gentleness, patience, tact, unselfishness, which would be to his greater honour and not to his discredit, but because he lacks the special virtues of manhood. And so a *virago* or masculine woman is not a *mulier fortis*, a brave, just, courageous, truth-loving woman, but one who fails in the graces that are the peculiar ornament of womanhood.

Again, as mother of his children, she helps man, not only in conceiving, bearing, nursing, and tending their bodies; but in perfecting the image of God in their souls, which is as much part of their natural perfection as the growth and maturing of their bodies. Her child is not fully born until it begins to be born to God, to learn from her lips to love and worship its Maker; nor is it weaned till it has learned in some way to walk alone and without her assistance in the way of God's commandments. And for this end God has made woman more spiritual-minded, more apt in the things of God, that she might be as naturally adapted for the nursing, rearing, and formation of the young soul as she is for that of the body.

And so we see that it is precisely because woman has a soul to save, that she is a help fit and worthy of man; a help in the great work of saving the soul first of her husband and then of his children; and that marriage, as God intended it, is not merely a carnal union, but principally a joining of souls; that its end is not to replenish and overpopulate the earth with animals *more canino*,[1] but to fill Heaven with saints; to multiply bodies for the sake of souls. And so far we have not been speaking of marriage as a sacrament instituted by Christ; but as ordained by God in the beginning, when he created man and sought out "a help meet for him" in the great work which he had to do, to praise, reverence, and serve God, and so to save his soul.

II.

"This is a great sacrament: I speak as to Christ and the Church."—Ephes. v.

"Every good and perfect gift," says St. James, "is from above and comes down from the Father of Lights;" that is to say, whatever there is good and perfect in God's works, whether in the kingdom of nature or in the kingdom of grace is a shadow, a type, an imperfect semblance, of that infinite good-

---

[1] St. Augustine, *De bon. viduit.*

ness and perfection, which is God Himself. "From Him," says St. Paul, "all fatherhood in Heaven and earth is named and derived." The Eternal Fatherhood, the Eternal Sonship, the Eternal Generation is the only good and perfect Fatherhood, and Sonship, and Generation; of which the natural and human are but distant, finite, immeasurably feeble and faulty imitations and figures; like all other creatures—frail steps by which our earthly mind can raise itself up some little way towards the infinite and everlasting archetypes. Similarly, if we wish to contemplate the heavenly type, the perfection, the ideal of marriage, we must raise up our hearts and gaze upon the great mystery of Christ and the Church.

A sacrament, as we learn, is made up of the outward sign and the inward grace signified and conveyed. If the grace were signified, but not conveyed, we should have no true and efficacious sacrament of the Gospel; no real, though mystical, application of one of the manifold fruits of the Precious Blood to our souls. In the beginning, matrimony, as ordained by God, was a sign, as it is now, of the union between Christ and His Church; of that which was to be the ideal of the relation subsisting between man and wife; but until it was made a sacrament of the Church, the marriage contract was not a *means* but only a *sign* of grace; it did not convey power to the man and wife to realize and carry out that ideal, to imitate in their conduct towards one another the intercourse between Christ and His Spouse the Church. For as the

Holy Eucharist helps us to mature and perfect, detail after detail, the image of Christ which the Holy Ghost prints on our soul in Baptism, by which Christ is born in us; as it helps us to grow up to the stature of the perfect man in Christ, so the Sacrament of Holy Matrimony produces in the soul of the husband a special likeness to Christ as Head and Husband of the Church; and in the soul of the wife a special likeness to the Church, as the Bride of the Lamb; and effects between both a mystical and supernatural union in the order of grace, over and above the moral and physical union of mere natural, non-Christian marriage—a union whose type is given us in the *fiat* "they shall be two in one flesh," whose archetype is the sameness, the oneness of Christ and His Mystical Body. And therefore, with St. Paul for our guide, let us look to Christ and the Church, that we may know better what the Christian husband and wife ought to be one to another; what the Sacrament of Matrimony alone can make them—and that, on the condition of its being well and worthily received, and co-operated with, and followed up.

"Let women be subject to their husbands as to the Lord; for the husband is the head of the wife, as Christ is the Head of the Church; for He is the Saviour of the body. But the Church is subjected to Christ; and women likewise to their husbands in everything. And let husbands love their wives, even as Christ loved the Church and gave Himself up for her, that He might sanctify her, having purified her with the washing of water in the word, that He Himself might present her to Himself a glorious Church, not having spot or wrinkle, or any such thing; but that she might be holy and blameless. So ought men to love their own wives even as their own bodies; for he that loveth his wife loveth himself. No man ever yet hated his own flesh, but nourishes it and cares for it, even as Christ does the Church; for we are members of His body. For this cause shall a man leave his father and mother and shall cleave to his wife, and they shall be two in one flesh. This is a great sacrament (but I speak as to Christ and the Church). But let every one of you in particular love each his own wife even as himself; and the wife, in such sort that she fear her husband."

First of all, then, Christ is the Head of the Church, which is His Body; and we ourselves are the various parts and members and organs, of which that Mystical Body is made up. · And although the body is subject to the head, and serves the head, and is ruled by the head, yet the head and body are not two distinct beings, but parts of one and the same being—each part necessary for the other; both necessary for the whole being. So Christ is greater than the Church, which ministers to Him, which is ruled by Him, which is His instrument and servant; yet He and His Church are not two distinct beings, but parts of one mystical whole, which we sometimes find spoken of indistinctly as Christ and sometimes as the Church. As the head needs the body, and the heart, and the limbs, and as it works and acts through their instrumentality;

so Christ needs the members of His Body, the Church, and works and acts through them. And again, as the body severed from the head is lifeless, sightless, motionless, and quickly falls to pieces by decay; so the Church severed from Christ would perish at once; the light of her infallible teaching would be extinguished; her sacraments would be empty outward signs, without life-giving power, her discipline and organization would fall to pieces, and her members would be severed and dispersed like dust before the wind. The head does not regard the body as distinct from itself, but as making with itself one personality. It does not rule the body selfishly, as though the two had diverse interests which might come into conflict, but as having only one common interest; and, for a like reason, the body does not obey the head grudgingly or of necessity, but gladly and willingly. So with Christ and the Church there is but one nature, one end, one desire, one operation.

Once more, it is one and the same spirit or soul which quickens the head and the body; it is the same vital spark which warms them both; the same blood which flows continually backward and forward from the one to the other; and likewise it is one and the same Holy Ghost, who dwells in His fulness in the God-Man and who was poured out by Him upon the Church at Pentecost flowing down from the Head to the furthest members of the body. It is the same Blood which courses through the veins and Sacred Heart of our Saviour, and which fills the chalices of the Church's daily Sacrifice, and which washes away the stains of sin in the Sacraments of Baptism and Penance. It is the fire of one and the same Divine charity which burns, with its all-but-infinite intensity and ardour, in Christ our Head, and feebly but truly in us His members; for it is kindled and fanned by the inspiration of one single Spirit.

"No man ever yet hated his own body," says our teacher, St. Paul, "but nourishes it and cherishes it, even as Christ does the Church." How tenderly Christ cares for this Body of His; how marvellously He nourishes it with the food of His own Sacred Flesh; how He refreshes its thirst and washes its soil with His own most Precious Blood. Surely we are bone of His bone and flesh of His flesh; taken out of His sacred side, when He slept the deep sleep on the Cross of Calvary, and built up, into a "help meet for Him;" surely, as far as was possible, He has *left* His Eternal Father, He has *left* His home in Heaven, He has *left* His Blessed Mother in tears for our sake, "for us men and for our salvation," that He might *cleave* to His Church, to His Spouse; for He was enamoured of us poor sinners, and His delight was to be with the sons of men.

It was the custom in the East, as we see in the story of Esther and Assuerus, that the monarch's bride, before she was presented to him for marriage, should undergo a long and tedious course of ceremonial preparation and purification, involving various ritual anointings and washings. It is to this St. Paul makes allusion when he tells us how

nobly and unselfishly Christ loved the Church, as
though some great and glorious prince, enamoured
of a poor, humble village maid, were to disguise
himself meanly and to serve her, and to labour and
suffer and bleed for her, that he might thus win her
love and raise her up to share his throne, his honour,
and his kingdom. So Christ loved the Church.
He did not send for her imperiously, but came to
her meek and lowly, came veiled in her own human
guise, came to seek and to save that which was lost.
He "gave Himself up for her," as the Shepherd who
gives His life for the perishing sheep, "that He
might sanctify her" with His sanctifying Spirit.
Nor does He leave it to His ministering angels to
prepare and purify her for His embrace; but He
Himself (αὐτὸς ἑαυτῷ), the King of Glory, must wash
and purify her with the water and blood that gushed
from His love-pierced Heart. And this labour of
love is going on day by day, as we, the members of
His Body the Church, are being purified and sanctified and prepared for the marriage of the Lamb,
when He Himself and no other will present to
Himself the Bride whom He has sought and
purchased, cleansed and purified, and made into
a glorious Church, not having spot or wrinkle or
other sign of her natural mortality and corruption;
but altogether "holy and blameless."

Was there ever a love-myth or romance that
would not read cold and colourless beside this
revelation of God's own passionate love and devotion towards His chosen Spouse, a cloud-wrapped
love shrouded in types and figures, which shoots

out a chance ray from the folds of its dark mantle—a hint and no more of the dazzling glory behind.

> "Behold thou art fair, O My love![1]
> Behold thou art fair!
> Thine eyes are the eyes of a dove;
> As a lily among thorns,
> So is My beloved among the daughters.
> Arise! Make haste, My love, My fair one,
>   and come.
> Thou art all fair, O My love,
> And there is no spot in thee.
> Thou hast wounded My heart, My sister, My
>   spouse,
> With one glance of thine eyes.
> One is My love; My faultless is but one.
> Who is she that cometh forth as the rising
>   morn,
> Fair as the moon, bright as the sun, terrible
>   as an army set in array?
> Who is this that cometh up from the desert,
> Flowing with delights and leaning on her
>   Beloved.
> Put Me as a seal upon thy heart,
> As a seal upon thy arm;
> For love is strong as death.
> Many waters cannot quench it,
> Neither can the floods drown it;
> If a man should give all the substance of his
>   house for love,
> He shall despise it as nothing."

[1] Canticles, *passim.*

And the Bride of the Lamb, the Church, His blessed
Spouse, makes answer:

"I am dark but comely, O ye daughters of
    Jerusalem,
As the tents of Kedar,
As the hangings of Solomon.
Do not consider that I am brown
Or that the sun hath altered my colour;
For it is because the sons of my mother
    have fought against me,
And have made me keeper in the vineyard.
Show me, O Thou whom my soul loveth,
Where thou feedest Thy flock, where Thou
    liest in the mid-day,
Lest I begin to wander after the flocks of
    Thy companions.
As the apple-tree among the trees of the.
    wood,
So is my Beloved among the sons.
I sat down under His shadow whom I
    desired,
And His fruit was sweet to my palate.
Stay me with flowers, compass me about
    with apples,
For I languish with love.
His left hand is under my head and His
    right hand shall embrace me.
My Beloved is mine, and I am His
Who feedeth His flocks among the anemones,
Till the day break and the shadows flee
    away."

It is, therefore, according to St. Paul, as an adumbration and prefiguring of the oneness of Christ and His Church that marriage was first instituted as a great sacrament or sign; a " mystery," or inarticulate hint, as the word means.

But as the sacrifice of the Old Law fell short of that of the New; so does the marriage of the Old Law fall short of the sacramental marriage of Christians. The Mosaic sacrifices looked forward to Calvary, the Eucharist looks back upon it; they obscurely, as to an unknown future; It distinctly, as to a well-defined past. They proclaimed the need of a victim; It supplies it. They signified; It fulfils and effects. So of Christian Matrimony; it figures the espousals of Christ and the Church, not as a thing that has yet to be, but as a thing which is already virtually accomplished; not as a thing altogether hidden and conjecturable; but as a thing to some extent revealed and more clearly delineated. It not merely points to Christ and the Church as to the heavenly archetype and ideal of the matrimonial relationship, but effectually confers grace whereby the earthly is conformed to the heavenly, and becomes its created expression and utterance.

Or, to illustrate the same idea again, God in the beginning gave man corn and grape, bread and wine. And from the beginning bread was a " great sacrament," a sign of God who is the life and support of man's soul and heart; a sign of the yet undreamt-of mysterious Bread which came down from Heaven to give life to the world, and was laid

in the manger, in the House of Bread; a sign of the
gathering together of the corn of God's elect from
the four quarters of the earth into one bread and
one body; a sign of the Christian antitype, the
Eucharistic Bread of Life, which was given us by
the Bread of Life—Himself by Himself,—" He gave
Himself with His own hands." Yet who could have
read this great mystery, this sacramental meaning
in God's good gift; who but God Himself or His
prophets, to whom His secrets were in part revealed?
But to us it was revealed in its fulness when Christ
took the bread of our natural life and changed it
into the Bread of supernatural life, and said, "Take,
eat, this is My Body." Similarly he took the
marriage of nature and changed it into the marriage
of grace; and to the contract, which was already
an outward sign, He attached the inward grace
which it signified; and to the manifold natural
bonds he added a supernatural bond higher and
holier and more insoluble, saying, "Whom God
hath joined together, let no man put asunder."
It is God who ties soul to soul by this mysterious
communication of supernatural grace, of which
neither alone is the complete recipient, but both
together, each having need of the other, each having
power over the other; and even if ever the law of
nations could permit the breach of the moral and
physical bond, tied by the parties themselves, it can
never give a right or power to sever the bond of
grace, which they have tied, not in their own
person, but only as ministers of the sacrament, as
mere instruments in the hands of God, the principal

author. Divorce from this perfected marriage bond is as the sin of schism—a rending asunder of the Mystical Body of Christ.

Christian sacramental marriage, therefore, confers grace on man and wife to set forth more and more perfectly in their conduct with one another the wedded life of Christ and the Church. The two together are to be one body and one spirit; not one body only, but one spirit, one life; and man's life is not mere animation, but intelligence. Still more, he has a supernatural life of grace; and in this the two are to be one, as in what is highest and best in both. Short of this we have a merely human, natural, unsacramental union; short of this again, there is a less than human and purely animal marriage, which is not even an empty sign of grace. For if the natural man has a two-fold nature and work, animal and spiritual, the baptized has a third and supernatural life and function, the life of grace, to be developed and perfected and exercised in the practice of supernatural virtues. And it is in this third and highest work that he is to seek a help meet for him in the Christian wife, in the mother of Christian children.

As one being, man and wife have one and the same supernatural and spiritual interest. The head does not use and rule the body as distinct from itself; nor is the supremacy and authority of the husband over the wife to be compared to that of parents over their offspring, who are subjected to them as totally distinct personalities. He must not sacrifice or postpone his wife's bodily welfare to his

own.   The head is well when the body is well; and
when the head suffers, the body suffers with it. The
head must think for the body and the body must
labour for the head, each living for the other as for
itself.   Husband and wife each must live for the
other as for themselves; for the spirit first, and then
for the body; as Christ's first care is for the
Church's sanctification, and then for her temporal
peace.   Still there is a true, natural, and willing
subjection of the body to the head; and the Church
sits ever at the feet of Christ, to learn His will and
to hear His words; and so too the wife's oneness
with her husband does not free her from a willing
submission to him—a yoke which is for her liberty
and honour and not for her degradation, and which
only galls so far as it is unlawfully resisted.

Once more the head and body are inseparable,
save by death; Christ and His Church are eternally
united; for He is the King immortal, "of whose
Kingdom there shall be no end." He is the mediator
of an everlasting covenant or marriage-contract
between Himself and His Church, a contract sealed
with the Blood of the New and Eternal Testament.
So man and wife whom the God of grace joins
together by a supernatural tie in the Christian
sacrament, no man may put asunder.   It is for God
alone, the Author of life and Lord of death, to
sever by the sword of death the band which the
breath of His Spirit has fastened.   There is no
power on earth which can undo what is done by
Christian marriage; and all pretence at such power
is founded in blindness, ignorance, or blasphemous

denial of Christ and His Church. Moreover, one head and one body, and no more. Two heads and one body; two bodies and one head, were a monstrous violation of nature. Christ has one Church and only one, "One is My dove, My faultless one;" and the Church has but one Christ, one Life-giver, one Law-giver. And the Christian sacrament forbids and nullifies absolutely, what the law of nature forbids all but absolutely, the simultaneous union of one man with more than one woman; so that adultery, which was always a sin of deadliest dye, is in a Christian a sacrilege also—a profanation of a great sacrament.

Again, the Church, the Virgin Spouse of Christ, through the overshadowing power of His Holy Spirit, is the joyful mother of His children, "Who maketh a barren woman to keep house, a joyful mother of children." "Then shalt thou see, and abound," is foresaid of the Church, "and thou shalt say, Who hath begotten me these?" "Thy sons shall come from afar, and thy daughters shall rise up at thy side." And of Christ it is said: "Thy wife as a fruitful vine, on the sides of thy house. Thy children as olive plants, round about thy table." It is of the new birth in the font of Baptism that wondering Nicodemus asks, "Can a man when he is old enter into his mother's womb and be born again;" and he receives for his answer: "Amen, I say to you, except a man be born again of water and the Spirit he cannot enter the Kingdom of God."

The Christian parents are not merely imitators, but in some sense co-operators in this fertility of the

Church. They, together with the ministers of baptism, are the means by which the Church increases and multiplies and replenishes the earth and subdues it. They should, therefore, be conscious and intelligent agents of Christ in this matter. The Christian mother should remember that her child is not full-born until it is born to grace; that the fruit of her maternity is not the child of wrath, but the child of grace; and that the care, nurture, and education of her offspring has for its principal aim the formation of their early consciousness to the knowledge, love, and grace of God—not merely their *natural* spiritual perfection, not merely their intellectual and moral development, but their engracement and supernatural sanctification.

Such being the type, the ideal of Christian marriage, what shall we say of the reality as we see it around us in this de-Christianized country, where Catholics find it so hard, so impossible to keep mind or heart free from the infectious pestilence of unbelief, misbelief, and moral corruption; a country where the true idea of a sacrament of any sort has been lost to the people at large for three centuries; where the nature of the Church and of her mystical union with Christ is wholly unknown; where the Catholic teaching concerning purity and chastity is simply ridiculed as Manichean in theory and impossible in practice; where the law of the land sanctions an adulterous remarriage of those who have been divorced, and permits marriages which in the Church's eyes are incestuous, null, and void; whose religion despises virginity and celibacy, and holds but lightly to the perpetuity or unity of Christian marriage.

Surely it is only too evident that Protestantism has done its work thoroughly; that it has first rationalized the notion of marriage and robbed it of all its mystical and spiritual import; then secularized what was a sacrament of the Gospel, and betrayed it into the hands of Cæsar; and by these means has finally succeeded in degrading and profaning an institution on whose elevation and purity the whole fabric of true civilization depends. Nor can the tardy penitence of a few of her children ever undo the sin of the Established Religion of England, or ransom that Sacrament which has been sold into slavery for silver; and for whose honour and liberty Catholic bishops have ever been ready to go to prison and to death.

III.[1]

It only remains to add a few words on the subject of the intellect and moral equality of man and woman as bearing on the Catholic conception of domestic society. Here, while we have to guard on the one hand against the false principles on which the modern movement in favour of the intellectual and social emancipation of woman is based, and the excesses to which it is carried, yet on the other there is a danger lest we suppose the Church to be altogether hostile to certain conclusions because

---

[1] This is condensed from an article which appeared in the *American Catholic Quarterly*, July, 1897.

Q

she is hostile to the premisses from which they are drawn, or to the spirit in which they are enforced.

In this, as in other matters, we must distinguish between the practice and sentiments of certain Catholics and the principles and teaching of the Catholic religion; we may not conclude that the condition of woman in any Catholic country or at any particular epoch is the product of Catholic principles unless we can clearly trace the connection. For the leaven of an idea works its way slowly. The Church will tolerate much, and will connive at many inevitable evils attendant on imperfect stages of social development, if only she can secure the essentials of religion. She "has many things to say" to the semi-pagan and semi-barbarian, but they "cannot bear them yet." The natural growth of subjective truth cannot be hurried, else it will have no deep root; and this is as true of the collective, as of the individual mind.

It need hardly be stated that the two principles of self-sufficient individualism and rationalism are essentially uncatholic and anti-catholic. Although the Church abhors the socialist extreme which enslaves the unit to the multitude, making society an end in itself and not a means to the good of its several members, yet she holds firmly to the truth that it is only in and through society—domestic, civil, or ecclesiastical—that personality can be duly developed. In the mystical body of Christ she finds the archetype of all society, whose unity she accordingly concludes to be rather that of a living organism than that of an artificial aggregate of independent units bound to one another by the force of self-interest. *Nemo sibi vivit*—"None for himself," is the law of the former association; "Each for himself" is the law of the latter. Together with this conception of society as a natural organism goes the doctrine of the right of authority and the duty of obedience. If the subjection of members to the head, of parts to the whole, is demanded by nature, it is therefore commanded by that Personal Power in and above nature. Hence obedience to lawful authority becomes a duty to God, and the right of that authority is, in some sense, Divine. On the other hand, if all society originates in a free contract, whereof the motive is self-interest; if no unit cares for the universal good except so far as it is a means to his own isolated advantage, then the submission is really to self-imposed restrictions, and eventually one obeys oneself; which is only a wrong way of saying he follows his own will, and not the will of another. In a word, with the artificial or contract-theory of society, the very notion of obedience must vanish.

As, in the Catholic view, the family is the simplest social unit, so the conjugal association is the simplest and germinal form of the family. In that society of two, as in all society, the distinction between head and body, ruler and ruled, is essential, because where a conflict of wills in morally indifferent matters is possible, social life requires a power of determining and ending such controversy; a right of decision on the one hand and a duty of acquiescence on the other. We say "morally indifferent matters," for where it is a question of right and wrong and of God's law, the decision of a higher court has already been given. This right of social superiority in the conjugal society the Catholic religion has always attributed to the husband. She has regarded it as the postulate of nature, and therefore as the command of God. She finds it confirmed by revelation in the account of the primitive and Divine institution of marriage, and further, in the restoration of that institution by Christ to more than its pristine dignity; in its elevation to the rank of a sacrament signifying and effecting a relation between husband and wife analogous to that which subsists between Christ the Head, and the Church, His body, the archetype of all social organism. "As the Church is subject to Christ, so let women be to their husbands in all things;" for "the husband is the head of the wife, as Christ is the head of the Church." Obedience in all matters pertaining to that little society, and when nothing is ordered contrary to any higher authority, is the wife's duty; and to command in such matters and under such limits is the husband's right. And it is not, as contract-theories conceive it, a right which the unmarried woman possesses over herself and which in marriage she gives over to her husband, as she might give over her fortune; but one which springs into existence for the first time together with the contract. As I cannot obey myself, so neither can I command or force myself; and, not having that power myself, I cannot give it to another. But I can posit the conditions on which he receives it from the very nature of things; that is, from God. In every free promise I put myself in another's power; yet the power exercised over me is not and was not mine, but it is the binding power of *truth*, or of that Lawgiver who forbids me to lie and commands me to fulfil my words. In this sense, all lawful authority is Divine, even as truth is.

It is, however, important to notice the distinction between social or official superiority and personal—a distinction ever insisted on by the Church in the interests of liberty. Just as, in her ministers and priests, she bids us discern between the man and his ecclesiastical office, and assures us that the personal unfitness of the minister in no way affects the validity of his ministrations, so, in the question of jurisdiction, ecclesiastical, civil, or domestic, she admonishes those in office not to credit themselves with personal superiority, or to govern, as it were, in right of possessing greater wisdom, or holiness, or ability than their subjects; nor to imagine that an appointment necessarily carries with it an infallible guarantee of aptitude, present, past, or future. Thus Ignatius of Loyola, who expresses the common doctrine of the Church in a form peculiarly distressing to the pseudo-liberal mind, says, in his well-known Letter on Obedience : " For indeed it is not as though he were endued and enriched with prudence or benevolence or other divine gifts, of whatever kind, that a superior is to be obeyed, but only on this account that he holds the place of God, and exercises His authority, who says : ' He that heareth you, heareth Me.'" The tyranny of individualism in government is altogether opposed to Catholic theory; and we cannot conclude at once that, because the husband has authority over the wife, therefore the man is superior to the woman; but, at most, that there is in the man, as such, a certain aptitude for that particular office which is not found in the woman. Let it suffice, by way of illustration of our last remark, to refer to the Catholic veneration for the Holy Family of Nazareth, where St. Joseph, as the husband of Mary, held the office of superior over one who, in the Church's estimation, was almost immeasurably his better in light and wisdom and divine grace. Official superiority, therefore, does not involve personal superiority, any more than personal superiority in one point or more, means superiority in all.

Still less is it in keeping with the Catholic conception that the subjection of the wife should be slavish, or the government of the husband despotic. For matrimony is a true " society," and the wife is *socia*, and not *serva*; that is to say, she is, as a person, both intellectually and morally her husband's companion and friend, and the end of their association is not the repression, but the fuller development of her personality. And this is the Church's ideal of government everywhere, in home and state, so far as men are sufficiently imbued with unselfish and social instincts to profit by it. The law and the spirit of fear is for the infancy of races; the Gospel and the spirit of love for their maturity. Where the less ideal state of domestic society prevails, the Church may tolerate it as expedient or necessary under the circumstances, but she is never satisfied with it.

Now all this is wholly unintelligible if we accept the contract-theory of society in general and extend it to the matrimonial bond. There is, in that view, as little assignable reason why the wife's place in the association should be one of inferiority, as why, in a partnership of any two free individuals for a common advantage, one should preside over the other; and where there is no authority there is no place for obedience.

Thus an American advocate of Woman's Rights, in a chapter headed Obey,[1] tells us how he protested one day to a clergyman against the "unrighteous pledge to obey," used in the Protestant marriage service:

"'I hope,' I said, 'to live to see that word expunged from the Episcopal service, as it has been from that of the Methodists.'

"'Why?' he asked. 'Is it because you know they will not obey, whatever their promise?'

"'Because they ought not,' I said.

"'Well,' said he, after a few moments' reflection, and looking up frankly, 'I do not think they ought.'"

The writer goes on to say: "Whoever is pledged to obey is technically and literally a slave, no matter how many roses surround his chains"—from which we must conclude that soldiers and sailors, civil servants and all subjects are slaves, or else that they are perfectly free, morally and physically, to do as

[1] *Common Sense About Women,* by Thomas Wentworth Higginson.

they like in everything. Finally he says: "Make the marriage-tie as close as Church or State can make it, but let it be equal and impartial. That it may be so, the word *obey* must be abandoned or made reciprocal." The idea of "reciprocal obedience" is hard to grasp, but, as far as we understand it, it does not augur well for domestic peace. But, in truth, all obedience is to a superior; and just so far as there is equality, obedience is impossible. In fact, on equalitarian principles the matrimonial relation is essentially different from what it is conceived to be, not only by Christianity, but by the hitherto unsophisticated reason of mankind. There are still, even for the equalitarian, certain prudential motives which make monogamy desirable and divorce undesirable within given limits, but those limits are soon reached.

It is absurd and futile for would-be orthodox writers to contend against the inevitable weakening of the marriage-bond, which is the necessary result of certain false social principles, unless they are prepared to repudiate those principles altogether. If all authority, civil and ecclesiastical, is only by delegation from the people, with whom it rests inalienably; if they not only designate its holder, but create its binding force; if it represents only their preponderating wishes and appetites, and not their judgment of what is eternally and divinely right and just,—whether they judge for themselves or choose others to judge for them; if it is merely self-interest that binds the members of society to one another; if obedience is only an indirect following of one's own will, subjected to that of another freely and revocably; then the self-interested association of man and woman must be conceived in the same way, and the word " obey " either expunged from the Protestant marriage-service or explained away. Indeed, we must freely admit that the most advanced and extravagant ideas of woman's position are but the logical outcome, a necessary product of equalitarianism. That philosophy tends to deny any difference between the sexes that is not strictly physiological. It refuses to admit that, morally and intellectually, they are complementary one of another; that the perfect humanity, the complete mind and character is divided between them; that human parentage includes the mental and moral formation of the offspring, to which both parents are instrumental and necessary each in their own way. Beyond the limits of physiology it regards all differences and inequalities as artificial and iniquitous, and it tends logically to the eventual abolition of matrimony in any recognizable sense of the term.

And now we may inquire in what, precisely, consists that inequality which, in domestic society, gives the husband headship over the wife. Those who make no distinction between what is and what must be, between what must be and what ought to be, will freely grant that in the state of rude savagery the wife depends for protection on the superior physical force and liberty of the husband, and that such dependence puts the reins into his hands. But as social evolution relieves her of this dependence more and more, it may be asked, What basis remains for the old relationship? If woman is not intellectually and morally inferior and dependent, why should she be the one to submit?

Now it is most necessary to observe that "superior" is here a relative term, implying some end to be secured. The end in question is the government of the domestic society, the government of the members only in matters pertaining to their common good, and in no others. For example, when we agree that in the savage state the man is more fit to govern the house or wigwam than the woman, we mean that he is superior in fighting power, being physically less encumbered. We do not mean that even physiologically he is a superior being all round, but that, having some attributes which she has not, he can secure an end which she cannot—just as, in many matters, she is superior in virtue of capacities which he has not.

If, then, woman's subjection in more developed domestic society is founded on a certain intellectual or moral inferiority, it does not mean that she is in all points intellectually or morally inferior to man, but only other than man; it does not mean that she is less fit for high intellectual or moral attainments, but only less fit for government, less endowed, as a rule, with the qualities, positive and negative, required for that trust. Whether those qualities are of all others the most admirable and enviable may be questioned. Widespread intellectualism is not a condition favourable to social tranquillity and progress; far more important are the stolid, practical qualifications to which the Teutonic races owe their steady progressiveness, and the absence of which makes free government almost unworkable in more fervid nations. Where idealism, imagination, and emotion prevail very widely, they are fatal to that stability which is needed for social order and growth. It was not without a touch of humour that Plato looked forward to the rule of philosophers as an ideal government; nor should we choose a civil president on account of the fervour of his piety or the sublimity of his political conceptions, although allowing these gifts to be far superior to an insight into the theory of taxation. What, then, is this peculiar characteristic which naturally fits man for the headship in domestic society? Aquinas tells us: "There are two kinds of subjection, servile, and domestic or civil. The latter is the kind of subjection whereby the woman is by nature subject to the man, *because of the greater rational discretion which man naturally possesses.*"

The whole human character in its adequate perfection is put into commission between the two sexes. Morally and intellectually, no less than physiologically, they are complementary; and that not merely as companions or associates, but as parents and educators of their offspring. It is on this natural and necessary diversity of mental and moral character that matrimonial society is founded. But when we reflect on the qualities needed for direction and government, chief among them seems

to be that *discretio rationis*, or reasoning discernment of which Aquinas speaks—a power of taking
a cold, impartial, abstract view of things; a gift
immensely useful, if not very attractive. Not, of
course, that every man possesses this pre-eminently,
but that he does so normally in so far as the masculine character is duly developed in him. Where, on
the other hand, it is the wife who excels in this
talent, there usually results a disturbance of due
domestic harmony, or else a complete inversion of
the matrimonial relationships, which confirms the
theory of Aquinas very satisfactorily. It is not,
however, the actual possession of this reasoning
discernment that constitutes or measures the
husband's right to govern, any more than the
authority of any other ruler depends on his
aptitude. The presumption of such aptitude is the
implicit condition of his designation, but the designation is not invalidated by the falseness of the
presumption.

The scope of marital government, as we have
already said, is confined to matters concerning the
common domestic good, and the subjection of the
wife is not servile, but social: "for the servant
knoweth not what his master doeth," but the wife
is governed in domestic matters, not despotically,
without reference to her views and inclinations,
but politically, as a person, and with the greatest
deference to those views and inclinations which is
compatible with the common good. *Nemo sibi vivit—*
"None for himself," is, as we have said, the ideal of
all Christian society. The husband is not made for

the wife, nor the wife for the husband, but each for the twain.

It will be already evident that there is nothing in the Catholic view favouring a belief in the *general* intellectual or moral inferiority of woman ; and how perfectly in accord with the mind of Christianity is her highest development in both respects will presently appear. Of course, we make a distinction between *necessary* and *actual* inferiority. The former may be repudiated very plausibly, the latter cannot. As we have said, the division of labour and of domestic cares which was needed in rude social states, and which is now, and perhaps always will be, needed among the unleisured classes, requires for the majority of young girls a training which will fit them for their probable after-work; a training which concentrates the mind on small, practical details, and which tends, apart from precautionary measures, to produce narrowness, except so far as religion raises the mind to greater and more universal conceptions. Indeed, the very existence of the movement for woman's intellectual emancipation is a confession of an actual and widespread inferiority. Again, it may be taken for granted that the un-natural will never so far prevail, but that the majority of married women will always be involved in the cares of maternity. This, as a heavy tax not only on the time but on the physical energy necessary for severe intellectual work, will put them at a serious disadvantage. In a word, equality of opportunity, which is essential to fair competition, can never be accorded to that same majority, owing to conditions fixed, not by custom, nor by male tyranny, but by nature.

But those who would contend for an altogether essential inferiority of intellect on the part of women have a very difficult thesis to prove, for the simple reason that all their instances are met either by denying equality of opportunity, or by the contention that diversity of intellectual gifts is not the same as inferiority. In proportion as equal opportunities are given from the first, we see everywhere a practical refutation of their view.

How much the Catholic religion, which exalts a Woman to the highest place in creation, favours and furthers her intellectual and moral development and ignores any such essential difference, is plain from a retrospect of the past. Let me quote the results of an admirable article in the *Catholic World* for June, 1875, none the less appropriate because written in reply to Mr. Gladstone's taunt to the effect that the conquests of the Catholic Church in England were " chiefly among women," and there- fore of no account. After noting the homage done to woman's intellectual power by the religions of Greece and Rome in the worship of a woman as the goddess of wisdom, and patroness of just and humane warfare; in the *cultus* of Vesta, of the Muses, of the Fates, of the Graces, and in the honouring of such names as Rhea, Alcestis, Ariadne, Alcyone, and so forth, the article goes on to notice her place in the Old Testament, as exemplified in the prophetesses and wives of the patriarchs; in Sarah, Rebecca, Rachel, Miriam, Deborah, Ruth,

Esther, and many others. Then we are reminded how it was among women that Christ found His most numerous, apt, and constant disciples when on earth, thus coming under the lash of Mr. Gladstone's sarcasm. St. Paul speaks of the women who laboured with him in the Gospel. Timothy learnt the Scriptures from Lois and Eunice. St. Thecla[1] was skilled in profane and sacred science and philosophy, and excelled in the various branches of polite literature. St. Apollonia preached the faith at Alexandria, and converted many by her eloquence. St. Catharine devoted herself to the study of philosophy, especially that of Plato, and confuted the ablest Pagan philosophers of her day. She is honoured as the patroness of learning and eloquence and of scholastic theology, and art represents her as the Christian *Urania*. After remarking that "the increasing demand which we have on every side for a more substantial and scholarly training of the sex does not look forward to that which they never had, but backward to what they have lost or abandoned," the writer reminds us how it was St. Macrina who taught SS. Basil and Gregory; how SS. Cosmas and Damian were instructed by Theodora. "Even as early as the second century," writes a distinguished scholar, "the zeal of religious women for letters provoked the satire of the enemies of Christianity." St. Fulgentius was educated by his mother, who made him learn Homer and Menander by heart. St. Paula stimulated St. Jerome to some of his greatest writings, and St. Eustochium was a faultless

---

[1] St. Paul's disciple.

Hebrew scholar. St. Chrysostom dedicated seventeen of his letters to St. Olympias; and St. Marcella's acquirements won her the title of the "glory of the Roman ladies." The convents of England in the seventh and eighth centuries vied with the monasteries in letters. St. Gertrude was skilled in Greek, and it was a woman who introduced the study of Greek into the monastery of St. Gall. St. Hilda was consulted on theology by Bishops assembled in council. Queen Editha, wife of St. Edward the Confessor, taught grammar and logic. St. Boniface was the teacher of a brilliant constellation of literary women.[1] We are told of women who were familiar with the Greek and Latin Fathers; of an abbess who wrote an encyclopædia of all the science of her day; of a nun whose Latin poems and stanzas were the marvel of the learned; of the injunction of the Council of Cloveshoe (747) that abbesses should diligently provide for the education of their nuns; of the labours of Lioba in conjunction with St. Boniface; of a convent school whose course included Latin and Greek, Aristotle's philosophy, and the liberal arts; of women in the Papal University of Bologna eminent in canon law, medicine, mathematics, art, literature; of Prosperzia de' Rossi, who taught sculpture there; of Elena Cornaro, a doctor at Milan; of Plautilla Brizio, the architect of the chapel of St. Benedict at Rome. In the eighteenth century we find women taking their degrees in jurisprudence and philosophy at the Papal Universities. In 1758 we have Anna Mazzolina professing anatomy

[1] "Valde eruditæ in liberali scientia."

at Bologna, and Maria Agnese appointed by the Pope to the chair of mathematics. Novella d'Andrea taught canon law for ten years at Bologna, and a woman succeeded Cardinal Mezzofanti as professor of Greek. Still more abundant and overwhelming is the evidence for woman's moral and spiritual equality with man in the Church's esteem. If fortitude is in question, we have SS. Thecla, Perpetua, Felicity, Agnes, Lucy, Agatha, Cecilia, Apollonia, Catharine, and innumerable hosts of women who faced the torments of martyrdom. If men have forsaken their homes for the Gospel's sake in their thousands, women have done so in their tens of thousands, though for them the wrench, as a rule, is far more violent and painful. In self-denial, in austerity, in patient endurance, in silence, in unselfish devotion to Christ's poor, in all that is rightly supposed to demand the highest degree of courageous self-mastery, they have shown themselves, if not superior, at least fully equal to the other sex.

If the number of men saints exceeds that of women, it must be recollected that the canonized represent but a handful of the saints, and chiefly those whose sanctity was notorious and before the public gaze; a fact which lessens the chances for the official recognition of female sanctity. For the same reason it is observable how far more frequent is the canonization of bishops than of simple priests, although no one would suppose that saintly priests were less numerous than saintly bishops, considering the numerical proportion of one order to the other. Again, it may be plausibly contended that sanctity

R

in men is more evidently miraculous and out of the common than in women, who, in a sense, are naturally devout and spiritual-minded.

It would be tiresome to enumerate the religious orders and congregations founded and ruled by women. Indeed, the extent to which the Church has entrusted women with jurisdiction and right of government would seem opposed to the doctrine of Aquinas, referred to above, were it not that this jurisdiction was very rarely exercised over communities of men, and was usually dependent on higher authority vested in bishops or prelates.

In the light of all this, it is impossible to deny that where the Church has her way, and is not trammelled by local prejudices, she desires the fullest possible mental and moral development of women compatible with the discharge of the social duties required by nature and God's law. Here, as elsewhere, the natural organization of society forbids, and will always forbid, absolute equality of opportunity. But it is the aim of sane progress to eliminate all unjust and unreasonable inequalities, and to secure the least possible waste of those spiritual energies in which the true power and wealth of every society consists. Nor must we suppose that it is only in the leisured and unmarried that the Catholic religion desires culture. The Church knows far too well the power and influence of the wife and mother not to see that their elevation means the elevation of both husband and children, and that eventually it is they who give the moral tone to the whole community. Woman is naturally the guardian of the spiritual wealth of the family, and for that trust, especially in these days, mere piety, which is not also educated and intelligent, is of little avail. The first formation of the mind is from the mother, and the impressions which she leaves are indelible. It may truly be said that whatever the Christian religion has done for the elevation of public morals, it has done through the instrumentality of women. A brief study of Mr. Devas's admirable little book on *Family Life* will confirm what perhaps no one with any knowledge of human history will dispute, and will prove that where woman is debased and basely thought of, there, in proportion, public morality is at a low ebb.

We must not credit the Catholic religion with the sentiments of certain recluses of the desert who, under the bias of Oriental influence, consider a fierce contempt for women to be a great point of virtue; who insist much on the priority of Eve's share in our racial disaster, forgetting that theology regards it as quite insignificant compared with that of Adam, and more than abundantly counterbalanced by the part of Mary in our redemption; who look upon all the immorality in the world as an evil brought upon man by that creature which God made to be a "help meet for him"—a little touch of Manicheism, such as induces some to regard wine as essentially demoniacal because men choose to drink too much of it. A moment's reflection will show that it is in the reverence for and not in the contempt of woman that purity must look for its only reliable safeguard; and it is with this in her mind that the Church counsels a devotion to the Virgin Mother in the interests of that virtue.

In conclusion, if we contrast the Catholic ideal of womanhood with that of modern irreligion—one the fair fruit of sound reason enlightened by Catholic faith, the other the base issue of crude equalitarianism and sense-philosophy—there is little difficulty in seeing that the former conception is strong and full of energies yet to be developed, while the latter contains within itself the principle of its own decay and death. The downfall of the family, the profanation of marriage, means the downfall and profanation of woman. Whether she likes to allow it or not, it is only in virtue of a waning survival of that chivalrous spirit which Christianity created and fostered, that the " new woman," as she is called, is able to elbow her way to the front as she does. If man is ever rebarbarized by the withdrawal of the softening influence of home, if woman becomes nothing more to him than a competitor in the general struggle for wealth, she will eventually be forced down to that degradation which has always been her lot under the reign of pure selfishness and brute force. If it is her greater unselfishness which has caused her so much suffering in the past, it has also been the cause of her great power for good. Selfishness is brute force ; unselfishness a spiritual force. She can never compete with man if the contest is to be one of brute force. It is the Catholic Church who has raised her, and, through her, has raised the world, though both processes are still struggling but slowly towards completion.

THE WAY OF THE COUNSELS.

I.

"If thou wilt enter into life, keep the commandments; if thou wilt be perfect, go sell what thou hast, and give to the poor, and thou shalt have treasure in Heaven; and come, follow Me."—St. Matt. xix. 17, 21.

As there is a growing disposition on the part of some to speak disparagingly of what is called the "religious state" as though it were something merely adventitious to the Catholic religion; something useful and perhaps necessary for past ages but rather out of place in our own times; a desirable ornament when not procured at too extravagant a cost; it may not be amiss to say a few words on the nature of this institution, its place in the Church and its relation to the Christian religion. As intelligent Catholics, such knowledge ought to interest us for its own sake; but living as we do among non-Catholics who are continually crying down the life of perfection and the practice of the Evangelical Counsels, it is doubly necessary that we should have a firm grasp of the truth both for their sake and for our own, to silence if not to convince them, and to satisfy ourselves. And be it noticed that our present scope is to defend, not religious orders in the concrete, nor monasticism, but the religious state in general, that is, the profession of the three

Evangelical Counsels,—whether independently, or in a society with others; whether in the world, or in the cloister, or in the hermitage. The religious state is a permanent and essential feature of Catholic Christianity; whereas the particular orders or institutions into which religious have at various times enrolled themselves for corporate action in the Church's service, are contingent and transitory, varying with the necessities of the age and locality: "They have their day and cease to be." But the religious state lives with the life of the Church, of which it is an essential manifestation.

St. Paul boasts—and he is a great boaster—that the world is crucified to him and he to the world; and "God forbid," says he, "that I should boast in anything save only in the Cross of Christ." The Cross has become so outwardly honoured since those days; such an object of worship and adoration; so rayed round with secular glory from the labours of poet and painter, that his words do not sound so mad in our ears as they did in the ears of those who looked on crucifixion as we do on hanging or penal servitude, and who felt as little reverence for the Cross as we do for the gallows or the tread-mill. To get the full flavour of his sentiment we should have to put the word *gallows* instead of *cross*, and *hanged* instead of *crucified*. His meaning is that, as far as we are permeated with the spirit of the Gospel, so far shall we feel an ever-growing contempt for the life and conduct and aims of the spirit of worldliness wheresoever manifested; in Catholics or non-

Catholics; in Christians or non-Christians; in its professed votaries or in its professed enemies. It is not the world but worldliness which is hateful to God—a subtle leaven of unbelief and selfish egoism lurking in all our hearts; and breaking out like a plague over the millions of humanity. And as our contempt of worldliness increases, so too will our reverence for the "Evangelical Counsels" and the religious state increase. For just as the Church of Christ took the hated gibbet and lifted it above her altars, and taught men to bow down and worship what the world spat upon and trampled under foot; so by the existence of her religious she continually sets the world at defiance; and teaches men to love and honour and—when it is God's will—to embrace what the world hates and despises and flies from,— namely, poverty, self-restraint, mortification, obedience, submission, humility.

Our Divine Saviour is rightly said to have sanctified and exalted and imparted a sort of sacramental dignity to whatever He touched, or used, or made in any way His own. It is the instinct of love to choose the lot, to imitate the ways of those we love. "Lord," says Peter, "I will go *with Thee* to prison and to death." It was the purpose of God to govern and reform the world, not by theories and philosophies, but by this imitative power of personal love; to draw men's hearts to Himself so that it should be their chief glory and joy to live as He lived, choosing and loving the lot which He chose and loved; walking in the paths trodden by His blessed feet.

But the world into which He came was a world where riches, wealth, possessions were worshipped and idolized to the ruin of souls and the dishonour of God. " Idolized," because they were sought as an end in themselves; or sought in a spirit of selfish individualism, not for the common good, but for the exclusive good of the unit; where accordingly wealth was acquired by fraud and oppression of the poor; where the labourer was despised by the capitalist as the vanquished by the conqueror. For it was not only the little world of Judea two thousand years ago, but the great world of all the nations and ages that He came to heal. It was in answer to the cry which to-day goes up to the ears of God from the oppressed millions of humanity no less than to the cries and groanings of past ages that He has come down as Emmanuel—God, one of ourselves; Jesus, the Carpenter of Nazareth.

To poor and rich alike the love of wealth is the most fruitful source of misery, spiritual and temporal.

Superabundance on the one hand is a snare to the rich, making them feel independent of God in so many ways, like the fool who said, " Soul, take thy ease; thou hast much riches laid up." Furthermore, it is the key to endless pleasures and enjoyments the appetite for which, when unduly indulged, grows insatiable and tyrannical; and breeds that sensuality which blinds the understanding to every spiritual conception and makes the heart cruel and selfish. It is no less the passport to vain honour and to influence, which also come quickly to be desired as ends in themselves with a spiritual hunger less degrading but really more soul-destroying than the craving for luxuries and enjoyments. The mere possession of superabundant wealth is no sin in itself, no injustice, as socialists pretend it must necessarily be; but it is a continual occasion, almost a proximate occasion, of such tendencies and temptations as we have just spoken of. For it is all but impossible for ordinary souls to possess wealth and yet not to love it; and "the love of money is the root of all evil." How few are they who not only believe but who realize that their wealth is given them by God only for the *common good;* and that if they are allowed certain superfluities and enjoyments as the fruit of their own or their parents' industry, it is only because the *common good* requires that there should be such reasonable differences, and that there should be a stimulus to industry; and because social unity requires that we should share often both good and evil, wealth and poverty, reward and penalty for which we are not personally responsible. Hence it is not against the poor but for the poor that the rich hold their wealth; insomuch as the poor are members of the same body. It is in the power of doing good that the true privilege of wealth and position lies.[1] "Let him that sitteth at meat be as him that serveth," says our Saviour, who was at once Lord of lords and Slave of slaves. To rule is to be great, because to serve is to be great; to have is happiness,

---

[1] "He wished to reign," says Wilhelm Meister, speaking of Hamlet, "only that good men might be good without obstruction."

because to give is happiness. "It is more blessed to give than to receive." And besides all this, it is the tendency of superabundant riches to ruin the spiritual independence of man by making him the slave of imaginary necessities. History everywhere testifies to the social and national decay consequent on the selfish accumulation and selfish use of wealth. We must not find fault with productive expenditure; nor even with such as promotes the moral, intellectual, and physical development of individuals. For society is helped and strengthened by the multiplication of healthy, intelligent, and moral citizens. We are not Vandals or Puritans to deny the refining pleasures of fine art to those who can afford them; nor are we so narrow-minded as not to see that there is such a thing as useful leisure; and that the existence of a leisured class is not necessarily a source of corruption, but might be and ought to be a helpful factor in the general well-being. It is against the enervating effects of luxury that we protest; against the indulgence of sensuality; against the squandering of possibilities of happiness and of true utilities, to no purpose or to an evil purpose.

Again: to the poor, no less than to the rich, the love of wealth is a source of misery. For not all who are poor in fact, are poor in spirit; and grasping avarice is confined to no class of society. No doubt where there is real insufficiency and destitution it is impossible—apart from miracles of grace —but that the heart must be eaten up with cares, or hardened with despair. On such poverty, the

fruitful mother of vice, our Saviour has pronounced
no blessing; but only a curse on those who are
responsible for it. But it is often the comfortable
poor who are most enslaved to a desire of accu-
mulating; to a thrift that has become an end
itself, instead of reasonable means to a reasonable
end.

It was therefore needful for us that our Saviour
by embracing poverty should make that state of life
more honourable and more lovable to His followers.
He knew that it was as difficult for a rich man to
use his riches unselfishly as for a camel to go
through the eye of a needle; He knew that for the
majority it was far better, safer, happier to be
actually poor, to have less rather than more, and
to be content with that less. And that they might
be not only content but better pleased with that
lot, He made it His own. To the anti-social,
selfish spirit of worldliness nothing is more hateful
than poverty; none are more contemptible than the
poor; and so, to condemn and defy the world and
to show His contempt for its judgment, our God
came among us as a poor man, labouring for His
daily bread in the sweat of His brow. He embraced
poverty and thereby made it something divine—
Holy Poverty, the Bride of Christ:

> With Christ she climbed the cross of woe,
> When even Mary stayed below.[1]

He shared it with His Blessed Mother, with
St. Joseph, with His Apostles, and with His closest

[1] Dante, *Paradiso*, xi.

friends. To them He says, speaking of that perfection which is counselled though not commanded:
"If thou wilt be perfect, go, sell all that thou hast
and give to the poor . . . and come and follow
Me," the Son of Man who have not where to lay My
head. And let us notice in passing that the spirit
of poverty is not a spirit of economy or parsimony;
not a spirit of keeping, but of giving. It sells all,
in order to give to the poor; after His example,
"who, though He was rich, yet *for our sake* He
became poor," and "emptied Himself of His glory."
It is the spirit of devotion, self-sacrifice, self-forgetfulness; the very antithesis and antidote of the love
of acquisition.

Again: it was not well possible for our Saviour
to choose any but the harder lot and the lot of the
majority. Which of us could bear to go well-clad
or to feast sumptuously, or to make merry, if one
most near and dear to us were in destitution and
pain and poverty? Even though we could in no
way by self-privation relieve his misery, yet love
and sympathy would make the inequality intolerable
to us, and we should be restless and miserable till
we were on the same level as he. True, common-
sense has no justification of such a sentiment; but
there is something in us, thank God, much diviner
than common sense; something that is a spark
from that fire that burns in the Human Heart of
God Incarnate. It was not merely to guide us,
to encourage us, to feel with us and for us, that our
great High Priest was tempted and tried with all
our temptations and trials; but because love is

miserable until it shares the sorrows of the beloved; it feels itself false and disloyal if it enjoys any advantage in solitude. *Pauperes semper habetis vobiscum;* He knew there would always be poor while the world lasted; and, furthermore, that the poor would always be in the majority. For, whatever economists dream to the contrary, the rich will be few and the poor will be many. But our Saviour was necessarily with the majority; for the few are for the many and not the many for the few; the rich are for the poor and not the poor for the rich; the gifted for the needy and not the needy for the gifted.

Again: He had come on a mission of reparation to make atonement for the sins of the world. He saw, as none other saw, the torrents of iniquity and corruption that streamed from this one source of avarice or the selfish love of wealth; and therefore, despising what the world loved and loving what the world despised, He willingly and freely chose to be poor rather than to be rich.

And the Church, His Spouse, has faithfully guarded His doctrine in this matter of poverty; and she proclaims it not only by word of mouth, but by the continual object-lesson given by the professors of voluntary poverty. She allows and encourages her children, if only they are called thereto by God, to make obligatory on themselves by vow what is of counsel and free to all; to seal a contract with poverty and to make her their bride as she was the bride of Christ.

Let us pause to notice that the sacredness of the marriage tie and the specific distinctiveness of conjugal love depends on the bond being irrevocable at will and perpetual. So he who gives himself to poverty irrevocably, who locks the fetter and casts away the key, loves her with a devotion far higher in kind and degree than he who embraces her at will or takes her on trial or with the possibility of a divorce in view. And so of religious vows in general. It is excellent to practise continence or obedience; but far more excellent to vow oneself to the practice.

The very idea of a vow is somewhat discordant with many of the dominant notions and sentiments of modern life. Any voluntary sacrifice of liberty is looked upon with suspicion as savouring of fanaticism. But this suspicion is at root akin to that which looks askance at every form of asceticism or self-imposed mortification on the grounds that what God has given us to enjoy He cannot desire or intend us to forego—a fallacy which destroys not only mortification, but all self-restraint and morality. It is no violation of our liberty to be bound by the law of God to do right instead of wrong; nor is it a violation of our liberty when by a self-imposed law we bind ourselves to do better instead of well. Nothing curtails our liberty but what restricts our power of doing well or doing better. There is no such prejudice against the notion of a vow where the service of God is not in question. History and romance and poetry abound with instances of heroic self-devotion to noble causes and enterprises sealed by vow, which elicit unqualified admiration from all who do not wish to be thought void of right senti-ment. Who will find fault with the hero of a recent

fancy sketch of considerable merit,[1] who vowed his
life and labour to the task of bridging a mountain
torrent which had for years exacted its toll of
human life? We are told how "he toiled day after
day, and the pains of loneliness and poverty were
ever with him; but the pain which had brought the
man's vow to birth spurred him on and helped him
to that endurance which is always heroism." And
then we read how later he awoke to the existence
of life's pleasures and of his own latent capacities
for enjoying them which his vow had doomed to
death; how he "had mingled with his fellow-men—
with women too; he had seen their pleasures, their
hopes, their loves, their happy lives, and he craved
the same;" . . . how his humanity "revolted against
the self-appointed dreariness of his existence" when
"in one hour he realized that hope and love were
not for him. He had vowed a vow that swallowed
up all gentler obligations; which demanded all his
strength, all his days. . . . He had paid out the
grandest years of his life for an impulsive whim,
and what had he gained? Was he obliged to yield
his own life—the life he could never live again . . .
for the sake of a few lives in a far-off corner of the
land, a few pangs in hearts which had quite forgotten him?" But ever the thought of his vow
comes to the assistance of his better self. He lives
till the necessary wealth is realized at great sacrifice;
he returns to his country after years; and on the
threshold of home he himself falls a victim to the
same cruel torrent whose foe he had sworn himself,

[1] *Man.* By L. Q. Couch.

and ere he sinks overcome, his last gaze rests on the bridge of his dreams, built easily long before by the wealth of others.

Few perhaps will care to withhold their praise from such an act of heroic self-devotion, even though in the issue it was fruitless of the results it aimed at so nobly and at such cost. But when it is a question of devotion to the service of God, to the salvation not of a few lives, but of many souls, to the maintenance of the cardinal principles of the Gospel and of the Eternal Life here and hereafter, then and then only are men alarmed for the interests of liberty and fearful of the encroachments of fanaticism. It has never been suggested that there was aught of servility in the profession of knighthood in the days of chivalry, when men bound themselves

> With such vows as is a shame
> A man should not be bound by, yet the which
> No man can keep.

Even though it be allowed that

> The vow that binds too strictly snaps itself,
> And being snapped,
> We run more counter to the soul thereof
> Than had we never sworn,

yet the fact that a profession is high and difficult, and that therefore a greater percentage of those who make it must fall short, and falling from a greater height make greater havoc, in no way argues against its lawfulness or rightfulness, unless we are prepared to carry the principle of dishonourable safeness to the repudiation of Christianity itself and of the baptismal vows.

It is then in sympathy with the intentions and motives of Jesus Christ that souls here and there are drawn to the profession of poverty; loving it first of all for His sake, that is, because He loved it and made it His own; and then, more intelligently entering into His mind, they love it for the sake of mankind because it is the harder lot and the lot of the many, and because they see that the love of riches is the source of all kinds of social misery and injustice; and therefore they give themselves to the preaching of poverty by their life and example, giving up freely the wealth, or the opportunities of wealth, they might otherwise have lawfully enjoyed. And finally, in a spirit of reparation for all the dishonour done to God by the worship of money, they do not merely accept the poverty that may be laid upon them in the course of Providence contentedly and cheerfully, but they freely make themselves poor for ever.

But against all this doctrine economists urge that the love of money, the desire to procure comforts and to raise the standard of enjoyments, is the root of all good, that is, of all progress and increase of national wealth which eventually redounds to the relief of destitution and poverty. Christ says: "Sell all and *give to the poor.*" He desires that poverty should be relieved. He regards it therefore as an evil. He insists strongly and frequently on this duty. Plainly, to find the causes of poverty and to remove them is the truest and most universal

s

kind of charity. May it not be said, they urge, that He is preoccupied rather with the evil of super-abundant riches, that is, of capitalism, than with the excellence of poverty; that it is only freedom from those particular evils which makes poverty *preferable*, in spite of other evils of its own.

To this there is but one answer. It is most true that where there is no love of money or of comforts there will be industrial stagnation, much poverty, and widespread destitution, and it would be wrong and mischievous to allow that Christianity is in any way hostile to true and rational progress; or that the *real* interests of this world and the next were incompatible.

The world is one thing and worldliness another. The latter is an enemy of the interests of Christianity; but it is also an enemy of the interests of the world. For though Christianity seeks first the Kingdom of heaven, it seeks *ipso facto* the advent of that Kingdom upon earth; and that God's will may be done on earth, in the individual, in the family, in the State, in things temporal as it is in things eternal, "as it is in heaven." Truth, justice, equity, charity, happiness, liberty, fraternity—what are these but the will of God? And what are they but the rational ends of progress, the truest interests of this world which God so loved that He gave His only Son to die for it? "What God has joined together let no man put asunder." This world and the next are related as body and soul. The body is subordinate to the soul; but it is not its enemy, not even its slave, but its companion, its helper, its friend.

Both, we believe, are to be glorified together; and we also believe that in some undreamt-of way the kingdoms of this world are to become the kingdoms of God and of His Christ; and that a renewed and purified heaven and earth will supervene upon the old.

It is absurd and narrow-minded to regard modern progress and civilization as being the pure result either of Christian or of anti-Christian principles and tendencies. It is a mixed product containing much good and much evil inextricably intertwined, as are the roots of wheat and tares in the Master's field. All that is really good in it is the fruit of the eternal and necessary principles of the Gospel; all that is evil is from the selfish spirit of worldliness. Were it possible to root out the tares, the wheat would grow more freely and fruitfully. What chokes and retards civilization is the same weed of worldliness which strangles the Gospel and forbids its full development and expansion. What do socialists and individualists revile one another with, except with the disregard of Gospel principles; with avarice, with luxury, with injustice, with tyranny?

Many glib talkers are zealous to prove that the Church's influence must be altogether in the interests of progress and civilization; but they never pause to define the nature of true progress and civilization, or to question whether what passes for such really deserves the name. That we live in an age of commercial and industrial progress cannot be denied; but it must not be assumed that the best and truest wealth is material, or that the multiplication of comforts and conveniences is the measure of culture. We cannot determine the nature and direction of true progress till we are agreed about the nature of man, the purpose of human life, the character and conditions of true happiness. If this world is the best we have to hope for; if it is our brief home; if pain, sorrow, and affliction are unmitigated evils; if our only wisdom is to gather, multiply, and hoard whatever little enjoyment can be crowded into a few years, then, indeed, it cannot be denied that the current notion of progress and civilization is satisfactory. But if this life is chiefly a school of suffering in which man is taught to master himself and to endure all things for the love of truth and principle and right, for the love, that is, of God and God's cause; if sorrow, pain, and affliction are evils only under certain conditions, but are as often, or more often, the very food and medicine of our spiritual and moral development; if conscience, and faith, and divine love, if purity, unselfishness, patience, meekness, compassion be the highest exercise of man's highest faculties, then indeed the civilization which the Church could encourage and sympathize with would be very different from the frankly godless and animal civilization of our times.

We do not deny that amid the prevalence of grosser principles and motives, the "Power that makes for Righteousness" strives unceasingly to assert itself and to mitigate the shameless impetus of the rush for comforts. But in proportion as a tendency is downward rather than upward and ideal,

it is strong, and universal and persistent; so that
from the very nature of things an ideal civilization
is something indefinitely far away, and, therefore,
although the Church is not only the ally but in
some sense the mother of true civilization, and
of whatever good there is in the•present civilization, yet historically speaking she has always
been, and will always be, at war with that which
calls itself civilization and progress, but is not. She
can never acquiesce in the view that as selfishness
is, so it ought to be the dominant motive of human
conduct, upon which alone we can calculate, with
scientific certainty. She will not purchase the
stability of civilization by contenting herself with
aims that are safe and facile because they are low.
She prefers to fail for ever rather than lower her
standards one inch. For she knows "How far high
failure overleaps the bound of low successes."

Let it be granted then that if the Gospel forbids
us to seek more than bare sufficiency of food and
raiment; or to make provision for the future; or to
compete with others in the race of life; if its ideal
is a life in the desert apart from all human interest:
if it inculcates mortification of every sense and every
affection as an end in itself in the spirit of Buddhistic
pessimism; if it teaches us to despise the great
drama of human history as an unmeaning "tale told
by an idiot"—as though He who cares for the
individual life cared naught for the life of cities and
nations—if all this be the essential tendency of
Christianity, then indeed it is the enemy of civilization and progress. But this is an ignorant travesty

of the Gospel which has never been accepted by
the Catholic Church, however favoured by certain
heresies which have arisen within her and broken off
from her. We are forbidden to seek temporal things
first, that is as the profane and worldly-minded seek
them, who regard them as ends and not as means;
we are forbidden—not foresight and prudence—but
anxiety and fretfulness in these matters; we are
forbidden to advance ourselves at the expense and
to the injury of others; to seek our own good at the
sacrifice of the common good; we are forbidden
even in temporal matters to seek the lower in preference to higher necessities and enjoyments; to
indulge in senseless display and luxurious, wasteful
sensuality; we are forbidden all that degrades and
enervates the individual and thereby weakens society;
we are forbidden such aggrandizement as causes
atrophy and anemia in the lower members of the
body-social, and hypertrophy and plethora in the
higher—a double cause of social decay and death.
But nowhere does the Gospel teach us to despise
any good creature of God's which used in due
measure and season promotes human happiness and
leads us to serve and praise Him better than before.
If a corrupt and luxurious civilization deadens and
debases the soul; yet it cannot be denied that of
itself civilization tends to the development of man's
spiritual faculties, and thereby renders him a more
fitting instrument of the Divine praise. Even knowledge has deservedly come into certain disrepute in
an age where it is worshipped merely as eventually
productive of multiplied comforts. But this perver-

sion does not make it less true that knowledge feeds and ministers to wisdom; and that extended knowledge is one of the principal fruits of civilization. Civilization is a good thing; one of God's helps to salvation; it is therefore a grace to be sought and laboured for. Starvation, destitution, suffering are not ends in themselves, and if, when endured or embraced in obedience to God's will, they are means to the very highest end, yet charity bids us imperatively relieve them in others, however gladly we might put up with them ourselves. Fight these miseries how we will, yet the very nature of things will always secure their prevalence, for we are but as children building sand walls against the tide.

But there is, thank God, an unselfish love of riches that can more than supply all that energy which is requisite for progress and civilization. As it is, when a man works for his family he usually works harder than for himself alone. But it is the tendency of Christian charity to throw down the barriers of family and clan, and without lessening the measure of our love for our immediate kin, or destroying its due gradation, to allow our affections to stretch indefinitely to the furthest limit of humanity. Indeed the extent to which the wavelets circle out depends on the force of the central disturbance; and it is the deepest love that spreads most widely with least diminution of intensity. Our Blessed Saviour, whose love reached to every son of Adam, past, present, and future, loved His Mother and special friends with an intensity proportioned to the same infinite reach of His world-wide love.

Is there not enough evidence in the past and present, of the existence of nobler and wider hearts which have preferred the general good to their own; of men who have, like the Good Shepherd, laid down their life for their flock; is there not enough heroic unselfishness even now in the world to bid us hope that what family-love can do, a love of humanity fed by Christian faith and hope and charity may effect one day more abundantly? As the false philosophies of pagandom prepared the world to receive the truths after which they were vainly groping; so the pseudo-humanitarianism of our day seems to be making possible a fuller declaration of the Christian doctrine of fraternity and love than would have been listened to last century.

Therefore as a man who understands that to rule is to serve, may ambition rule simply out of love of the many and a desire to serve them; so a man may ambition wealth just because it increases his power of doing good, of perfecting himself and those who are connected with him in due gradation from the nearest to the furthest, within a sphere which is increased by every accession to his riches.

In no sense, therefore, is the love of personal poverty hostile to civilization. It is compatible with the love of riches; provided this be an unselfish love. Plainly it is compatible with a keen desire to get money in order to give to the poor. "Let him that stole," says St. Paul, "steal no more; but rather let him labour, working with his hands, that he may have wherewith to give to him that is in need;"[1]

[1] Ephes. iv.

let him no longer seek wealth selfishly at the expense of others, but let him for the love of others get all he can by honest endeavour in order to make himself useful and not hurtful to society. All wealth that is reasonably and unselfishly used is for the general good and redounds to the relief of the poor. Yet, as has been said, it is easier for a camel to pass through the eye of a needle than for a rich man to use his wealth unselfishly. With God it is possible; and Christianity has multiplied and will yet multiply these miracles of grace. Still we are far off from the ideal; and the poor if not the destitute will be with us always. The love of the poor will lead us not only to individual, but to corporate and social efforts for their relief. It will urge us to study the laws of economics, to seek out the causes and remedies of want and suffering. And the love of poverty, what is it after all but the love of *the poor*— that compassion for the weaker members of the body-social which should counteract the corruptive tendency of competition.

By embracing the state of the poor, the Religious of the Catholic Church keep before the world His example who was poor Himself and has chosen the poor to be His representatives; and they choose what He chose, they love what He loved—not blindly, for love of being like Him exteriorly; but intelligently, for the same reasons as He; being like Him in their mind and in their heart.

II.

" No man could say the canticle but those hundred and forty-four thousand who were purchased from the earth, for they are virgins. These follow the Lamb whithersoever He goeth."—Apoc. xiv. 3, 4.

The second great vice of the world is sensual licence and impurity. We need scarcely enlarge on so unsavoury a theme. Commenting on the words: " Behold the Lamb of God who taketh away the sin of the world," some have thought that this sin of the world is nothing else but impurity. Be that as it may, it is certain that it has at all times been the commonest form of sin; and that those who pass through life untouched by its contamination are few and far between. We know, moreover, that it is the gravest and most persistent of social evils; the chiefest hindrance to collective happiness. It is not only the conditions of civilization but the exigencies of Nature herself that demand restraint in this most difficult matter, and that, for most men, and at most times. It is not our intention here to explain this apparent anomaly, but simply to take it as we find it. Look at it how we will, we see that restraint is one of the necessities of human life, as much as labour, or sorrow, or death.

It is the harder lot and the lot of the many; and He who would have His friends feel for that lot and make it their own, came among us, not as an example of conjugal perfection, but as a virgin, born of a Virgin; His foster-father, a virgin; His herald, a virgin; the friend of His bosom, a virgin; His heavenly body-guard, virgins—virgins not in mind only, but in body. It was that He might sanctify and exalt virginity that He embraced it and gave it to His choicest friends to embrace; so that a weak and impure world might be strengthened to honour and reverence virginity; to see in it the very crown of human dignity, the absolute mastery of the spirit over the most imperious exactions of the flesh; to emulate it and approach as near to it as possible by perfect chastity and spotlessness according to each one's state of life; or even to embrace it, if called thereto, as a higher and holier state than that of matrimony. For it is higher and holier to serve the many than to serve the few; to forsake home and kindred for the Gospel and the Kingdom of God on earth, and thereby to find a hundred-fold even in the present life.

Here, as in the case of poverty, Christ took what was bitter and sweetened it by making it His own. For the love of being like Christ and His Mother and His friends, thousands in every age have embraced freely and gladly that hardship which is imposed upon so many whether they will it or no. And still more do they resemble Him when they do so for like motives, amongst which, though not principal, is "compassion for the multitude." With what face can the wealthy preach contentment to the poor? and with what face could the Church preach continence to the world, did she not practise it in the persons of her priests and religious?

A married clergy may preach chastity by word of

mouth, but not by the most effectual method of preaching. By marriage a man does not overcome · in the conflict, but simply withdraws from it. Plainly the mere fact of marriage does not infuse the difficult virtue of chastity into one who was previously unchaste. Indeed, there is some fear that even matrimonial chastity will prove too severe a yoke for such a one. One who was a coward while the battle raged does not instantly become brave because peace is proclaimed. He may talk more valiantly, even as a father, forgetful of his own unmarried days, may treat the delinquencies of his son with the austerity of a Stoic.

Always and everywhere, even in the most corrupted ages the Church has preached an object-lesson to the world by the existence of her voluntary celibates of both sexes, who by vow have wedded themselves to the conflict for life. Were it not for such examples men might well say that the yoke of chastity was impossible, as many do say, who like to think that the abuses of certain times and places prevail everywhere among professed celibates, only better concealed. On the other hand, it is no less falsely said that they who fly to religion or to the altar are as cowards who flee from the danger to safety; rather they stand firm, that learning the tactics of the enemy they may be able to help others; and, having suffered themselves, pity the sufferings of others. God, says St. Paul, "comforts us in all our tribulations, that we may be able to comfort them who are in any trouble with the same comfort wherewith we ourselves are comforted of God." Nay, more, if we may believe the mystics, they "fulfil the law of Christ" by bearing the burden of others; even as the Ransomers of old who as free hostages embraced the captivity which would have endangered the faith of their weaker brethren. They do not escape temptation, but they face it and bear it. And, moreover, it is in a spirit of reparation to God's injured honour that they willingly forego what is lawful in order to make˙ atonement, in union with Christ, for the lawless indulgence and sensuality of others, and to turn away God's anger from many a sinful city or state, as the ten just men needed for the salvation of Sodom.

The more we understand the social and practical importance of an *idea*, the more shall we be convinced that, apart from all Christian and supernatural considerations whatever, the mere existence of voluntary celibates and voluntary mendicants is of incalculable importance; that as a living object-lesson they drive home truths simply and effectually, in a way which no amount of verbal insistence could succeed in doing. Hence, as we saw before, the spirit of worldliness is socially destructive, while the Catholic and eternal principles of the Gospel are conservative and progressive.

III.

" He came to Nazareth and was subject to them."
St. Luke ii. 51.

Once more; Christ came into the world where
unqualified independence, self-direction, self-government were worshipped as ends in themselves; where
obedience was viewed as at best a necessary evil—
the less of it, the better. He knew that each member
of the body was healthier, happier, and more useful in
its own place; in subjection to the superior members
and to the head; in concord and agreement with its
fellow-members; that independence, separation, isolation, meant death; death for the intellect, for the
heart and affections; for all that belongs to man
as a rational and free agent. Neither in home or in
city, in Church or in State could there be progress or
happiness without order, harmony, and subjection.
He knew also the strength of man's self-assertive
instincts,—useful and needful when restrained and
pressed into the service of higher instincts and
principles, but destructive of social life when suffered
to run riot in the form of lawless, self-regarding
ambition, grasping at the reins of government for
purposes of self-aggrandizement and self-glorifica-
tion; caring for private gain, not for the common
good. It is one and the same anti-social spirit
which manifests itself as tyranny in the ruler and as
insubordination in the subject—*omnes quærentes quæ
sua sunt et non quæ sunt Jesu Christi*—seeking themselves and not the community; and in seeking

themselves, losing themselves; even as they who lose themselves and suppress their egoism find themselves again.

For it is in proportion to the perfection of the social organism that the individual can enjoy perfect liberty and full mental and moral development. "He that seeketh his life shall lose it; but he that loseth his life for My sake shall find it." It was, then, the spirit of obedience that needed to be cultivated; obedience inspired by charity, that is, by love of the common good, of the interests of Jesus Christ; the spirit that obeys no created will, but only the will of Him who has care for the whole. It is in obeying rather than in ruling that the majority of mankind are tempted by the anti-social, self-assertive spirit; and though the temptation is far stronger in the case of those who rule, yet it was to lighten the lot of the many that our Saviour came, not merely to point out the expediency and necessity of obedience by word of mouth, but to teach us to love obeying for His sake; to prefer, should it be God's will, to obey rather than to rule; to sacrifice more liberty rather than less to the common good; to look on preeminence and authority as in some sense the less Divine and sanctified lot.

In the same spirit and for the same motives the religious of the Catholic Church have by their free and perpetual self-devotion to a life of obedience, maintained in all ages the true social principle so needed for the healing of the nations. They have furnished an object-lesson in the doctrine

of obedience as ever taught by the Christian
Religion.

Doubtless the ideal society would be one in
which the common good and greatest interest of all
would demand the fullest development of each,
securing to the several members all the conditions
requisite for the perfect realization of all their latent
capacities; one in which charity would entail no
suffering or sacrifice. But such a society is to be
found only in the Heavenly Jerusalem, never upon
the earth,—though it is a standard of approximation.
All human society, secular or ecclesiastical, entails
sacrifice and self-repression upon its members; nor
has any individual just cause of complaint if in
many ways his liberties are restricted, his talent
injured and left idle, his capacities squandered,
sometimes through force of inevitable circumstances,
sometimes through the blunderings or the faults of
those in command, sometimes through the selfishness and blindness of his fellow-members. All these
inconveniences are inseparable from our finite conditions; and by submitting to these, out of deference
to the common advantage and public peace, a man
realizes what is best and noblest among all his
capacities. Not but that he may and should vindicate
himself by all constitutional methods, and never
submit to any violation of his conscience; but that,
when all things point to the duty of self-repression,
he should yield himself courageously. It is this law-
loving self-denial, which is the strength of armies
and nations, and of the Church of Christ, whereas
it is the decay of this principle and the confusion of

licence with liberty which is rotting every European state to-day.

These, then, are the three counsels of the Gospel; the three nails, as some will have it, whereby Religious are fastened to the Cross of Christ, and held up to the derision of this foolish, near-sighted world. " Near-sighted," for, as we have said, all true progress and enlightenment which the world has so far seen is traceable to the prevalence of these three great principles, to the silent preaching of which Religious devote themselves in life-long sacrifice; while all the failure and defeat which progress has met with is due to their neglect.

We can hardly expect those outside the Church of the Saints to enter into the secrets of the saints, or to understand how, in the eyes of every true Catholic, poverty, chastity, and obedience are looked upon as the better part, the luckier lot; as beautiful and lovable for their own sake; for the sake of Christ and His saints who embraced them; for the sake of the multitudes of mankind to whom the harder lot has fallen. Still less can we expect them to enter into the more mystical and esoteric principles which, apart from all other reasons, would make the way of the Counsels the better way. Yet even outsiders have recently discovered that religious vows and even religious Orders are exceedingly useful and economical institutions; that it is desirable to have people banded together and organized for the prosecution of certain philanthropic and charitable purposes, who should be

content to receive for themselves only strict neces-
saries from a common fund, and not look for any
salary or remuneration. So far voluntary poverty is
an excellent thing. Likewise a married clergy is
rather an expensive institution, and one absorbing
in family cares a large fraction of the available
clerical energy of the country. And as for obedience,
of course some must obey, just as some must be
poor and weakly and unfortunate. For what would
become of the Government, the army, the navy, the
family, without obedience ? And who does not
see that the masses should be kept in subjection,
and that ideas of liberty and equality are fraught
with danger to public security ? Use, economy,
convenience,—these are the non-Catholic standards
and tests. Not poverty for poverty's sake; nor
chastity for chastity's sake; nor obedience for
obedience' sake; not out of reverential love of the
lot which Christ and His saints have made their
own and embraced and sanctified; not for any
sympathy with Christ's love of humanity, for whose
well-being, here and hereafter, these three counsels
are so needful; not for any scorn and contempt of
the spirit of worldliness which nailed Christ to the
Cross, and crucifies His little ones daily by the
million,—the mortal enemy of God and of humanity;
but for narrow, economical, mercantile reasons such
as appeal to souls from which all that is ideal,
spiritual, catholic, eternal, has been driven by three
centuries of egoism in religion, in politics, in philosophy, and in morality.

IV.

" Mary hath chosen the best part."—St. Luke x. 42.

Whatever toleration the world may have learnt for the religious profession, it is only in so far as it secures conditions favourable to a life of active usefulness and practical charity. For the higher life of contemplation it has rarely a good word to say. St. Simeon on his pillar, the hermits of the Thebaid are its classical examples of perverted piety and of the early defection of Christianity from the philanthropic and utilitarian spirit of its Founder. *Ut quid perditio hæc?* Why this waste of energy and time which might be turned to good account and given to the poor? How is society or how is the Church the better of such an existence? or how is it compatible with the very conception of charity, which means association, co-operation, mutual service?

Here again, though particular orders and institutions are contingent and transitory, yet the greater excellence of the contemplative life, viewed in the abstract, is a constant and unchangeable part of the Church's teaching. For, indeed, the eternal life of Heaven is a life of contemplation and praise; and man touches his highest here on earth when for some brief moment he anticipates Heaven and dwells in loving wonder on the features of Divine Truth. All the labour of man done under the sun is directed to some few spells of restful contemplation and enjoyment, which make life

worth the living; even the pleasures and amuse-
ments of the most degraded and perverse are found
in the last analysis to consist in gazing upon or
witnessing something that interests the mind or the
imagination; but only when our taste is schooled to
delight in the beholding of God and of things
Divine do we attain the end of our creation. As
each single soul must be stifled to death if from
time to time it does not rise to the surface for a
breath of the upper atmosphere; so it is needful for
the corporate life of the Church and of the community that there should be those who, being fitted
by natural gifts and supernatural grace, are set apart
for the direct cultus and service of truth, and for the
exercise of Divine praise; whose office is to keep
the sacred lamp burning while others immersed in
active charity slumber and sleep for very weariness
and heaviness of the eyes. Strange that an acute
thinker of our day,[1] one keenly alive to the organic
conception of society, should not have seen that the
division of labour involved in separation of contemplative from active life is a consequence of
that very conception. St. Simeon Stylites in the
desert, was as actively a member of the Christian
community as St. Paul. By the perfection of each
part the whole is perfected, and he who recognizes
himself as part of a whole often serves the whole
best by being rather than by doing. If in no other
way, at least in proclaiming by his very existence
that man's last end, his highest work here and
hereafter, is eternal rest, the love of truth, the

[1] Dr. E. Caird, Master of Balliol.

contemplation and praise of God, a work which produces nothing, which is worth doing for its own sake, and for whose sake alone all other work is profitable,—were it only to keep this idea alive in an insane world of aimless rush and unrest, the professed contemplative in these days would be in one sense the most valuable and useful member of society.

Obviously the contemplative life, even more than the religious life, is an exceedingly rare vocation, demanding many natural gifts of no common sort as a basis for grace to work upon; while the needs of the Church in a given locality or age might plainly require the sacrifice of these aptitudes to more urgent calls of duty. There is a common fallacy about equality which has done much harm to the Church by supposing that because all are equally called to be perfect in their own line, therefore all are called to and capable of equal perfection. It is as untrue to say every one can be a saint or a religious or a contemplative, as to say he can be a hero or poet or a genius. The Church is always warring, by her legislation, with the indiscretion of those whose haste and inexperience would hurry them to profess willingness for prison and death when they are not capable of following even from afar, and still more with the indiscretion of those who, for one foolish reason or another, would play the part of the Holy Ghost to others in the matter of vocation. Yet, while readily admitting the call to be rarer than is supposed in practice, we cannot but justify the judgment of the Catholic Church in her esteem for the profession of the Evangelical Counsels, as well as for the higher life of contemplation.

It is not then to new social systems that we can trust for the remedy of those evils which weigh upon the public conscience of these times.   It is to the character of the people before all else.   Doubtless this in its turn is conditioned by environments ; and it may well be questioned if under the existing social organization any universal amelioration through religious influence is possible.   Still whenever such favourable conditions are secured it is religion and religion alone—nay, the Catholic religion alone, that will be able to effect and maintain that elevated moral tone which is essential for all veritable progress.   It is by her continual insistence on the three Evangelical Counsels, illustrated and brought home to the public mind by the lives and examples of her Religious that she will keep alive that flame of charity kindled by Him who is at once the " Light of the nations and the Glory of His people Israel."

THE DIVINE PRECEPT.

"Whoso loveth not God how loveth he his neighbour as himself, since neither doth he love himself?"

"How then doth Christ love us but to the end that we may be able to reign with Christ? To this same end let us love one another."—St. Augustine, Tract 83, in Joan.

"My Beloved is as a bundle of myrrh." Our Divine Saviour is that same "Beloved," laid in our bosom to heal the corruption of our affections; to purify the gold of human love from all its dross and defilement; He comes to lay His Heart against ours, and to heal them; not to freeze them or still them into death, but to calm and regulate their wild wayward pulsations, to teach them a rhythm from Heaven; from the Heart of God Himself. This was His precept, the summary of His doctrine; not that we should merely love one another—that was commanded from the beginning, when the human heart was first moulded—but that our love should be after the pattern of His, *Sicut dilexi vos*—"As I have loved you." It was a method and manner of loving He came to teach us; a devoted, a passionate love, yet restrained, severe, and seeming cruel; a suffering and a dying love, which could find no exercise, no expression, no relief, but in pain; not merely in serviceable and useful pain, but at times in pain for the mere sake of expression; because pain is the very language of love, which even God Himself had to speak before He could persuade our hearts.

Seeing the oceans of sin that deluge the world through the perversions of human affections, men might well be excused for thinking that the love of God and of creatures were incompatible and antagonistic, except so far as the latter were loved not spontaneously, or for themselves, but only from a sense of duty to God. Yet our Lord will have no such safe charity, but bids us at His word launch out into the deep, and face the peril inseparable from our lot. *Et Verbum caro factum est,*—Divine love took flesh and embodied itself in a throbbing human heart, that we might learn what our affections may rise to, by the infusion of the Holy Spirit. The object of His love is man, not the soul, but the whole man, body and soul, the whole nature which He assumed, in which He suffered, in which He was transfigured and glorified. And He loves us, not for any merely extrinsic reason, but for the very lovableness which is inherent in us, which He Himself has given us; for every participation of His own Divine excellence and beauty. When we think how infinitesimal this is, we might wonder how His love is so great; but we no longer wonder when we remember that the infinite force with which each particle of created goodness is drawn back to the Creator's bosom as to its origin and end, is the force of God's self-love. Even when we see what God sees, we cannot see it in the way He sees it, nor therefore love it in the way He loves it. Greater minds and hearts are penetrated and rapt away by what to others seems ordinary, perhaps "common and unclean," and each one feels that his soul's inner growth is shown in a keener appreciation of the unnoticed goodness that lies round him on every side. The vulgar can see no beauty except in perpetual novelties and sensational surprises; they must go abroad; while the trained eye and delicate affection see delights everywhere without end. Therefore God's love of finite goodness is infinite; though not in every way, as is His love of His own infinite goodness. He delights infinitely in those beauties of mind and heart and form which stir our feeble affections to their roots; and, moreover, He who looks into the darkest corners of the soul often sees there a thousand lovablenesses hidden from us. Nor in any two are these beauties combined in the same assortment or proportion, that they should be classed together and loved under some universal kind. He knows His sheep individually, and calls each by its name—that is, He draws it to Himself in its own individual way, and no two in the same way.

The Father Himself loves us by the very necessity of His nature. He was free to create us, to give us more or less lovableness; but having made us lovable, He is not free to do other than love us; for He must love His least image as necessarily as He loves Himself. And the Incarnate Son, whose human will and heart is dominated by that same infinite love, and thrills in the most perfect and intelligent sympathy therewith, loves not merely *what* the Father loves, blindly, extrinsically, but loves it for the same reason, looking on us with the same eyes, with an understanding, sympathetic love. *Sicut dilexi vos,*—This is how He loved us, this is how we are to love one another, according to His precept, and His commandment is not grievous.

Many speak as though the Divine love of our neighbour differed from the natural, in that the former is wholly extrinsic and relative, the latter intrinsic and absolute. God has bid us (they say) to despise and put aside that love whose motive is inherent lovableness, and to foster that only which has no reference to intrinsic qualities. God might have ordered us to love so many stones, for some mysterious reason or other, connected with His service; and we should have been bound to love them (or rather, to act as if we loved them, for real love essentially supposes intrinsic attractiveness in its object). And were He capriciously to change His mind, and order us to love stocks instead of stones, we ought to have no difficulty in at once transferring to them whatever exterior courtesies we had previously been bestowing on the stones. "No difficulty," because there was no real personal affection to uproot, whose only possible soil is inherent lovableness. This is what they call "spiritual," as opposed to "carnal," or "natural" love. To love our parents "spiritually," means, with them, to disregard the natural instinct of filial affection, and to pay them only such service and duty as we are bound to give to any stock or stone that God has told us to love; not because it is what "nature" prompts us to do, but because God has ordered it for some reason of His own. This, they say, is what is meant by loving God alone, and all things else only for His sake. We are to look on them simply as fetiches, as arbitrary tokens, withdrawing from them any love they might absorb into themselves that we may transfer it all to their Creator, and so loving them for His sake that, without any change in them, we should be equally ready to hate them for His sake, should He tell us so to do. "Whatsoever you did to the least of these you did it unto Me," is interpreted to mean that fraternal charity is purely relative, a fiction as far as our brethren are concerned; that God is its sole object, just as the obeisance made to the Queen's empty throne is accepted as personal to herself.

The meaning, however, is not so much: Forget them, and think of Me, as: Forget Me, and think of them; as is plain from the wondering reply of the just: Lord, when saw we Thee hungry, and fed Thee? It is the same spirit which is embodied in the command, "Weep not for Me, but weep for yourselves and for your children."

We do not say that this doctrine of extrinsic charity has ever been so explicitly formulated as we have formulated it here. But holy men and even canonized saints have at times unconsciously implied its principles, both in practice and in precept. Nor is this scandalous or wonderful, to any one who understands rightly the tedious process by which the golden grains of truth are sundered and sifted from the chaff of errors and fallacies. Still less, when we find these same holy men just as often implying in precept, and far more in practice, principles diametrically opposite and inconsistent with those we complain of. For it is only when they are explicitly separated and stated that principles can be judged and compared. Not one of the Saints was ever sanctified or sanctified others in consequence of the incorrect principles, but in spite of them. As a matter of fact we find that all the greater Saints were men of large and tender affections, who drew others to them by the cords of Adam; who, however imperfectly they may have analyzed and formulated their love, loved truly and directly by the very instinct of the Holy Ghost. For a Saint is not necessarily a philosopher, any more than a philosopher is a Saint.

Nor is it wonderful that in so subtle a matter much inaccuracy should creep in; for the very words in which the erroneous theory is embodied, are the words of Christ and of His Apostles, and of such a master of spiritual things as St. Ignatius of Loyola. Evidently they are ambiguous words; but heaven and earth are not more distant and opposed than the two meanings of which they are susceptible. One is by implication the doctrine of the dualism of Zoroaster, and of the Gnostics and Manicheans, which in its open form has ever been regarded as the most pestilential error, but which, as the parasitic corruption of a truth, has ever and again subtly interwoven itself with the ascetic teachings of saints and doctors, and has sprung up from time to time to choke the good seed and impede its fruitfulness and vigour. The other is the Catholic teaching of reason and revelation, the canon by which all other teaching must at length stand or fall. Dualism gives us practically two gods; a principle of good and a principle of evil. Spirit, it tells us, is the work of God; matter is the work of the devil. The conflict between these two, ending in the victory of spirit and the subjugation of matter, constitutes the drama of creation. This is only the perversion of a great truth, a perversion slight in itself, but portentous in its consequences. We too hold that the subjugation of matter to spirit and of spirit to God is the consummation towards which all things move. But matter, no less than spirit, is God's dear creature; and as spirit is not destroyed, but perfected and elevated by its subjection to divinity; so matter is transfigured, glorified, and exalted by its impregnation with spirit. God's conflict with matter and spirit is not that of an enemy, but of a parent with a wayward child whom he chastens in love—*Quem diligit, castigat.* Evil spirits and evil men play their part in this work of evolution and purgation, but only under the permission and direction of God's most wise and loving, though mysterious, providence. Seeing how large a part the subjugation of the flesh to the spirit plays in Christian asceticism, and how the great bulk of men's more patent sins are due to the insubordination of the animal passions, it is a natural exaggeration of the truth to suppose that the interests of the body are wholly and always hostile to those of the soul; that spirituality requires the death of the

senses and emotions; and that because the pre-
eminence of mind over matter is good, therefore it
may be with advantage carried to infinity. This
seems to be Plato's view, who regards the body
simply as the prison-house of the soul, a mere
impediment to its expansion, a hindrance altogether,
a help in no sense; though it must be confessed
that he credits the pure spirit with an emotional
fervour and passionateness which an acuter analysis
recognizes to be dependent on the senses. How
great an influence Plato had with St. Augustine and
other Christian writers, and St. Augustine, in his
turn, upon the Western Church is notorious. Still
Aristotle, as interpreted by Aquinas, supplies a
salutary antidote to whatever insidious poison may
have been imbibed in regard to this matter. His
doctrine is altogether in sympathy with the mysteries
of Christian revelation touching the origin, office,
redemption, and glorification of the body. It is not
in the extinction of the feelings and passions and
instincts, but in their culture and restraint that
man's spirit reaches its fullest development. As
body and soul are complementary principles of our
substantial nature, so senses and intelligence, imagination and reason, feeling and volition, are co-
principles of our perfect operation; the one material,
the other formal; the one embodying, the other
embodied; neither perfect, except so far as duly
proportioned to the other. Evil is not matter, or
anything absolute, but a discord, a disproportion;
and to secure concord and proportion is the aim of
Catholic and Christian asceticism, so far as it is

identified with moral training and perfection. But, as we have said above, it is easy to misunderstand and pervert the true principle of mortification so as to fall into implicit gnosticism. Christianity insists on chastity, honours celibacy, approves fasting and bodily penance. Gnosticism does the same, but on a different assumption, and does much more besides, dishonouring the body, forbidding marriage and the use of animal food. And in a sense the erroneous principle is simpler and more easily apprehended and embraced than the truth, which is a nice balance between the two extremes of an exaggerated spiritualism on the one hand and of gross sensuality on the other—the latter being the inevitable reaction and final issue of the former.

For this reason the Church's watchful guidance is continually needed to keep her children's feet in the narrow track of truth, deviating neither to right or left; or rather, since the deviations are incessant, it is her office to recall us now from one excess, now from another. Hence she is credited by her enemies with the most opposite vices; at one time she is the friend of publicans and sinners, eating and drinking, a glutton and a wine-bibber; at another, she comes before the world fasting, and "behold she has a devil."

Besides this natural misunderstanding of the relation of body to spirit, a kindred source of the error we are combating is found in the misconception of the relation of nature to grace. This error is a perversion, not of a natural truth, but of a dogma of revelation. No Christian can believe that the devil created human nature, but many believe wrongly that he has so perverted and corrupted the essence of humanity, that God has practically made him a present of it; that as a cracked reed can only give forth a harsh and broken note, so every action and operation, every thought and desire and impulse proceeding from our fallen nature jars upon God's ears, is hateful and discordant to Him, as reminding Him of the ruin of His fair handiwork. This is Lutheranism and Jansenism; and so far as the writings of St. Augustine or even of St. Paul present obscurities "which the unwary and unstable wrest to their own damnation," it happens that at all times there have been unauthorized Catholic teachers who have implicitly, by precept or practice, admitted a similarly false conception of the nature of original sin; and who have allowed it to tinge their ascetical theories so that "natural" and "wicked" have come to be synonymous in their language. "If we love from natural motives, such love," they say, " must be wicked. God has no pleasure in the moral perfection even of a Socrates, but regards such unbaptized virtue with disgust."

Here, as the truth is subtler, its perversion is the more easy. Human nature in its essence has suffered no deterioration through original sin. It is still the image and likeness of God, and He, seeing Himself mirrored therein, pronounces it "very good;" and since it is He who works in its every movement, and causes it to think truth and to love goodness, and to do righteousness, that which He works in us and through us as free instruments is also " very good," and " shall in no wise lose its reward." Yet it does not receive the same reward as when our soul and its faculties are permeated, transfigured, and elevated by supernatural light and grace; which, without destroying or removing our natural goodness, shines through it like the sunlight through stained glass, giving it a glory and radiance which is in it, but not from it. Grace is not another soul over and above our natural soul; but it is a new radiance given to the soul by a new indwelling of God. We have not one set of actions which are natural and another which are supernatural; but when the soul is supernaturalized, its faculties and operations, as it were, its leaves and blossoms, are characterized like the root from which they spring. Grace is given us not to destroy but to fulfil, to perfect nature in its own order and to add to it a perfection of the Divine order. Supernatural love presupposes perfect natural love as its subject and basis. It breathes into it the breath of divinity and makes it instinct with eternal life. It is not too bold to say that grace is for nature, and not nature for grace; for every subject or substance is the final cause of its own properties and endowments; clothes for the body, and not the body for clothes. Grace is given to us for the healing and perfection of our nature, in order that our natural intelligence and our natural affections may be raised to a perceptible preter-natural excellence and infused with an imperceptible supernatural dignity and merit. Natural love is the raw material which grace works upon or is wrought upon. Crush natural love, and grace must remain idle.

U

Here, again, it is evident how fatal a false dualism must be to ascetical doctrine. And yet the fallacy as before is an easy one; for the natural mind, and will, and heart are perfected by the gentle restraint of grace, and reach their culmination through obedience to law and at the cost of "many tribulations;" and from this fact we are prone to conclude hastily that what needs to be conquered, needs to be slain. Some confusion moreover is due to the double sense attaching to the word "natural." Besides the ordinary and scientific sense there is a specialized use of the word, in which it signifies, not merely what is not transfigured by grace, but that which, owing to its positive deformity and unreasonableness, is *incapable* of being so transfigured. "Natural" love in this sense—or "carnal love," as it is sometimes called—is really "unnatural" if we use "natural" in the proper sense of reasonable. It is love which is selfish, disorderly, unrestrained; bestowed on some unfitting object, or on some fitting object in some unfitting way.

It is plain, then, that we need not be surprised if many good and holy men have been wanting in clearness of perception and precision of expression in regard to this obscure matter, where so much caution is required to steer straight between the Scylla and Charybdis. "Love me, love my dog," sounds a very straightforward and easy principle, yet it can mean two very different things. It may mean that, however much I may naturally and justifiably detest my friend's pet, I cannot con-sistently with his friendship ill-treat or abuse it, and may even be bound to bestow upon it the outward signs of an affection which I do not feel. This is mere extrinsic love, whose motive is no excellence I see in the dog; but only the excellence I see in my friend. Yet a deeper friendship will make me wish to go further; to enter into complete sympathy with my friend's tastes and inclinations; so that I shall try to love what he loves with him, seeing in it what he sees. I may not be able to do so altogether, and so far my friendship is imperfect (supposing his taste correct) and my soul is out of harmony or not in the fullest harmony with his. Similarly, when we speak of loving others for God's sake, we may mean one of two utterly different things. We may mean loving them with a merely extrinsic love whose sole motive is God's own intrinsic goodness; or we may mean loving them in sympathy with God, seeing them as far as we can with His eyes and loving them for what we see in them. There can be no doubt whatever as to which is the true conception, that, namely, which means the most perfect, and intelligent, and sympathetic love of God. We can never hope to see in others all that lovableness which He sees; or that our heart shall be drawn towards the little we do see with a force not infinitely less than that of the Divine Heart; but the measure of our approach is the exact measure of our growth in the love of God.

The more we understand and love God, the more shall we enter into sympathy with His love of men; and the more we get to understand and love men, the sooner shall we be able to enter into the mind of God. For all true and spiritual friendship is founded on and requires community of tastes, the appreciation and love of the same things. God, hungering and thirsting for our affection, knows well how slowly that affection must be won; how our taste must be gradually formed and raised until it can find delight in the Divine beauty, which is the common object of knowledge and ecstatic love whereby God and His saints are bound together in a single life of joy and praise—even as two friends may, in some common object of loving adoration, be tied together heart to heart. Were there one whose capacity we doubted not, and for whose fuller love we craved, with what care should we not lead him into completer sympathy with ourselves, bridging over the distance between us. So it is that God leads us to Himself through creatures; step by step purifying and raising our love; giving it an ever-increasing breadth, and depth, and height, till at last we love nothing in creatures but what is truly lovable and Divine; and are, therefore, in proximate readiness to love Divinity itself, not to the exclusion of others, but indefinitely above them all.

Then, indeed, what we love in them is Him; not His substance, but His image. Nor is our love of the image a merely relative love whose sole motive is the excellence of the thing imaged; as though the image were but an arbitrary sign; but it is an intrinsic love founded on the real and inherent beauty of the image; it is a love distinct from, though subordinate to, the love of **the** archetype to which it leads us.

And what we love in Him is them; for we have no proper concept of God, but only a concept built up from creatures, amongst which man is principal, as the microcosm, the epitome of creation. All **the** Divine perfections that draw our love to God are those that we have gradually learnt to love first in our fellow-men— justice, truth, purity, gentleness, mercy, and the rest. As far as we are blind to these excellences in our neighbour, as far as we steel our hearts against their attraction, so far is the Divine beauty hidden from our eyes and impotent over our affections; we may hear and we may assent to the truth that God is good, and gracious, and holy, and just, but these words kindle no fire of enthusiasm or devotion within us; for our affections are dwarfed and stunted for want of food and exercise; we have no heart to give; we have crushed our love of man, and have not found the love of God; we are unloved and unlovable; unloving and unable to love. Nor can we ever know, or at least realize, God's passionate love for us if we ourselves have never felt the hungering affection of the mother for the child, of friend for friend, or some one of the nobler forms of suppliant, self-denying love and devotion. Else what does it avail to tell me that God's love for me is that of father, mother, friend, and spouse, all in one and carried to infinity? Or to tell me that I should aspire to love Him back as father, mother, friend, and spouse, if I have never given any one of these affections play; never developed and purified my power of loving? In brief, it is through man alone that we can know or love God as long as we see Him only through a glass darkly, and before we are face to face with Him.

To love our neighbour as Christ loves us, means, therefore, to love him as far as possible in sympathy with God; loving him for what is really best and divinest in him; seeking to bring out more fully the hidden image of God in his soul. It means the perfecting of our instinctive affections; recognizing in them the impulse of the Divine will drawing men first to one another, and through one another to Itself, as the Supreme Lover and centre of all attraction. It means restraint and sacrifice and the sword of separation, for *Sine dolore non vivitur in amore*—"the life of love is a life of sorrow." It is the love of Abraham for Isaac; the love of Christ for His Mother; the love which is ready to stab and thrust and slay; which shrinks from no present pain for the sake of after bliss. It is the love of St. Paul for his children, heedless of present ingratitude and misunderstanding; spending itself gladly, "though the more I love you the less I be loved." And it will show itself in ceaseless toil and labour for the beloved; in endless endeavour to communicate with him our choicest treasure; to get him to see what we see and to love what we love; to break down every wall of separation or unsympathy that stands between soul and soul; to find ever richer treasures ourselves that we may have more to share, more costly and precious fuel to feed love's flame;

to learn new arts and sciences that we may impart them to the beloved; to wean our hearts from all that is spurious, untrue, lest we hurt so much as a hair of his head, every one of which is numbered and dear to us; to find in God alone that pearl of great price, that common Friend who is the bond of all friendship, in whom all other pure and noble sympathies are united.

This is how Christ has loved us; and His precept is that we should so love one another, or rather labour so to love one another; for it is the work of our life to educate ourselves out of our selfishness and sensuality and to learn the lovableness of God's children. If we can study God only in His works, man is the epitome and summary of His works; and it is there we must seek Him and love Him. *Omnes in eo, et eum in omnibus*—"All in Him and Him in all." The second great precept is not different from the first, but only another expression of it.

Whether we consider our Saviour's human love of His Blessed Mother, of the Baptist, of His Apostles, of His own people, of His betrayer, of His murderers and enemies, we see everywhere the characteristics we have described above. It was no mere extrinsic love indifferent to the inherent lovableness of its immediate object, and therefore equal towards all. He loved all equally in the sense that He loved each, so far as each was beloved by His Father and made lovable. But God's gifts are manifold, in no two cases the same. He has no unjust preferences; but He loved His Mother

immeasurably beyond all; and His Apostles who
were "with Him in His temptations" beyond His
other disciples; and Peter, and James, and John
more than the other Apostles; and John of these,
with the peculiar love of special friendship. And
He loved Lazarus and his sisters, but especially
Mary. Plainly His love was not merely extrinsic,
but was motived by what He saw in each; and
since His estimate was perfectly true and just, and
His affections pure and noble, His human love was
in the most perfect sympathy and accord with His
Divine love. And how very naturally His love
manifested itself is also clear. He wept over the
grave of Lazarus; He wept over His beloved city
of Jerusalem; He sought at times to be apart with
His friends; He revealed to them His special
secrets; He sought their sympathy and their
prayers; He was grieved by their coldness and
slowness to believe in His love; by their cowardice
and treachery. Altogether, if His love for them was
Divine and supernatural, it was at the same time
thoroughly natural and human, and therefore *Quod
Deus conjunxit, homo non separet*—"What God hath
united let no man put asunder."

Yet if it was deep and tender "beyond the love
of women," it was not soft or selfish, but austere and
restrained; a love that could rebuke, and chasten,
and hold aloof with a severity proportioned to its
tenderness. How abrupt with His Blessed Mother
at times; how seemingly cold and indifferent; how
ruthless with Peter; how cruel in the very tenderness of His reproaches! None could sit at His

right hand or lean upon His bosom, who had not drunk deep of His chalice and been baptized with His baptism and pierced through and through with the dividing sword of sorrow.

And if it is the part of love to give itself, to empty itself out to the last drop of blood; to humble itself to the dust, who ever loved as He? "Greater love hath no man than this that a man lay down his life for his friends;" only a God-Man can go beyond this and say, " Take and eat: this is My Body. Drink ye all of this, for this is My Blood." Yet it is only the same natural longing carried to a greater extreme,—*usque in finem;* it is the passionate craving of all true love, divinized and lifted above the clouds. Nay, it is rather God's Love made flesh and dwelling among us; Divine, yet altogether human. And this is His precept, that as He has loved us so we also should love one another; for if a man love not his brother whom he hath seen, how can he love God whom he hath not seen?

THE MYSTERY OF FAITH.

I.

"O sacrum convivium in quo Christus sumitur;
  Recolitur memoria passionis ejus;
  Mens impletur gratia;
  Et futuræ gloriæ nobis pignus datur."
                                        St. Thomas Aquinas.

IN these words the Blessed Eucharist is offered to our consideration, first, as a sacrificial banquet; that is, as being at once a sacrifice and a banquet; then, as a memorial or commemorative feast; finally, in its effects as a means of grace in the present, and a pledge of glory in the future. Let us then first dwell upon it under its sacrificial aspect.

God is a spirit, and they that adore Him must adore Him in spirit and in truth. Man, on the other hand, is not spirit alone, but spirit and body, and therefore his adoration, internal and external, private and public, is an embodied adoration. He is bound by the necessity of his double nature to picture God to himself, and to speak of Him after a human fashion; to conceive Him in his own image and likeness. And God who has made man, and knows whereof he is made and remembers that he is but dust, not only permits it and tolerates it, but wills it to be so. Had He wanted us different, He would have made us different. And so He wills that we should utter our prayers and praises with voice and tongue, as though He heard with mortal ears and could not read the secrets of the heart; that we should lift up our eyes to Him, as though He were seated in the clouds far above us; that we should kneel and prostrate ourselves as at the feet of a mortal monarch; that we should hold up our joined hands, as it were begging release from our fetters—in a word, that we should embody our inward worship in outward signs and symbols, and speak of spirit in the terms of sense, of the infinite in the language of the finite. Nor is there in these practices, as some foolishly think, any real ignorance or superstition, so long as the inadequate and merely symbolic character of such utterances is adverted to.

Still more needful are such symbolic manifestations where men meet together for the public worship of God, and where their internal concord in thought and desire can be expressed and secured only by means of outward expression.

Chief among those rites whereby in all times and places men have embodied their worship, is the offering of sacrifice, in which food is brought and laid as a gift on God's table, as a sign of praise and adoration, of gratitude for favours received, of sorrow for sins committed, as the price of protection and assistance and grace. As the

word is now understood, sacrifice is said exclusively
of an offering made to the one supreme God in
attestation of His supremacy and oneness; so that
it can be offered to no other being, however great,
without the guilt of idolatry and blasphemy. But
if we look back to early times for the derivation of
the rite, we find apparently that food-offerings
were made by way of tribute and homage to the
father or patriarch or monarch, to symbolize
such a relation between the offerer and receiver
as exists between children and their father, from
whom they derive their life and support and food;
who spring from one body, eat of one bread,
drink of one cup, dwell in one house, look to one
heritage. We see that it was directed to the
confirmation of the rights of sonship where they
already existed; or to their renewal, when broken
off by trespass; or to the creation of an adoptive
sonship, where no such tie had existed before. It
was, therefore, the sign or seal or outward formality
of a solemn contract, or covenant, whereby the
rights and duties of fatherhood on one side, and of
sonship on the other, were created, renewed, or
ratified. And accordingly, when men needed to
enter into relation with God, the universal Father,
to be received as His adopted sons, to be allowed
to sit at His household table and eat of His meat,
it was in keeping with our necessity of conceiving
Divine things humanwise, that we should bring
food-offerings to Him, and solemnize our covenant
with Him, according to the rites and conventions of
similar human contracts.

That the offerer should partake of the victim after it has been accepted is the natural, though not necessary sequel of sacrifice. It is a complementary act to which the act of sacrifice is in some sort directed. To accept the offering, is to admit the offerer to the rights of sonship, whereof the sign and evidence is a seat at the household table, a share in the household meal. Thus, when the prodigal is restored to the forfeited rights of sonship, a banquet is prepared for him by his father, as we read in the parable. The food which one offers as a supplicant and servant or slave, he receives back as a child from the hand of his father.

That this is the earliest notion of sacrifice and communion, seems fairly evident from a careful study of the sacrifices of the Gentiles and of the pre-Levitical sacrifices, recorded in Holy Scripture. Those of the Mosaic law are too complicated with prophetic symbolism to permit the root-idea to stand out in all its clearness and definition. We find God rebuking the Israelites for offering food libations to false gods instead of to Him; and St. Paul sums up the whole matter briefly, where he says: "I speak as to the initiated; judge ye what I say: The Cup of Blessing which *we* bless, is it not the communion of the Blood of Christ? the Bread which *we* break, is it not the communion of the Body of Christ? Look at Israel after the flesh. Are not they that eat of the sacrifice partakers of the altar? I would not have you to be partakers with devils. You cannot drink the cup of the Lord and the cup of devils; you cannot share the table of the Lord and the table of devils."[1]

Whether, then, we speak of Gentile sacrifice, or Jewish sacrifice, or Christian sacrifice; of the altar of devils, or of Jehovah; the notion of sacrifice, of food-offering and libation, is one and the same— it is a solemn covenant-feast, an expression of absolute subjection and submission on the one side, and a pledge of protection and fatherhood on the other. The former is symbolized by the offering, the latter by the communion which follows acceptance,—"They shall be My people and I will be their God." Thus our Saviour says, expressing the fruit of His own sacrifice: "I ascend to My Father and to your Father; to My God and to your God."

But like every outward expression or symbol, a sacrifice may be true or false according as the inward homage it signifies is present or absent. Self-oblation and subjection is the soul and quickening principle, without which the sacrifice which symbolizes and embodies it, is worthless or worse than worthless before God—for we insult Him with a spotted and blemished victim instead of honouring Him with an odour of sweetness. Of such lying sacrifices God says: "Shall I eat the flesh of bulls or drink the blood of goats?" and: "Obedience is

---

[1] "Ut prudentibus loquor, vos ipsi judicate quod dico. Calix benedictionis cui benedicimus nonne communicatio sanguinis Christi est? et panem quem frangimus nonne participatio corporis Domini est? . . . Videte Israel secundum carnem! nonne qui edunt hostias participes sunt altaris? . . . Nolo autem vos socios fieri dæmoniorum; non potestis mensæ Domini participes esse et mensæ dæmoniorum." (1 Cor. xi. 15, seq.)

better than sacrifice, and to hearken than the fat of rams;" and David: "If Thou hadst desired sacrifice I would have given it Thee, but Thou delightest not in burnt offerings." Not that God here rejects the form of worship which He Himself had approved and enjoined; but He reminds us that the form is not the reality, the sign is not the thing signified, the body of sacrifice is not the spirit of sacrifice.

Thus, gathering up our results so far, we see that sacrifice is an offering of food made to Almighty God to testify our submission and subjection to Him as to the Author and Giver of all; to express our desire to be received or retained among the number of His children, to sit at His table, and to share His meat. It expresses our love and reverence for His glory and majesty, our thankfulness for all His goodness towards us, our consequent sorrow if we have offended one so good in Himself and praiseworthy, one so good to us and thankworthy. It is an earnest of our desire to repair the wrong we have done singly and collectively—for as an act of public and social worship, it is an offering for the sins of the people, for the sins of the world. We implore by it all those helps and graces needful for ourselves singly and collectively, for the spread of His Kingdom, for the extension of His glory. And God in accepting it, and in inviting us to partake if we will, thereby signs and ratifies the covenant between us, and engages to be to us a Father, if we will be to Him true children.

And all that is contained in this notion of

sacrifice we find verified in a higher, more excellent, and truer way, in the great sacrifice of the Christian Church, which is the full and adequate expression of that worship which the sacrifices of Jew and pagan strove vainly to utter in lisping, stammering accents, *Lex habens umbram futurorum bonorum*— "the law being but the shadow of good things to come:" the substance being Christ. For the praise and gratitude and contrition of every soul that ever lived, the perfect self-oblation of the whole race, could never satisfy what is due to God in the way of love and worship; much less could such internal dispositions embody themselves in an offering adequate to their expression. Therefore, that the human race might be able to offer Him an acceptable and adequate sacrifice, God gave His only Son to be the second Adam, that all who received Him and were incorporated with Him, might through and with Him offer a supreme and sufficient worship in spirit and in truth. He alone, who in virtue of His Divinity was eternally in the bosom of the Father, could comprehend the infinite lovableness of God; could measure the depth and height and length and breadth of His mercies towards the children of men; could fathom the abyss of the malice of sin, knowing each several sin of every son of Adam; could sorrow for it, as if it were His own by imputation; and could make amends for it so ample as to blot it out of the Divine memory, as some faint discord is drowned in a great burst of harmony; He alone could intercede with infallible wisdom and efficacy for the glory of God, for His Kingdom and His will upon earth; for the needs of mankind—spiritual and temporal; for the averting of Divine anger; for help in temptation and deliverance from evil. And being the Son of God by nature, and also the Son of man, He alone was the fitting Mediator of that New and Eternal Covenant between God and man, whereby the human race under Him as their Head was adopted as the son of God and entitled to a place at the banquet of Eternal Life—a Covenant sealed with the sacrifice of His Body and the libation of His Blood—His Blood of the New and Eternal Testament. Moreover, if the inner submission and self-oblation of all men and angels together could never equal the infinite adoration due to God, or atone for the indignity offered to Him by a single wilful insult or rebellion; not so the self-submission of one who in point of personal dignity was equal to the Father and of the same nature—His beloved Son in whom He was well pleased. Nor was the sacrificial offering, wherein that worship was embodied, something of mere conventional worth, an inadequate symbol of the supersensible reality, but, Priest and Victim in one, He offered that same priceless self, the Body and the Blood of the Incarnate Son of God as a true food-offering, on Calvary and on the altar. As a true food-offering, for He is the very Bread of Life, not such manna as Israel ate in the desert, but the true Bread from Heaven; the bread of grace, of the spiritual life, nay, of the Divine life.

v

Now, plainly, God, who is the Giver and Pre-server of that Divine vitality, stands as little in need of this spiritual and heavenly food as He does of bodily food. "If I were hungry," He seems to say, "I would not tell thee; for mine are the cattle on a thousand hills;" for "the earth is the Lord's and the fulness thereof." Yet though He was rich, for our sakes God has become poor and needy and dependent. He knows well that love is starved where it finds no indigence, nothing to bear, or to give, or to suffer; that it seeks rather to minister than to be ministered to; to give than to receive. And so He has framed Himself round, as it were, with a halo of created glory in the creatures which He has made and loved; and His love makes their interests and needs His own, so that in the order of nature no less than in that of grace He seems to say: "Inasmuch as ye did it to the least of these My brethren ye did it unto Me." And therefore He who needed nothing in Himself, in the person of poor fallen humanity hungered and fainted for the Bread of Life. "God so loved the world" that its miseries were His own; "so loved the world that He gave His only-begotten Son" for it. Far be it from us to picture an angry God reluctantly dis-suaded from vengeance through the intervention of a more placable Son. There is but one nature and love and will in the two. "I and My Father are one;" "He that hath seen Me hath seen the Father;" "The Father Himself loveth you." Let us rather enter into the eternal council of mercy and hear the Father's compassionate demand,

"Whence shall we buy bread in the desert that these may eat?" and the answer of the Son of His Love, *Ecce ego, mitte me*—"Lo, here am I; send Me," the true Manna, the Bread that giveth life to the world. Sacrifice and offering Thou wouldst not, then said I: Lo, I come to do Thy will, O God; to be obedient unto death, even the death of the Cross.

And now what was this "will" that He came to do; of which He says: "My meat is to do the will of Him that sent Me, and to perfect His work"? What was this work that was perfected when He bowed His head and said: *Consummatum est*—"It is perfected"? What was the commandment of the Father which He came to obey and fulfil? Even that commandment whereof He was the great teacher and example; of which He says, "A new commandment give I unto you; even that which you had from the beginning." "This is My precept that you love one another in the same manner as I have loved you." And in what manner? Even unto death. Christ was made for us obedient to the new and eternal precept of fraternal love, "unto death, even to the death of the Cross." The Good Shepherd layeth down His life for His sheep. It was, then, in obedience to that precept that having loved His own who were in the world He loved them to the uttermost, and took bread and brake and blessed and gave to them, saying: Take ye and eat, this is My Body which is given for you; and the cup, saying: Drink, this is My Blood of the New and Eternal Covenant of Love; love between man and God, love between man and man. And just as when for God's sake one gives alms to the poor one gives it to God; so in the same act whereby Christ offers Himself to us for food in obedience to the Father's precept of love, He first offers Himself to the Father, and in so doing offers an infinite sacrifice of praise, thanks, expiation, and prayer.

And of this act of sovereign worship we are made sharers and fellow-offerers as often as we gather round the altar to hear Mass and, as it were, to lay our hands upon the head of the victim and to make His offering our own. For as the act of the lips or the heart is not the act of those organs alone, but of the whole body to which they belong; so the praise and worship of Christ our Head; the words of His lips, the love of His Heart are not His alone, but ours also, as often as by hearing Mass we make ourselves one body with the priest, His vicar and representative. Little as our self-oblation is worth apart from His, yet if in union with it we offer ourselves up at Mass a living sacrifice to obey, if need be, the precept of love even to death, our offering is merged into one with His, and His with ours. And though our knowledge of sin be childish and our grief for God's dishonour feeble, and our efforts at reparation ineffectual, yet if we heap them together with this infinite sacrifice of expiation and satisfaction, they will not be rejected or despised. For it is only in harmony with His praise and thanksgiving that ours have any meaning or value in the ears of God. In His Heart is gathered up all the love and joy of creation, of angels and of men, and thence welling upwards to His lips, finds utterance in one burst of Eucharistic praise, of which the Church sings: "It is truly meet and right, that we should always and everywhere render thanks to Thee, Holy Lord, Almighty Father, Everlasting God." And how? "*Through* Christ our Lord," "*through whom* the angels praise Thy majesty, Dominations adore, and Powers tremble; . . . with whose voices we supplicate that ours may be mingled in one song: Holy Holy, Holy," and again: "Through Him and with Him and in Him is to Thee, O God the Father, in union with the Holy Ghost, all honour and glory for ever and for ever. Amen."

II.

"O sacrum convivium in quo Christus sumitur.'

We have already dwelt on the Blessed Eucharist regarded as a sacrifice. We have roughly traced the notion of sacrifice from its first beginnings to its full development and realization in the perfect sacrifice of the Christian Church. We have seen that a food-offering made by way of homage and tribute was a symbol and expression of dependence and subjection such as exists between the children and the father of the household to whom they owe their existence and preservation, to whom they look for their heritage; and that this offering was directed to the strengthening of the family tie where it already existed; to the renewal of it where it had been sundered by sin; to the creation of it where it had not existed before. We have seen that when offered to God, the Father and Creator of all, it was a confession of our absolute dependence on Him as the Author and Preserver, not only of our natural, but of our supernatural life, the life of grace, "eternal life"—as the Scriptures call it; that it was a creation, or else a renewal, or else a confirmation of our claim to be called the sons of God by adoption, and to take our seat at His table with His sons and with the Eternal Son of His love; to eat the bread of angels. Finally, we have seen that as no man could offer any sacrifice adequate to the majesty of God, the Eternal Son, first-born of every creature, came down as Manna from Heaven, the living Bread of the soul, the Food of Immortality—and in obedience to the Father's eternal precept of love, loved us even unto death, and gave Himself to be our food, saying: "Take and eat, This is My Body," and that in that same act whereby in obedience to the Father He offers Himself to us for food day by day on a thousand altars, He first offers Himself a true food-offering and sacrifice to the Father. And of this great sacrifice of praise and thanks and prayer and expiation, we are fellow-offerers and sharers as often as, by assisting at Mass, we make one body under Christ our head. For the action of the head is not of the head alone, but of the whole body in subjection to it.

Let us now dwell on the Holy Eucharist viewed more strictly as a sacramental communion, as a *convivium in quo Christus sumitur*. For though sacrifice and communion are closely connected—the latter being the complement and, in some sense, the end of the former—yet they are separable and often separated; as we see, for example, in many of the Levitical sacrifices, which were not partaken of by the offerers, for symbolic and prophetic reasons. It is only so far as the sacrifice is accepted, that the offerer has a claim to partake of it; and the right thus purchased need not be exercised here and now. Those who sit down as *convivæ*, or guests, at] the sacrificial banquet are fed as children at the hands of the same father, who, as he has given them their life, so also fosters and increases it. They derive their life and nourishment from a common source; they spring from one body, they eat of one bread, they drink of one cup, they dwell in one house, they look forward to share one inheritance. And so of the Eucharistic feast. The chalice which we bless is it not the communion or sharing of the Blood of Christ? the Bread which we break is it not the sharing of the Body of Christ? For we, being many, are one bread and one body, as many as are partakers of that Bread. We being many, distinct and separate units, are one bread, for even as the grains of corn are ground up into flour and welded together in the dough and hardened together in the oven; so in this mystery of love and charity all that separates man from man, tends to be obliterated, all the dividing lines are erased under the amalgamating force of love, which seeks to give all and to receive all; to absorb and to be absorbed, staying only at the limit of personal distinctness.

"We being many in one bread, as many as are

partakers of that bread." We are one bread, because we live by one bread, deriving our life from the same principle. What bread is this? "I am the Bread of Life." It is not because He gives Himself under the semblance of bread that He calls Himself the Bread of Life; but conversely, because He is the True, the Spiritual, the Heavenly Bread, the stay of eternal life, therefore He gives Himself under that defective semblance to signify that truth. Yet how imperfect is the symbolism! Of those who live from one loaf or who drink from one cup, no two receive the same identical part, but similar parts, once united, now divided. Nor are they transformed into the nature of the bread they receive, but rather it is transformed into their nature. And so of the sacramental symbols or outward appearances, no two receive the same part from the hand of Christ; and it is "one bread" only so far as it is one in kind and received from the same hand. But the underlying reality, the True Bread of Eternal Life, Christ who is received, is not multiplied or divided, but remaining in Himself one and the same, yesterday, to-day, and for ever; removed from all limiting conditions of time and place, is communicated to all; nay, rather, draws all to Himself, as to a common centre; changes all into Himself—all, that is, all who receive Him worthily at any place or in any time. For our *convivæ*, or fellow-guests, are not only those who kneel beside us to receive Him here and now; but all those who in any difference of place or time have received Him or shall receive Him. This

Sacred Banquet, though set forth on innumerable altars and prolonged age after age to the end of the world, is morally one single feast in which we "communicate with, as well as commemorate" the Glorious and Ever Blessed Virgin Mary, the Blessed Apostles and Martyrs, and all the Saints. In Christ time and place are gathered up as into their cause—the centre from which they radiate; at the creative words of blessing,

> Earth breaks up ; Time drops away
> In flows Heaven with its new day
> Of endless life.

The substance of His Sacred Body being present after the manner of a spirit, is present to each receiver, as our soul is present to each part of our body; not part to part, but wholly to each part; not multiplied with the parts, but one and the same in all. For the substance of the bread in each host is not transformed into a different Christ, as though His Sacred Body were multiplied in place and time. He is not changed into it; but it is changed into Him. The appearance is multiplied and divided; but the reality is one and the self-same. Nor is that Eternal Bread changed into us, but we are changed into Him; united with Him; and thereby changed into and united to one another; being all merged into the same reality. We are all "one bread and one body."

Of this mysterious union we can speak only in the figures and images of revelation itself. "As the living Father hath sent Me and as I live by the

Father, so he that eateth Me the same also shall live by Me." **It** is from the Father that the Eternal Son originates and, in some sense, derives His Divine being, and nature, and life. One and the same identical life is possessed by both, but with an order of dependence such that **one** is called Father and Begetter, the other **Son** and Begotten, and while **we** may say that the Son lives by the Father, we may not say that the Father lives by the Son. The **Son** is the Image and Likeness of the Father, but the Father is not the Image and Likeness of the Son. The creatures which proceed from **God,** need to be preserved and watched over by His providence, to be fed by His fatherly bounty and care; but that Eternal Life, communicated to the **Son** is unfailing, unchanging, needing no conservation **or** feeding. So that **one** and the same eternal act is both generation, and conservation, **and** sustenance in a simple and ineffable sense. The Father is at once the Giver and the Bread of that life which is communicated to the Son. "As the Living Father," the Father who is Eternal, "hath sent Me," hath uttered Me His Eternal Word, hath sent Me forth proceeding from Him; "and as I live by the Father," who is the Giver and Sustainer and Bread of My uncreated life; "so he that eateth Me the same shall live by Me." "So," *i.e.,* plainly, not in the same **way,** but in some analogous way of which the mystery of the Trinity is the archetype. Christ lives in us and we live by Him so far as He communicates His nature to us, and assimilates us **to** Himself, conforming **our** mind more and more to the pattern of His; bringing all our sympathies and affections into accordance with those of His own Divine Heart. For this is the way in which spiritual union manifests itself; eliminating all distance and diversity and opposition of thought and sentiment. As the Eternal Father and Son have but one identical nature, operation, thought, and love; so Christ and the sanctified soul have, not indeed identical, but altogether similar thoughts and affections.

This is the manner in which our sacramental union with Christ *manifests* itself; though what it *is* in itself is veiled in mystery. We can only say that a new life-principle is infused into us; and that as the life of sense differs from that of mere growth, and the life of reason from that of sense, so Eternal Life—which is a participation of Divine Life, differs from that of reason. We can also assert that, unlike the life of reason, though it is *in* us it is not *of* us; even as the warmth we receive from the fire differs from that which is generated within us and by us. Hence it is ascribed to a principle which is in us yet distinct from us; which is said to dwell in us; which, like a guest, can come and go without prejudice to our natural faculties and attributes. Christ, the Bread of Life, is the Fire which warms us and illuminates us with the life of grace; and is so far said to dwell in us, and to make His abode with us. He that eateth My Flesh dwelleth in Me and I in him." "I in them [Father] and Thou in Me, that they may be made perfect in one."

"Perfect in one," for in proportion as we are all drawn into union with the same Divine substance, we are united one to another; and as the minds of men become more conformed to the pattern of Christ's mind, and their affections and sentiments are corrected by the same standard, the barriers to perfect sympathy and fraternity are broken down, and "we being many are one bread and one body, as many as are partakers of that bread;" and the four quarters of the earth are knit together—as Peter saw them in his vision of the Catholicity of his Church—into one brotherhood in Christ under our Father in Heaven. Many shall come from the East and from the West and shall sit down to eat bread in the Kingdom of God with Abraham and Isaac and Jacob.

Hæc est vera fraternitus! This is, indeed, the true brotherhood, whereof the brotherhood of nature, of our common descent from Adam, is but the dim figure and suggestion. What tie of affection is it between men to descend from a common ancestor, five or six generations back; what, from one distant from us by thousands of years? But at the altar of the Catholic Church, all nations meet together at the table of the Father of their Eternal and Divine Life, and eat of the same spiritual meat and drink of the same spiritual drink. At that table there is no distinction between Jew or Greek, Barbarian or Scythian, bond or free, male or female; there is no respect to riches, or talents, or birth, or colour; there is no distinction of classes and masses; but Christ is all and in all. There they alone are great who are great in His eyes and receive most abundantly of His fulness. He fills the hungry with good things and sends the rich empty away. A man may be great in talent yet poor in possessions; great in learning but little in birth; great in influence, little in virtue. But he who is great in the court of God is alone absolutely and truly great. At that table men are ranked as they are in the eyes of God, the mighty are put down from their seat and the lowly are exalted; to the former He says: "Give this man room," to the latter, "Friend, come up higher."

It is the mission of the Catholic Church to direct, and foster, and supernaturalize that progressive evolution, whereby the whole human family tends to knit itself into one brotherhood and society. False philosophies have fought skilfully and persistently against her, backed up by the Gates of Hell. They have taken the most sacred ideas of the Gospel, and under specious perversions, have used them in the interests of servitude, tyranny, and oppression. They have associated so much that is odious with their canting use of these sacred words, they have put forward such crafty counterfeits, that there is danger lest the wheat be rooted up with tares, and that in rejecting the perversion and distortion of the truth we reject the truth itself.

The history of the Christian era has been the history of the development of the dogma of the Fatherhood of God and the brotherhood of all men in Christ; of the liberty of the sons of God, of their equality, not merely as men, but as the sons of God in destiny or in fact, of the slow vindication of inalienable rights founded on this equality. So far as the movement has been directed by Catholic dogma it has prospered; so far as sophistical and counterfeit notions of liberty and fraternity have intruded themselves, it has been impeded. But the chief factor in its progress has been this " Sacred Banquet wherein Christ is received "—*O sacrum convivium in quo Christus sumitur,* where high and low, rich and poor, master and servant, emperor and beggar, have knelt, side by side, century after century, in their common nothingness before Him who in obedience to the Father's precept of Fraternal Love gives Himself for all and to all indiscriminately; and who says: " I have given you an example," that, " as I have loved you, so ye also should love one another;" where, we being many are one bread and one body, as many as partake of that Bread: of the Bread of Life.

III.

" Recolitur memoria passionis ejus."

Having previously dealt with the Blessed Eucharist as a sacrifice, we considered it in the light of a sacramental communion, whereby we being many were made one bread and one body in virtue of a mystic transformation into one and the same Bread of Life. We saw that this incomprehensible union—this infusion of Eternal Life—tended to bear fruit outwardly and manifest itself in a continual conforming of our hearts and intelli-

gences to the human heart and mind of the
Incarnate God Himself; that hereby our nature
and life became so saturated with His, that we
could truly say, "Now I live, yet not I, but Christ
liveth in me;" as He Himself has taught us when
He tells us, "As I live by the Father, so he that
eateth Me shall live by Me." We saw that the
great end of this *convivium* or banquet was to draw
the four quarters of the earth into one, to knit them
together into one great brotherhood in Christ under
God, the universal Father and Food-giver in the
order of nature and of grace.

We must now revert to the sacrificial aspect of
the mystery, and consider it, not merely as a true
sacrifice, but more particularly as a memorial
sacrifice or feast of commemoration. We know
that, year by year, the Israelites offered the paschal
lamb in thankful remembrance of their deliverance
from the destroyer, through the blood of the first
paschal lamb. Each annual offering was in itself
as truly a sacrifice as the first; yet it was also a
commemoration, which the first was not. It was a
relative as well as an *absolute* sacrifice. It was not,
however, merely the commemoration of a sacrifice,
as it were a dramatic and fictitious reproduction of
it, but a sacrifice of commemoration. So the Holy
Eucharist is not merely a symbol or fictitious
representation of Christ's sacrifice on Calvary, but
is itself at once a sacrifice and a commemoration of
a sacrifice. We commemorate the event by repeating
it, renewing it—just as we sometimes commemorate
a first meeting with a friend by meeting again on

the anniversary; or as we like to retrace the walks of some happier days, not in memory alone, but in fact. So our Saviour loves to renew Calvary as far as possible; to give Himself again and again; to enjoy as nearly as possible that ecstasy of love and pain once more.

Were it merely a calling to mind of a past event, and not a real renewing of it, then indeed a Passion play, or a crucifix, or the reading of the Gospel would be a far more effectual provision than the breaking of bread and the pouring out of wine. But, as we have seen, Christ truly and indeed gives Himself to us in every Eucharist to be our food; and in offering Himself to us, first offers Himself as a food-offering or sacrifice to the Eternal Father. It is a commemoration of Calvary because He does here really, though sacramentally, what He did there visibly and sensibly—He gives Himself to be the Bread of Life. In both He gives Himself; and gives Himself as food: as the Bread of God. For there are two means whereby grace or Eternal Life is conveyed to the soul—prayer and the sacraments; two ways in which we apprehend Christ, the Bread of Life. Of this non-sacramental feeding He says, " He that cometh to Me shall never hunger; he that believeth in Me shall never thirst." To come to Christ, to believe in Him, to submit to Him, to receive Him, is the condition whereby we feed upon Him outside the sacraments. " As many as received Him to them gave He power to become the sons of God; to them that believe in His name." It is not in asserting this, but in denying the sacramental reception of Christ, that heretics have gone astray. God has not tied His grace to the sacraments, and as there is a baptism of desire, so there is a spiritual communion. Yet where access to the sacraments is possible, none may with impunity despise such easy and abundant sources of grace, or vaunt a more spiritual religion than that instituted by Christ.

Christ crucified is indeed the food of the soul, the cause of its growth and of its development in intelligence and in love. As God, He is the life of the soul, *Ego sum Veritas et Vita;* as God-Man, He is the Bread of Life, the means of life. For the mind and heart need gradual preparation for the full face-to-face revelation of God. It is the function of the Word made Flesh to show us the Father, step by step, leading us from light to light, and love to love, till we are prepared to attain our spiritual maturity in the possession of the Source of all light and love. Thus the soul is fed and fashioned in the dark womb of time, ere it is born into the day of eternity. As a book feeds the mind and forms it, so the fact of the Incarnation and Death of Christ is an inexhaustible store of spiritual food, whereby we go on from strength to strength, till we appear before God's face in Sion.

What Christ does in the sacramental sacrifice of the altar, that He did in the visible sacrifice, which began with His Incarnation and ended with the shedding of His Blood on Calvary; and that He will continue to do for all eternity:

Se nascens dedit socium
Convescens in edulium

W

> Se moriens in pretium
> Se regnans dat in præmium.

Dedit se: He gave Himself for us—*usque ad mortem* —even unto death. In the same sense, every new gift of Himself in the sacrament is a reminder of that past self-giving, of the life-sacrifice ending on Calvary; it is a pledge of that future self-giving referred to in the words, *Se regnans dat in præmium.* And of the absoluteness of this self-giving, of the utterness of this devotion, bread is a more eloquent symbol than any other kind of food. For the animals or fruits that we use for food have, in themselves, and apart from such use, sufficient reason for their independent existence; but bread is something wholly and entirely consecrated and devoted to the service of man, and destined to no other end. Wherefore God spoke to us better of the love He bore us, and which we should bear one another, when He gave His Body and Blood neath the semblances, not of corn and grape, but of bread and wine.

But more than this; in the very form and manner in which Christ gives Himself to us in the Eucharist, His Death on Calvary is set forth and expressed and thereby called to mind. St. Paul tells us that in the celebration of these mysteries we show forth the Lord's *Death* till He come. It is not merely a commemoration of Christ, but more particularly of Christ slain. It was in the severance of His Body and Blood on Calvary that His obedience to the precept of love culminated, and His life-sacrifice was completed in loving us unto death. And it is of

this extremity of love that the Mass is a memorial
—a reminder to us, and a reminder, if we may so
say, to the Eternal Father. Therefore under one
species He has given us His Body sacramentally
separated from His Blood, the "body of the Pasch"
"as it were of a Lamb slain;' and•He has said,
"This is My Body which shall be given for you, do
this for a commemoration of Me." And then that
we might consider His Death under another aspect,
as fulfilling another prophetic type, after supper He
took the cup and gave us His outpoured Blood,
sacramentally separated from His Body, saying,
"This is My Blood of the New and Eternal
Covenant"—referring to the sealing of the ancient
Covenant by the sprinkling of sacrificial blood. For
the Old Law which conditioned the contract between
Israel and God was now fulfilled and absorbed in
the New Law of that Fraternal Love, which is
"the fulfilling of the Law."

Each part of the sacrament then is, according to
the Gospel, a commemoration of His Death. But
though they seem very independent of one another
according to the account there given us, where
a considerable interval of time seems to have
separated the offering of the Sacred Body from
that of the Precious Blood, yet the Church has
always joined the two as forming together in one
sacrifice a fuller and more perfect memorial of the
Death of Christ. For the destruction of any unity
is brought home to us more forcibly when we see all
its severed fragments together, than when we see
any one of them singly. But however essential the

two-fold presentment of Christ's Death may be for
the integrity of the commemorative sacrifice, yet
the Church has never insisted on the necessity of
two-fold reception for the validity of sacramental
communion, and in the West has had reason to
insist on its non-necessity. For though bread and
wine answer symbolically to the severed Body and
Blood of the slain Christ, and therefore perfect the
symbolism of the commemorative sacrifice, and
though the nutrition of the body symbolizes that of
the spirit, yet the distinction between food and
drink has no application to spiritual sustenance
which may be conceived equally under either metaphor; and as there is no distinct grace signified, so
neither is any distinct grace conferred—the hunger
and thirst of the soul being but two aspects of the
same thing. Thus Christ says: " He that cometh to
Me shall never hunger; he that believeth in Me shall
never thirst," where " coming " and " believing "
answer to eating and drinking, and yet mean one
and the same thing. Also He blesses those who
hunger and thirst after justice; where hunger and
thirst are but two figures for one and the same
spiritual craving. So, the grace signified and conveyed by either sacrament being one and the same,
one receives no more from both than from one; just
as one receives no more from two Hosts than from
one.

The Mass is therefore a commemorating of
Christ's Death, that is, of the extremity of His love.
And the end or object of this commemoration is
thanksgiving. It is the essence of gratitude to

remember the love bestowed upon us; to keep it always in mind, to linger on the thought and draw from it new delight, to stimulate our wavering trust, to feed our flagging love. As an absolute and independent sacrifice the Mass may be offered in gratitude for any or every favour; but as a commemorative sacrifice it was instituted as an Eucharist or Benediction whereby we bless and thank God, who gave us His only-begotten Son to be the Bread of Life. As at the Pasch it was customary to rehearse the long history of God's ancient mercies to Israel, culminating in the deliverance from Egypt, and in the institution of the feast itself, so in our Eucharist we commemorate our deliverance through the Death of Christ, preceded by the inauguration of the new Pasch; we lovingly record how " on the day before He suffered He took bread and broke and said : This is My Body which shall be given for you. Do this for a memorial of Me."

In what sense can we say then that the Blessed Eucharist is the same sacrifice as Calvary? Plainly He who offers is the same and what He offers is the same—namely, His Body to be the bread of our soul. Yet here it is eaten sacramentally, there by faith; as the mode of eating, so the mode of offering is different. There He was slain once and for all; here He becomes sacramentally present again and again, upon our altars. Yet we may not suppose that Christ left this earth with His sacrifice unfinished, and needing to be completed through the centuries of the Church's history. As far as the sacramental giving of Himself was concerned, He gave Himself at the Last Supper in virtue of the consecrating words once and for all. It is in virtue of that act and those words that every Eucharist is offered. Every host and chalice was before His mind at that moment. It is the distributing of the effects of that act which stretches to difference of place and time—even as a grant of royal bounty which is given in one word may take months before its effects are realized in every corner of the kingdom. Each hand which receives it, receives it from the King, as though he gave it then and there. And so every Eucharistic self-offering of Christ was included in that total self-offering which began with His conception and ended on Calvary. It is but a part of that gift of Himself which He gave at the Last Supper; the part that was put aside and reserved for us here and now, for you and for me. And though as a commemoration each Eucharist represents, expresses, and re-enacts Calvary, yet absolutely it is a different self-offering, or at least a different part of the entire giving of Himself from birth to death. It is, then, a renewal of the *memory* of His Passion—*recolitur memoria Passionis ejus*—not a renewal of the Passion itself. Being raised from the dead, He dieth no more.

And what is the Passion of Christ, if not the history of such a passion of love as the heart of man has never mastered—the passion of God for the soul of man, His Spouse, His Beloved; for her who will not believe in His love, but repels it and sins against it. That God should count man His friend and die for him, were mystery enough; but that we, being yet enemies, Christ should die for us to make us His friends, that He should not only shed His Blood for us, but for the remission of our sins against Himself, is a measure of love past all measure.

The word "passion" means suffering; and even when we speak of the passions of the soul we imply that we are to some extent passive and helpless under their influence; they seize hold of us, if we let them, and trouble us and shake our physical frame to its foundations, even as if we were possessed by an alien spirit for the time being. So it is with anger, or fear, or joy, or love, when they get the mastery over us. When we speak of the Passion of Christ we commonly understand the pains inflicted upon Him by His enemies—the blows and scourgings and wounds, the insults and indignities, the vinegar and gall. We forget too readily that all His Passion was self-inflicted. "Thou wouldst not have any power against Me," He says to Pilate, "were it not given thee from on high;" and: "I have power to lay down My life and to take it up again—no man taketh it from Me."

What is this Spirit that has mastered Him, and possessed Him, and driven Him on to death? What is it that has worn Him away, and tortured Him; and rent Him with scourges and nails and thorns; and parched Him with thirst; and broken His Heart; and deluged the earth with His Blood, if not the power of that love wherewith He loved us in obedience to the New and Eternal Precept of the New and Eternal Covenant, wherewith the Father

Himself hath loved us, and hath willed that we should love one another? This is the passion, the love which we commemorate; this is the theme of our Eucharistic praise; this is the love which we pledge ourselves and strengthen ourselves to imitate as often as we, being many, are made one bread and one body by partaking of that one Bread. Let a man prove himself, therefore; and so, let him eat.

IDEALISM, ITS USE AND ABUSE.

" Ah, but a man's reach should exceed his grasp,
" Or what's heaven for ? "

Browning.

AN idealist, as here understood, is a man of ideals.
An ideal is more than an idea, in two ways at least ;
for it stands in some sense for the archetype from
which things are copied, and to which they ought
to be conformed, rather than for a mental image
derived from things as they are. The proper *locus*
of ideals is the Divine mind; if they are in our
mind, it is thence we have borrowed them, and not
directly from experience. Again, an ideal is an
object of love no less than of thought. It is something whose contemplation rests,. satisfies, delights
the mind; and which the will longs to realize, and
make actual, wherever it should be realized and
made actual. For practical purposes of discussion,
it will be sufficient to say that " Idealism " is the
conception and the love of what *ought to be;* or
better still, it is the love of ideals, the aspiring after
perfection.

There are high ideals and low ideals, according
to the cast of various minds, and their greater or
less power of transcending experience and of rising
towards the spiritual and divine. And there are

right and wrong ideals, according as the conception is or is not duly founded in the nature of things. A high ideal may be chimerical and impossible. It may involve contradictions and absurdities, not apparent to our limited view. "Not all that is high is holy," says à Kempis, "nor is every desire pure." That a man should live in unbroken, conscious union with God here on earth, may be ideal, but it is not possible or desirable in the concrete. It is the state of angels and disembodied spirits, but not of flesh-clad mortals. A society of free agents in which every member should perform his part faultlessly and perfectly, and in which no energy or talent should be wasted or misapplied, becomes more and more chimerical in proportion to the number of its members, the complexity of its organization, the multitude and difficulty of its aims. Still, the "ideal" in such cases is not without its use, provided it be recognized rather as determining the direction of our efforts than as fixing a possible goal. It is a term to approximate to indefinitely without ever hoping to attain. Whereas were one to aim not merely at the perfect subjection of the flesh to the spirit, of the imagination to the reason, of the emotions to the will, but at the complete elimination of the lower in the interest of the higher, such an ideal would be positively false and wrong, since human perfection lies in an adjustment and harmony of the two. And the same is to be said of the relation of Nature to Grace, and of the State to the Church, and of the members to the head; where a false idealism is very possible, very frequent, very pernicious, fruitful in all manner of fanaticism, and followed usually by a reaction towards the opposite extreme.

A man may have an ideal for himself and for his neighbour; for individuals, and for associations of individuals.

With the first dawn of reason, conscience sets before us some more or less vague and imperfect notion of what we ourselves ought to be; and the unspoilt heart stirs itself to desire and realize this ideal. In some ways it is as yet a crude and childish ideal; especially as regards the remote future; even as the child's view of the world is hazy, imaginative, and even grotesque as to all outside the narrowest field of clear vision. It knows what it is to be a good child to-day; but it has no idea what it is to be a good youth or a good man. Conscience does not bewilder us with more light than we need for present emergencies; or terrify us with burdens we cannot bear now. Sufficient to the day is the evil thereof. When we follow its light faithfully it leads us ever nearer to its source, and therefore into clearer light. The ideal of the conscientious man grows each day fuller, higher, and more clearly defined, whereas he who violates conscience, even if, from a desire to justify himself, he does not, as usually happens, wilfully pervert his moral judgment, at least ceases to love, desire, and seek for further light. He *knows,* perhaps what he ought to be, and what he is not; but he has lost all love of his ideal. The light remains in his mind, but it is powerless to kindle his will; and since a man is what he wills, such a one is no longer an idealist.

As regards others, it is easier to retain one's idealism, even as it is easier to lay burdens on other men's shoulders than to touch them with one's own finger. It is pleasant to prescribe a *régime* for another, especially if we have power and authority to force it upon him. An ideal is not realized and born into the world without pain and travail; but when the pain is to be borne by another, and not by ourselves, the fear of it does not warp our judgment nor thwart our will. When our neighbour fails of his ideal, or rather of our ideal in his regard, we are not so tempted to justify him at the expense of truth, as we are to justify ourselves. Hence it comes to pass that one who is by no means an idealist in his own regard, may, like many a reformer, be enthusiastically ideal in relation to others, and may exhibit an apparently heroic unselfishness and benevolence in seeking for others those blessings on which he himself does not seem to place very much value.

It may be, indeed, that retaining a very clear idea of what people and institutions ought to be, a man is simply too selfish, too indolent, too unsocial, to care very much whether this ideal be realized or not; it may be that through sourness, disappoint-ment in self, or like motives, he may envy and grudge to others any excellence that he himself has not attained. But such a man is not an idealist, because, as has been said, his will is not kindled by his ideals.

When under the notion of a man's *ideal*, we comprehend all that he thinks *ought to be*, not only in himself, but in the whole moral world (where alone " ought " has its full meaning), it is plain that his ideal must, as long as he lives, be subject to a continual process of modification, either for better or for worse, or even for both under different respects. It is no less plain that, however men's ideals may agree as to certain simpler matters of detail, the chance of their agreement grows smaller as the matters become more numerous and complicated ; so that in the comprehensive sense of the word used above, no two men can have the same ideal. They may agree as to the general end of human life, as to the general nature of human perfection, individual and social, but they will differ when the picture is to be filled in in detail. Still more will they differ as to the means through which the end is to be effected, seeing that many divergent paths may converge to the same centre. Wisdom, therefore, no less than charity, demands great liberality and toleration in regard to such differences.

There cannot be much divergence of opinion as to the requirements of an ideal turnspit, but the necessary qualifications of a perfect cook are matter for endless dispute. And so, as we ascend upwards from the simpler to the more complex, from the shoeblack to the monarch, from the family to the Church or State, our ideals become more disputable as well as harder to realize.

Whence come our ideals ? They are evidently

not directly derived from those actualities and facts with which they are always contrasted in our thought. Yet they are undoubtedly suggested by facts. It is as when we guess the mind of one who stammers or expresses himself very imperfectly, and put his thought into exact language. God is everywhere striving to express the ideals of His Divine mind through creatures, and if the limitations of the physical world necessarily impede their full utterance, still more does the pervertible free-will of man mar the worthy expression of God's moral attributes in human life. Yet there is always some hint of the Divine intention from which we can build up our ideal, as we can complete a curve if we know the law of its formation. There is nothing in nature perfectly straight or perfectly circular, yet I have a clear and true notion of a straight line and of a circle. From the perfection of one feature, or one limb, or one characteristic, I can put together a notion of perfect beauty and grace and character, just as the palæontologist can ideally reconstruct an animal from the inspection of a single bone or tooth. Were every member in a society or a state to fulfil his office as faultlessly as a certain few do, we should be presented with an ideal society. Indeed, our notion of God Himself is in some sense an ideal built on our experience of limited and finite perfections. In fine, we may say that all our ideals are from God, who strives unceasingly to express Himself in our soul and as it were to reproduce the conceptions of His infinite mind in our finite mind; who, through the defective, stammering language of creatures and of human conduct, hints and suggests to our understanding that perfection which He has created us to attain.

And it is because in a measure He depends on our free co-operation for the realizing of His ideals and intentions with regard to human life, that He makes us thus sharers in His aspirations, treating us not as servants, but as friends.

Idealism is the motive power of all progress. It is the want of something better just dangling within our reach, which lures us on to exert ourselves, only to find, when we have attained it, that the satisfaction of one want gives birth to another, and that of receding horizons there is no end. In economics this " raising the standard of comfort '" is a necessary factor of progress in " comfort-production," which, in a materialistic and gross-minded age, is the ideal of national felicity. But whatever the true ideal be, it is through dissatisfaction with the present and the conception of a possible betterment that improvement is inaugurated. Christianity bids men be content with a comparatively low standard of physical comfort and of animal enjoyment, with the simple sufficiencies of health and strength, that their energies may be free for worthier ends. It strives to make them dissatisfied with the baser æsthetic, moral, and spiritual ideals, and to raise their aspirations indefinitely towards the best, and towards God. But in all cases alike, it is the idealists who draw the laggard multitude after them onward or upward, even as a man is slowly but surely drawn after his own ideal, so long as he holds to it.

It is most important by all possible means to kindle and foster, both in ourselves and in others, this fire of idealism which is the source of all spiritual energy; and so much the more because the world, the flesh, and the devil conspire in a thousand ways to damp and extinguish it. "Blessed are they that hunger and thirst after justice," is as great a paradox as any of the beatitudes, it is as diametrically opposed to the maxims of the world as the blessing on poverty, or meekness, or purity. The world solemnly warns us against idealism by precept and example, and brings all its forces to the work of lowering our ideals, blighting our hopefulness, perplexing our faith, till the last spark of enthusiasm has been smothered in the ashes of despair. *Fruamur bonis quæ sunt,* it says. "Enjoy what you have, and while you have it. Don't be ideal; take life as you find it; take yourself as you find yourself; believe me, I have had experience. I too have had my youth with its golden dreams and hopes; I too have chased the rainbow. Now profit by me, and don't make yourself miserable by chafing against the inevitable. Be average, if you like, but don't be ideal."

What and who is this world whom we thus personify, but the multitude of men which we come in contact with taken collectively, with its average opinions, views, sentiments, dispositions, modes of action? Everything about it is necessarily average and not ideal. It acts upon us by the force of universal and perpetual example; or if it formulates its principles, its only accredited spokesmen are those who represent the average mind and morality. It is only by the presence of a few idealists here and there, sprinkled through the multitude, that the average is slightly and slowly raised, or at least saved from sinking continually. They are the salt of the earth, and the leaven of the mass. The *ideal* and the *average* are deadly enemies, each trying to destroy the other, though working by different methods. A thousand idealists yield at last to the pressure of example and are dragged down to the level of the average, for one who resists and raises the average by an infinitisimal fraction of a millimetre. And what is true of the big world is true of every little world or society; the idealists are the few and the unideal are the many, and between the two a certain antagonism is inevitable.

In our tender years, when we are almost entirely dependent on example and tradition for the formation of our mind and character, it fortunately happens that our ideals are very elementary and imperfect, and our powers of discernment feeble; so that we are able to look on our seniors with a wondering worship as embodying and surpassing our highest notions of wisdom, goodness, and power; but day by day, as experience and reason assert their sway and we begin to observe and criticize, the support on which we lean fails us inch by inch, until it comes home to us with disagreeable clearness that if we are to stand high we must so far be ready to stand with a few or even alone, and that the more we depend on general example the lower we shall have to fix our ideal.

X

It was a shock to us, and a rude withdrawal of a trusted support, to find that those who were so rigorous in precept, so severe in chastisement, could be themselves so lamentably deficient in practice. One by one our idols fell flat on their faces never to rise again. New ones came to take their places for a time, but only for a time. Layer by layer the weakness and wickedness of the respectable average world was uncovered and exposed to our view; and what we first regarded as painful exceptions came to be recognized as general rules.

In the face of this gradual awakening, the consequence is frequently an abandonment of our early ideals and an acceptance of the standards of the majority. For this we are prepared in most cases by the failure to realize in ourselves that which conscience set before us as attainable. At first we rushed at the task with all the confidence of ignorance and inexperience. We thought that to know was to will; that to will once was to will for ever; that fervour was always at our command. We knew nothing of the slow growth of laboriously formed habits, of the irregularities of passion, of the obscurations of the moral judgment, of the protean diversities of temptation, of the burdensome monotony of perseverance. And so we flung ourselves on the task, to be flung back again and again, baffled, discouraged, puzzled, sceptical, bitter. While we still retained our belief in the majority, and regarded our own case as one of exceptional weakness and depravity, we were humbled in our own esteem by our failures and stimulated to be, and to do, what so many others seemed to be and to do. But when our eyes were opened to the fact that in our weakness we were with the many and not with the few, this wholesome rebuke and encouragement was withdrawn, and we were left to fall back largely on the authority and sanctions of conscience and faith.

If, however, these highest and most imperishable motives were absent or undeveloped, if the habits and opinions of others had secretly been our one rule of conduct all along, then we were rather relieved than distressed to find ourselves compassed by so great a cloud of witnesses to the expediency of an average rather than an ideal standard. We stifled our conscience with a *Securus judicat orbis terrarum*, we accepted the world as the best practical commentator on the Gospel, and we agreed that however excellent truth, sincerity, honour, purity, unselfishness, meekness, humility might be in the abstract, yet there were necessary limitations in practical life, and that one should not be extreme, fanatical, or ideal. Thus we were restored to good humour with ourselves and with our neighbour, and found a certain negative peace, not in the satisfaction, but in the extinction of our earlier aspirations.

This is precisely the scandal of which it is said, "Woe to the world because of scandals! It must needs be that scandals come; but woe to him by whom they come." That the world should be *average* is in some sort a necessity; and also that it should by the force of its example exert a downward drag on idealism. Under this aspect it is the enemy of the better, and the enemy of God, and to be at peace with it is to be at war with God; for it is to cease to struggle upwards and onwards; it is to let go and drift down stream. It is the old story of the conflict between the flesh and the spirit; between death and life; between nature and grace. In all cases alike, without resistance and conflict there is no life or growth; and the same lower forces which rightly managed are serviceable and helpful, become a cause of scandal and destruction when they are yielded to and obeyed. Those who resist the downward drag of the world and stand out against it, are strengthened and raised in the very exercise of resistance. If we can swim, the water will support us; if not, it will drown us. It is, therefore, no easy or common thing to carry our idealism through so many dangers unimpaired; so that our judgment shall not falter or recede from its high thoughts or our will relax the firmness of its purpose, for all the temptations that urge us to accommodate ourselves to things as they are, rather than to strive to accommodate things to our notion of what they ought to be.

But useful and essential as idealism is, it is not without its dangers. Of these we may notice first a tendency to a false optimism with regard to ourselves and to other things. For where we are half conscious of a distressing want of uniformity between facts and ideals, we may either remedy the evil by mending the facts, or we may get rid of the distress by ignoring or forgetting them. A sanguine, indolent disposition will be apt to believe too readily that its ideals have been realized, and to take a complacent view of things. It will refuse to face disagreeable truths, or to risk any shock which would rudely wake it from sweet dreams to sour realities. We often find Church history or the lives of saints written in this soothing *à priori* strain, taking for granted that what ought to have been, must have been.

But prejudicial as optimism may be to the truth, it is never nearly so prejudicial as pessimism, the child of narrowness and impatience of judgment.

Our ideals are sometimes absolutely and intrinsically chimerical; sometimes chimerical under existing conditions and circumstances. We often want hills without valleys; shade without sunshine; or else we want to run before we can walk; to be strong without exercise; virtuous without temptation; to know without learning; to reap without sowing. Above all, we are impatient and will not wait for the slow processes of growth and development.

From all this comes a readiness to condemn rashly and freely and universally, in the case of those who hold fast to their ideals and yet are too much in earnest to wish to be deceived as to facts or to live in a fool's paradise. In their anxiety to be sincere they are unjust; and wishing to be impartial, they fly from one extreme of unfairness to another. It is easier and simpler to pronounce things utterly rotten, than to sift and measure the true proportion of good and evil; it is easier and simpler to impute the evil to free and deliberate fault, than to discern the fractional part which

free-will plays from that which is played by necessary conditions and inevitable limitations; it is
easier and simpler to say that things are hopeless
and to do nothing, than to find out remedies and to
apply them.   Hence, also, a crude belief in violent
and radical remedies, in wholesale pulling down and
destroying, as a needful preliminary to constructing,
and a disbelief in gradual and noiseless reformations
effected by observing and co-operating with those
forces in nature and man which are ever making for
right.   When this temper of mind passes into the
will, it shows itself in the form of cynicism, bitterness, uncharitableness in regard both to ourselves
and to others, and in a sour habit of destructive
criticism, which is ever blind, one-sided, and
untruthful.

This embitterment is one of the commonest
parasites of idealism; for such as is our love of that
which *ought to be,* such will be our disdainful anger
and impatience with that which *is,* so far as they
are opposed one to another; unless, indeed, we
are partakers of a higher wisdom and a more
excellent way.

Of this way Christ is our example in His
relations to Israel, His chosen people, and to
Jerusalem, His chosen city—the people and the
city He had set apart to satisfy a Divine ideal.
The Sacred Scriptures are one unbroken record of
the resistance, active and passive, offered by that stiff-
necked nation to God's loving designs for its glory
and triumph.   " Stiff-necked and uncircumcised of
heart and ear," says St. Stephen, " you are always

fighting against the Holy Ghost; as your fathers did, so do you. Which of the prophets have you not persecuted as your fathers did?" God's spirit and ideal was always striving to realize itself in Israel, and striving in vain. In prophets and saints and men of good-will it found unimpeded utterance, and broke forth in warning, rebuke, and exhortation. But time after time the irritated pride of the mediocre, average multitude rose up in wrath against the idealist and silenced him for ever. Last of all, coming to them in His own Person, Christ was received with distrust and hostility, as an enemy of existing traditions; and was cast out and crucified. Surely if ever one had a right to be bitter and pessimistic it was He. Yet His love for His chosen people seemed to suffer no diminution from first to last. "O Jerusalem, that killest the prophets and stonest them that are sent unto thee, how oft would I have gathered thee as a hen gathers her chickens under her wing, but you would not!" These are the words of sorrow and disappointment, if you will, but not of bitterness; of grief, indeed, but of a grief born of love. Again, little as our Saviour could sympathize with the spirit and the tactics of the rulers of Israel, fierce as was His indignation against individuals and cliques, yet in no way was His loyal reverence to the law diminished in consequence of the unworthiness of its administrators or the perversity of its interpreters. Nay, it was for His fidelity to the letter and spirit of the law that He died excommunicate.

As He stood over the city and wept at the tragic

contrast between its present glory and its impending
ruin, when not one stone should be left upon
another, His thought was rather of that spiritual
ruin whereof the temporal was but the symbol; He
wept, as so many of His servants and prophets had
wept, over a shattered ideal. We may well pause
and ask ourselves what there was in Jerusalem as it
then was, that the Heart of Christ still clung to.
Was it merely the ideal Jerusalem that He loved
and longed for; or was the existing perversion of
that ideal still dear to Him? And the question has
more interest for us when we reflect that Jerusalem
is the type, not only of the Catholic Church, but of
every human soul which is by destiny a city of
peace, a spouse of Christ, a temple of the Living
God. For each soul God has His cherished ideal;
an ideal in all cases (save one or two) more or less
disappointed; in many, shattered beyond redemption; and yet while life endures, and until the instant
in which the soul steps by its last choice into its
unchanging condition, His love clings to it, follows
it, weeps and laments over it, and cries, "Oh, that
thou hadst known and hadst harkened," and, "How
oft would I have gathered thee, but thou wouldst
not!"

In spite, then, of all her errors, sins, perversities,
apostasies, it was no abstract Jerusalem, but the
concrete assembly of the sons of Israel, which was
so dear to God and to His prophets. He loved her
as being the offspring and growing embodiment of
an ideal, as tending in virtue of her nature and
constitution towards the fulfilment of that ideal,

even as the soul which animates the child in the womb strives to assert itself and clothe itself with the matured body of perfect manhood. A thousand circumstances may impede the work of development; but while there is life the imprisoned ideal is there, striving to become real. Nay, rather, it *is* the perfect realization in its infancy and weakness. So it was with Jerusalem, the City of the Great King, the dwelling-place of His Name; so it is with the Holy Catholic Church; so it is with the soul of every man. God loves the present reality for what it is and for what it tends to be and is capable of being. And the contrast between its present lowliness and imperfection and that final glory and greatness towards which it is borne by the force of its nature, rouses a tender pity in the Divine Heart, together with a fierce indignation against those rebel wills of ours which thwart so fair a growth.

Besides this, Jerusalem was (and is) dear to Christ for the sake of the fruits it had already produced, for the sake of Abraham and Isaac and Jacob and Joseph; for the sake of Moses and the saints and the prophets; for the sake of legions of her children whose names are unrecorded; for the sake of the continual incense of prayer, praise, and sacrifice which had ascended from her altars through so many centuries. Even had there been no vestige of such fruit, what time our Lord wept over the city; had she been then altogether a barren fig-tree, yet it was the same tree which in other seasons had yielded so rich a harvest, and which, in virtue of the vital principle within her, might yield a more abundant harvest still.

It was for these reasons that He loved and reverenced that fallen Jerusalem as His Mother; that He obeyed her law to the letter; that He clung to her until she consummated her wickedness by casting Him off. And in like manner He clings to the human soul in general, and to each soul in particular, until the treasure is wrenched with violence from His wearied grasp. Long after we have despaired of ourselves, and after the saints and angels, nay, after the Mother of God herself has despaired of us, He, "faithful and true," clings to us still, hoping while a spark of life is left.

Since, then, He is the sovereign and holiest rule of all right judgment and affection, it is in viewing things with His eyes that we shall find clear insight and peace of mind. From Him we learn to hold unfalteringly to our best and highest ideals of what things ought to be, and yet not to be embittered by the sad contrast often presented by things as they are.

In the light of His example let us ask ourselves what, for instance, would be the right attitude of mind for one living in the midst of the most extreme ecclesiastical corruption, such as may have prevailed here and there at the time of the sixteenth century revolt, or such as does now and then prevail where the usurpations and interferences of the secular power sever the local Church from free and healthful connection with the main body of Catholic Christendom, and impede the full effects of her discipline. Let us, for the sake of argument, make things about as bad as they can be—and that is very bad.

The fact that the tainted and rotten members, who are the principal agents of this corruption, should break away from ecclesiastical unity, and seek an independence favourable to their love of licence, that they should sell themselves to the secular power of Egypt for the sake of the flesh-pots, the leeks and the garlic, is altogether natural and reasonable. But a revolt led by such men could not live long for lack of that *species veri* and plausibility which can be lent to it only by the accession of seemingly good and moral men of strict and regular life, who have turned in disgust from patent wickedness in high places, and have joined themselves to what seems to them a movement of reform. More often, indeed, the reform movement is actually initiated by these men, and from these motives; and when so initiated, is at once utilized by the baser sort for their own baser ends. On the other hand, the corruption, which to many is a cause of ruin and scandal, is an occasion of strength and resurrection to not a few whose faith is proved and whose love and hope are deepened by holding out against the downward drag of universal example. Hence, as the richest flowers often grow from the foulest refuse, so the greatest saints have shone out in the darkest nights of the Church's history.

What, then, should be the attitude of mind of a good Catholic Christian under such painful circum-stances as we are imagining? Is he bound in any

sense to love, reverence, and obey the concrete
Church in which he finds himself? or will it suffice
that he retain a love and reverence for the ideal,
giving birth and strength to a hatred and detestation
of the contrasted reality? There can be but one
answer. Terrible as is the evil and perversion, yet
that which is thus perverted and degraded is by
organic continuity a part of the body founded by
Jesus Christ, a branch of that tree which He
planted, and watered with His Blood. While it
keeps the Catholic faith, and is as yet unsevered
from the centre of unity, it retains its vital principle
and root of recovery, even as does the most degraded
and fallen Catholic who still clings to the faith of
his baptism. It has that in its very nature which
tends, in due conditions, to the realization of the
Divine ideal of the Spouse of Christ. It is part of
the same body of which Christ is the Head, and of
which Mary, with all the apostles, martyrs, confessors, virgins, and holy souls on earth and in
Heaven, are members. That wild beasts have
preyed upon it and devoured it may fill us with just
indignation against those through whose fault such
corruption has come about; but for the body itself
our sentiments should only be those of Christ when
He wept over Jerusalem—sentiments of sorrow and
anguish, born of an unalterable love and affection.
Where one has both the power and Divine commission to act, and to apply remedies, one is bound
to move heaven and earth in the cause of God; but
where one is powerless or unauthorized one can but
stand by helpless with Mary at the side of the

Cross and pray. *Bonum, est præstolari cum silentio salutare Dei*—" It is good to wait in silence for the salvation of God." Ten thousand are strong enough to draw the sword with Simon Peter, and to rush into the midst of Christ's enemies hacking and hewing right and left, for one who has the strength to wait and be silent. Doubtless there is a silence and an expectation, which only means apathy or indifference, or timidity, where there is nothing to suppress and therefore no self-suppression; or there is the silence of the fatalist. But apart from such cases it is the weak man who gives way to violence in speech and action; whose first impulse is revolution, rebellion, secession; it is the strong man who keeps silence and waits and hopes and obeys. They that take the sword, be it the sword of the tongue or the sword of steel, perish by the sword; violence defeats itself; but the meek possess the earth because they are the really strong, and because they husband those energies which the passionate squander in fruitless impulsiveness. Theirs is the violence which takes the Kingdom of Heaven by storm.

Secession, when it is not a work of malice, is the child of crude thought and moral cowardice. It is to fly from a temptation which it is our duty to face and to conquer; the temptation of scandal, of seeing ourselves deprived of the support of public example and edification, and left in comparative isolation as idealists and dreamers. It is the act of a soldier who deserts, lest he should be involved in the defeat of his regiment which he foresees, or share the suspicion of having failed in his duty; or is it the act of a son who denies and disowns the mother that bore him, lest he should be partaker in her disgrace? It is, therefore, shirking the consequences of our contract of membership, which requires that we should be willing to share evil things no less than good things in common with others; and which holds, like the marriage-bond, "for richer, for poorer; for better, for worse; in sickness, or in health; till death us depart."

Little as we may like it, we are of necessity social beings, and our life and lot is bound up with the life and lot of others, whose burdens we have to bear even as they have to bear ours. We may secede from the Church because of scandals, lest we should be rated according to the average of its public, but we cannot secede from our membership with the human family, or disown our ineffably close brotherhood with the erring multitudes of our Father's children. If we isolate ourselves from the multitudes, we isolate ourselves from God.

But if the weak no less than the wicked fall away in such crises, the strong stand firm and by resistance become stronger; and the love that holds them back strikes root yet deeper in their hearts; even as true affection is called forth in its highest form by the afflictions, needs, sorrows, and sins of those we love. However their hands be tied through lack of the ability or the authority to correct others, they know well that the perfection of the multitude depends chiefly on the perfection of its component units, and that no change of regimen, no legislation will bring any remedy unless there be virtue and probity in those who administer it and in those who submit to it. Until each member is imbued with the true ideal of the whole, at least in outline, and is zealous for its realization in preference to all isolated and private interests, there will always be the disorders and diseases that spring from selfish-ness and pride. This, therefore, is the first and most essential work—the intellectual and moral betterment of individuals one by one—a work effected often quietly and noiselessly; at first very slowly, one here and there; then with geometrically increasing rapidity as each torch becomes a new centre for the dissemination of light and heat; and the whole face and tone of a community is changed, we know not how. For it is with growth as with decay; more depends on individuals than on systems; and men are led by their affections rather than by principles; by example and fashion rather than by theories and views.

This being so, there is no question as to the immediate task which it is in every true reformer's power to apply himself to vigorously, namely, the task of self-reformation; and this not in an exclusive, self-regarding spirit, as though, in despair of the republic, one had cynically resolved to live for one's own highest good, and let the world go its way; but in a spirit of true, universal apostolic charity, clearly recognizing that this is the nearest, the surest, the most imperative way to help others; and subordinat-ing one's own self-care as a means to that nobler and greater end. " First, keep yourself in peace, and then you will be able to bring peace to others; first be zealous about yourself, and then you will have some right to be zealous about your neighbour "—*Tene te primo in pace et tunc poteris alios pacificare. Habe primo zelum super teipsum et tunc juste zelare poteris etiam proximum tuum.* This is indeed no easy task, and the very attempt will teach a man to be more patient with others. "If you cannot make yourself what you fain would be, how can you force others to be as you would have them?" No man is fit to teach others with any effect who has not learnt what he is teaching by experience. He can give directions learnt from a book, he can deal in phrases, but phrases they are and nothing more. We do not deny the utility of such repeating-machines, which is precisely the utility of a book: but it is nothing comparable to the animating influence of one who has himself first tried and failed; and then tried and succeeded. This is the secret of à Kempis' *Imitation* or of Augustine's *Confessions*, and of the words of saints as contrasted with the words of scribes.

Speaking now in general of the way in which we should meet such difficulties and seeming scandals, whether universal or local, whether in the Church or in the State, or in particular institutions sub-ordinated to the one or to the other, the first question we are bound to ask ourselves is: Are things really as bad as they seem? Before we attempt to solve the problem, let us be quite sure that it exists. There is such a thing as subjective colouring; and to the jaundiced eye all things are yellow. It cannot be denied that the prophetic *régime* and mode of life, with its austerity and solitude, its introspection and reflection, its concentration on one only aspect of things, may tend to dehumanize and pervert the judgment; and prophets, whether of the study or of the cell, would often keep their spiritual vision all the keener and clearer for an occasional day in the country. Like round numbers, or sweeping statements and generalities, extreme views, whether optimist or pessimist, are much simpler; when we have neither the ability, nor the justice, nor the patience requisite for exact measurements, it saves a deal of trouble to include all things under a general anathema. Moreover, the appeal to sensation is not without its attraction. Mediocrity is uninteresting to contemplate, but extremes are thrilling. Again, it is just possible that the particular ideal which we are pleased to regard as the sole measure of what ought to be, may be but one of many alternatives, all equally good. It may be indifferent whether a man carries out his chief end in life as a doctor, or a lawyer, or as a merchant; and so of a government, or an institution, or an order, there may be paths indifferently converging to the same centre. All is not lost because the end is reached by some path I had not fixed on or dreamt of. Often our pessimistic estimate of facts has no other reason than this, that our own ideas have not been preferred to others equally good or better. A Tory will never allow that the country is prospering under a Radical Government; nor

Y

will a Radical Opposition be more generous in its turn.

If, however, there is still a heavy residue of evils that refuse to be resolved into phantasms of the imagination, the next question is as to what proportion of them is due to wilful malice, and what to inevitable circumstances and limitations over which even the Almighty has no control. Without weakening our belief in the existence of free-will, our self-experience and our experience of life tends ever to narrow the sphere in which free-will has action, and to make us see that the ocean of apparent iniquity which deluges the world owes far less to sin, far more to circumstances, than we had ever thought. Our early judgments are as a rule narrow and severe; and they become gentler and wider in exact proportion to our experience and reflection.

It would be well, for this reason, to consider that the end which a society or institution proposes to itself is sometimes very high and very complex, depending on a great number of individuals being each *ideal* in his own department; and on the exact balance of a very delicate organization, easily disturbed by the defection of even one member. A society for the manufacture of match-boxes or broom-sticks can be very easily organized. The gifts needed for membership are common and well-nigh universal. The stimulus to co-operation and labour is tangible, and one that appeals to the universal instinct of acquisition. Little marvel if such a society prospers; if it abounds in individuals who arrive at the highest degree of skill in their profession ; if all the members co-operate cordially each for his own interest ; or if there is little diversity of judgment as to the best mode of production.

If we turn, for example, to the Army, or the Navy, or the Civil Service, the end in view is much more complex, especially in the last. Still, the killing of men and the battering of ships—the proximate end of the first two—is a fairly simple end, however intricate the machinery brought to bear upon it. The gifts required for such a service are not so very rare. The motives in most cases are simply worldly advancement and a good position ; and were these insufficient to secure faithful service, the sanction of very tangible penalties is at hand to supplement their weakness. Nor has the Government to go begging for recruits, but has only to pick and choose the best from the eager crowds that are pressing into its service from all quarters of the empire. With these we may contrast the high and difficult end which the Church (to take the extremest example) sets before her, a work to be wrought upon the minds and hearts of men, of her own subjects and of those to whom they minister. Even were she only occupied with the secular education of youth, how difficult and complex are the problems suggested by that task, how far from solution, even in these days of pretended enlightenment ; and how few are the men with the requisite learning, how still fewer those with the more requisite skill to form the minds of the young ! But if in addition to this she aims at the moral and spiritual education

of all, young and old, and at other ends even more
public and universal, the difficulty becomes indefinitely greater.   What sort of men ought not they to
be who would minister to the very highest good and
happiness of humanity; what almost impossible
combinations of gifts and graces are needed!   How
scarce even the raw material fit to be shaped for
such purposes! how easily spoilt in the shaping!
And then the motives which draw men to work for
religion or spiritual ends, if they are higher, yet
being invisible, supernatural, distant, they appeal
to a smaller number, and to those, comparatively
feebly.   We must take men as we find them.   It is
only in our exceptional states of vivid faith and
spiritual exaltation that the supernatural tells on us
effectively and intensely, whereas temporal self-
interest, the love of gain and reputation, act upon
all men at all times.   Men of the world have at·all
times found cheap and abundant material for caustic
satire in the ludicrous contrast between the profession and practice of those who aim at higher and
more spiritual standards.   They forget how easy it
is to be consistent in sliding downhill; how hard, in
clambering up.   When there is no struggle, there is
no cause for weariness and failure; nor need he fear
a fall who lies flat on the earth.   As the height
aspired to is more exalted, so will the percentage of
those who fail in their attempt to reach it be
greater; and the failure itself be more lamentable
and disastrous.   Many a fallen priest would have
made a respectable layman, or at least would never
have fallen so low; and the rottenness of a Catholic

country is worse perhaps than that of a Protestant. For in these cases the forces disorganized are stronger, and the light sinned against, clearer.

The success of a religious society like the Church depends ultimately on the extent to which its several members are imbued with and possessed by the spirit and enthusiasm of its founder, and this spirit is difficult to enkindle, and more difficult to sustain. We have Gospel-warrant for saying that the children of the world are wiser, more watchful, more energetic in their interests than the children of God. In a way it must be so with mortal man; with this mixture of spiritual and animal, where the lower element is so often preponderant. The higher element in us is the feebler, and our whole task in life is to develop it laboriously and slowly. It is easy to be enthusiastic and successful in the things of the body; but hard in things of the soul. Just then as our self-experience convicts us of being subject to this law of sin in our own individual life, so we should expect to find it in the world around us. God's work will be done slothfully, meanly, unsuccessfully, while temporal interests will be sharply looked to. Those who enter the active service of the Church are not chosen by competitive examination from a crush of eager candidates; they have no salary which can be forfeited; nor can they be coerced to their duty by physical force or fear. All depends on spiritual fervour and intelligent spontaneity. Often, moreover, the public from which in particular localities the Church has to draw her recruits, is a very small one, and yet the work to be

done is extensive and diversified. The harvest is
great, but the labourers are few. It therefore becomes
necessary to accept as labourers many who are very
imperfectly qualified for the work, for sheer lack of
hands.

Finally, so far as the Church's work brings her
into relation with the world, the rapid changes in
her environment may demand continual adaptations
and modifications, which are hard to effect con-
sistently with the ancient traditions of a world-wide
and necessarily centralized institution which moves
slowly because of its very bulk.

These and a thousand similar reasons ought to
convince us that much of our dissatisfaction is rather
with circumstances than with persons; in a word,
our quarrel is with Almighty God, and with the
finite nature of things.

If, after eliminating what is due to these impersonal causes, we still find matter for blame and
censure, it remains for us to ask whether there may
not be much excuse for such wilful faults as we
seem to have detected; *humanum est errare,* and
perhaps a little self-knowledge would dispose us not
to be altogether surprised, if here and there others
misuse the liberty that we ourselves so often misuse.

If we ever expected, we never had a right to
expect to find an ideal state of things in this world.
The Church of the Saints is one in which men
profess to tend to sanctity, not to have attained it.
We are not scandalized at the inefficiency of a
hospital because we find that all the occupants of
the beds are more or less sick and disabled. We

only require that they should for the most part be on the road to recovery; or at least under medical treatment.

This world is not the place where we are to look for the ideal. Here and there little glimpses of it are given us to whet our appetite for higher things, and to lead us from dissatisfaction to dissatisfaction, and thence to a desire for the great archetype of all ideals, in whom at last and alone the Real and the Ideal are identified.

DISCOURAGEMENT.

"Great is the facile conqueror,
Yet haply he who wounded sore,
Breathless, unhorsed, all covered o'er
With blood and sweat,
Sinks foiled, but fighting evermore
Is greater yet."

Watson.

THE young and the inebriate, according to
Aquinas, have it in common that they abound in
hope; that is, so far as hope is classed among the
emotions or passions enumerated by Aristotle. The
reason in both cases is to be found in their inability
to estimate the difficulties to be encountered, and
the limits of their own powers and resources—an
ignorance due to inexperience in the one case, to
alcoholic influence in the other. Obviously this is
to be accounted foolhardiness rather than courage—
the body and semblance of hope without its soul
and substance. For hope as a virtue of the intelligence, and spiritual will is no blind optimism, but a
confidence that faces the cruelest facts, unmoved,
undismayed. Ultimately it is grounded in an
unshaken faith as to the eventual victory of truth
over error, of right over wrong, of good (that is, of
God) over evil. Its noblest opportunity is when
the manner of that victory is most obscure and the

odds against it most overwhelming. So far as its object is the triumph of God in our own soul, a triumph which depends upon the grace of God and upon our own co-operation therewith, hope excludes certainty; for though God is faithful, our will is incalculably mutable, as we have learnt by past experience. Yet hope requires that we should consider our salvation, not merely possible, but as most probable—nay, practically, though not intellectually, certain; and that the consciousness that we are "working out our salvation with fear and trembling" should itself allay that deeper fear which drives peace from the heart. We cannot be as certain of salvation as we are of to-morrow's sunrise; but it is not enough to hope for it only as for to-morrow's sunrise, which may be or may not be—who can tell? Rather, it should be as we hope for summer and autumn in due season, with a hope which ignores the scarce appreciable possibility of disappointment.

But on what is such hope grounded, since God's fidelity to His promise of needful grace is absolutely certain—a matter of faith rather than hope; while our own co-operation depends on the freaks of a will whose past history should incline us rather towards despair?

It is, however, from a closer study of our past that we draw sustenance for hope, since there we see how in all His dealings with us God is not only just and faithful, but better than His word, giving more and far more than He had promised. Day by day uncovenanted graces have been rained

upon us, and it is chiefly through them that we are
what we are; "it is the mercy of God that we have
not been consumed" and cast away for our sins.
And though we know not the measure or the law
of these quickening showers, we know that in some
sense they are without measure; that it is only
those who wilfully presume upon them that forfeit
the right to hope in them; while the very hoping
in them, without presumption, almost merits and
demands them.

If hope's counterfeit is easy when we are young,
when we still think that to know right is to will
right; and that to will once is to will for ever;
hope's reality is hard when we are older, when we
have learnt the wide difference between these things,
when time after time we have been beaten back
almost to the very starting-point, and when the
distant hills of our early ideals look further and
more inaccessible than ever; still more, when
from knowledge of ourselves and of others this
defeat of our hopes is felt to be the result of almost
natural causes, whether working in our own nature
or in the nature of things around us. "Was not
ignorance," we ask, "the ignorance of an untaught
mind, stranger to the notion of law, confident in the
omnipotence of free-will, the parent of our crude
hopes? Is it not ruthless knowledge, bitter experience, that has strangled them?" Our first repent-
ances and recoveries are easy and hopeful, for we
know not how sin has injured us and poisoned our
will; our next, more difficult, less hopeful; and so
of the successive efforts, until at last the **strongest**

stimulus can elicit from us no more than some sluggish response like faint stirring of a life flickering out.

Then it is that the lethargy of discouragement supervenes; and if a process of rapid decay does not follow at once, if the soul remains *in statu quo,* sulky and sullen, it is only because lethargy is not death; because the discouragement is not absolute; because there is still, unperceived save by God, a feeble pulse of hope which fights against death and despair.

This lethargy and state of supine inaction is often falsely confounded with that tepidity or half-heartedness which characterizes those caitiff souls which Heaven cannot stomach and even Hell disgorges. But the lukewarm, from the very littleness of his heart and paltriness of his ideals, is all self-satisfied; he winks inwardly for that he has made a sharp bargain with Heaven and has skirted the edge of Hell without slipping in. Discouragement, on the other hand, is never self-satisfied; it is the parasite of idealism. "Woman, why weepest thou? whom seekest thou? They have taken away my Lord, and I know not where they have laid Him." The discouraged soul sits weeping and disconsolate by the empty tomb of its hopes, bearing in its hand the evidence of its good-will in the idle spikenard and aloes ready for service and worship. It weeps for what it loves, for what it deems itself to have lost, and its comforter is never far, though hard to see through blinding tears.

But although discouragement or despondency

has none of malice and offence of tepidity, and although it implies good desires and high aspirations, still it is in itself something evil, the base progeny of truth and lie. It is known by its fruit— remissness and heavy listlessness, and perhaps a certain desperation and recklessness from which ruin may quickly result. Like a viper whose bite is death, it cannot be shaken off too soon.

Largely it is the child of ignorance; ignorance, that is, of the common psychological laws which govern the formation of the human mind and will. *Homo es et non angelus,* says à Kempis—"Thou art a man, not an angel;" yet we are ever impatient and wrathful with the limitations of this poor soul of ours, in which the highest of the animal order weds with the very lowest of the spiritual order. There are forms of sense-life so low that we can scarce distinguish them from vegetation; and so we might fancy God's angels puzzled for clear evidence of man's spirituality, yet because we can know very little and that with great labour, our wounded vanity spurns all knowledge with a *Quid est veritas?* and because virtue is slow and difficult of growth we lose patience with it and throw the task aside in anger. We cry out upon God: "Why hast Thou made me thus?"

Some conjecture, not unreasonably, that as the angelic intelligence, unencumbered by bodily conditions which would tie its movement down to time and space, is full-formed and enlightened in the first instant of its being; so, too, and for the same reason, its moral self-formation is effected, once and for all in the first exercise of its free choice. There is not, as with us, room for after-thought and repentance. Light breaks upon us slowly, and God presents Himself to our choice and love under a thousand partial aspects before our trial is ended and death seals our changeless doom. But in the angels, seemingly, virtue is not the fruit of repeated acts and elections and trials, but of one full exhaustive choice, one fearful purgatorial instant, one fiery trial in which self-love is to be wrenched out by the roots and burnt up in the flame of Divine charity.

But because we would be angels and not men, because we expect more of ourselves than God expects of us, because our pride revolts against the necessary limitations of humanity, we fall into sullen discouragement and since we cannot be all, and do all, and have all, we will be nothing, and do nothing, and have nothing, but will sit with knees relaxed and idly hanging hands.

Humiliating as it may be, yet we must accept the fact that it is the nature of man to learn through blundering, through making every possible mistake before the right method is discovered. We know it, whether as teachers or learners, in the acquisition of any art, or skill, or science, where we graduate our exercises so as to deal first with one then with another of the innumerable ways of going wrong. Again, we do not think it enough to have overcome the same difficulty once, but we repeat and repeat, till conquest has become a habit, and only then do we turn our attention to some other enemy.　By practice alone can any sort of skill be created, maintained, and increased; and so it is with that moral skill we call virtue.　It seems to some that they are deluding themselves, that they cannot be sincere in their resolves, because they are morally certain that they will fall again.　In other words, they think a habit can be created by one act.　Supernaturally it might be so, were the act one of intense and fervid love melting and moulding the soul in an instant—such a purgatorial act as that by which the angels fix their unchanging state; but ordinarily and naturally it is not so; and as one learning to draw, or to write, or to play, desires in all sincerity to succeed and not to blunder, and yet is morally certain that blunder he will and must, and that many and many a time; so it is with regard to the uprooting of any evil habit or the acquisition of any good habit.　We are not insincere because we are certain we shall fall again, if only at the present moment we do not want to fall and lament the prospective fall, and are resolved not to cease endeavouring in spite of a thousand falls.　For this is what perseverance means for us mortals—not an unbroken record of victories, but a dogged purpose of going on though we should stumble at every step; and of this it is said, that " he that shall persevere to the end shall be saved."

This very saying contains a thought which on the whole makes for encouragement rather than discouragement, and is well worth developing.　For it implies that in His judgment of us God looks not to the success, but to the endeavour; not to what we have attained, but what we would attain. The Samaritans would have nothing to do with our Lord because " His face was set as though He would go to Jerusalem; " not because He was in Jerusalem, but because He was as good as there, for He was there in will and purpose and firm resolve. And the world, in like manner, counts those lost to its own cause, and won to God's, whose face is set to go to Jerusalem, the city of peace. In this, as in many other things, the world's instinct and intuition is right, for God, too, takes the will for the deed. We *are* what we will. He who sincerely wills (that is, loves) purity and patience, or faith, or any other virtue, already possesses it as to its most essential and inward part; for all human virtue is primarily of the will. That it should pass beyond the will and embody itself in our outward conduct, in those faculties subject to the will; that we should be pure and brave and patient, not merely in sincere resolve, but also effectually in our words and actions, belongs to the integrity of the virtue; it is the body of the virtue, but not its soul. The soul is the principle of life, which slowly draws to itself apt matter from the environment and weaves it gradually and laboriously into a body meet for its own service and self-manifestation. The soul can live without the body, but the body without the soul is dead. And so it is with the soul and body of virtue; with the purpose and the attainment.

In this we are not countenancing "indifferentism" in morals, or approving the maxim, that it matters not what we do so long as we mean well. Because it matters less, it does not cease to matter very greatly; nor can any one who thinks it matters little be really said to "mean well." To "mean well" is to be sincerely resolved to procure the entire reformation and perfection of our conduct, so that the "body" of our spiritual and moral life shall be the exactest possible expression of the "soul." To mean the truth and yet to lie in ignorance is far better than to mean a lie and yet blunder upon the truth. But no one sincerely means the truth who speaks at random on the supposition that a material lie is of no consequence whatever.

Again, when we say God takes the will for the deed, we are not speaking of mere "velleity," but of what is called "efficacious" will, not because it actually effects its desire, or succeeds in its purpose, but because the failure is through no lack of will. A close prisoner may have a most efficacious will to escape. Stone walls and iron bars prevent his will from taking effect; but let these be removed, and the impeded force of his resolve at once becomes effectual. A "velleity" is not a resolve that actually exists in the soul, but one which would exist were it not excluded by some incompatible resolve. I want to possess a certain book, but I am not willing to pay the price, though I could do so. In short, I like the book but I prefer the money; and the resolve to keep my money excludes the resolve to get the book. I do not actually will to have it, but I *would* will to have it, were it not for this other will. Similarly a man may will patience or purity and fail to realize it, either because he could pay the price but is unwilling, or because, being quite ready to pay the price, he has not got it to pay, but must toil and labour and economize, and perhaps die, before he can effect his purpose. The former will is mere "velleity"—a will that might be, but is not— the latter is that "efficacious" will which God accepts for the deed.

Yet even the "velleity," though insufficient, is good; it is a spark of heavenly fire which can be fanned into a flame; or it is the light which God holds to the lamp of our heart that it may catch fire and make that light its own. But it is not enough to sit down with exiled Israel by the waters of Babylon and to remember Jerusalem in the midst of our tears; it is not enough to sit with the prodigal in rags and misery dreaming of the home we have lost through our folly and madness; we must arise and go; we must set our faces firmly towards Jerusalem, resolved to tread the weary way, albeit stumbling at every step, or even perishing on the road with our vow unaccomplished. This is an "efficacious" will, though outwardly it were to effect nothing, but were to fall back dead in the very effort to arise. In that instant watchful Love would be at our side from afar to bear us home in triumph to the "haven of our desire." Thus it was that Christ went forth, "knowing all things that were to come upon Him," to pass through Passion and Death to the bosom of the Father, to the haven of His desire, with His face set towards that Heavenly Jerusalem. *Posui faciem meam*, He says, *quasi petram*

z

durissimam—" I have set my face as it were a hard rock, firmly, immutably resolved to go through to the bitter end.

Man, says the Holy Ghost, looks at the outside of an action, considers the appearance: God looks at the heart, at the substance and soul of the act, at the set of the will.   Nor is this said to man's blame, since the surface is all his faculties enable him to take cognizance of; but it is to warn him off God's preserves, to remind him that he knows nothing or as good as nothing of the reality of his neighbour's conduct, that is, of the motive and merit.   In our judgment of human conduct, of the relative merits and goodness of men, we must be agnostics and positivists; we must keep ourselves to the observation and record of what appears, and relegate motives and merits to the region of the unknown and unknowable.   Much as God cares for the rectitude of our outward conduct, yet the " goodness " of men as such, that which makes a *man* good, is simply and only the goodness of his will. As he may be a good statesman or soldier or scholar or citizen without being a good man ; so, too, he may possess natural or acquired moral perfections without being really a good man, or as good as another who lacks all such ethical adornments.   The penitent in the first instant of his sorrow when, with all his vices and evil habits still clinging to him like rags, he rises and sets his face towards Jerusalem, may be before God a better man than one whose moral propriety is the fruit of happy temperament, of careful education, of easy

and graceful surroundings, of immunity from temptation. These facilities and natural graces are of
course compatible with the highest heroism of good-
will, but they must not be confounded with it. The
cripple may be able to stand without his crutch, but
it is hard to tell till it is taken away. Here at least
we can say: "Behold we know not anything." We
see two men struggling for life in the angry surf,
one sure of victory, the other of defeat; yet who
shall say that the will to live is stronger in the
former than in the latter; or that it may not be
precisely the reverse. And so God looks on ship-
wrecked humanity struggling for salvation against
lust and anger and sloth and weakness and all the
powers of evil, and where we see defeat He often
sees victory, for the will that is the least effectual is
sometimes the most "efficacious" and earnest.
We are safe in saying: "This man has fallen ten
times, the other a hundred times." But God may
know that the former fell at every temptation on
every occasion; while the latter resisted a thousand
temptations for the hundred he yielded to. Not
till we enter into the secret of a man's will, not till
we know all the antecedents of his life, the precise
measure of his knowledge and understanding, the
exact condition of every nerve and muscle, the lie
and correlation of all the cells of his brain, the
composition and heat of his blood, in fine, the
infinity of conditions under which he acts, can we
venture in our criticism of his action beyond a
"positivist" statement of what is external and
apparent. Human society rightly demands that we

should compare and treat men as good or evil in
the light of their outward behaviour, and legislates
to secure the outward act while careless about
good-will save as a means to that end; but we must
remember that this is after all a "legal" estimate
belonging to the *forum externum* of public opinion,
and is no guide to the ranking of guests at God's
table, where good-will is everything. "When thou
art invited," says Christ, "sit down in the lowest
place;" that is, be on the safe side and rank
yourself last before God, since you have absolutely
no certain grounds for a more flattering supposition.
"It will do you no harm," says à Kempis, "to place
yourself last of all. It will harm you much to
prefer yourself even to the least."

By introspection we can in some measure know
ourselves absolutely, but not relatively as compared
with others. We can be certain of much infidelity
to grace, of repeated falls and backslidings, of
habitual half-heartedness, of great need of God's
indulgent patience and mercy; but when we would
contrast ourselves favourably with Sodom and
Gomorrah, or Tyre and Sidon, let us withhold our
judgment, on the Divine assurance that it will be
more tolerable for them in the Day of Judgment
than for Corozain and Bethsaida and Capharnaum;
and let us forbear to "judge before the time." The
only thing that God has told us of the issue of that
day should seal our lips: "The last," He says,
"shall be first, and the first last;" all our conjectures
and anticipations shall be confounded and set at
naught.

But will not God judge men by their works, and not by their aspirations and wishes? Is not Hell paved with good intentions? With inefficacious intentions, yes; with "velleities" never brought to the birth, never shaped into resolutions and determinations. The works of man, like his nature, are compounded of inward and outward; and the inward is principal. It is by the acts or works of our will we are saved and judged; nor do outward acts or works count for aught save as quickened by the inward act; while the latter can subsist alone, where the former are impeded or distorted.

God, therefore, looks to what a man would be at, to the direction in which his face is set, to the sincerity of his endeavours and struggles; and not to where he is on the road, or to the extent of his success.

In all this there is contained both warning and encouragement; warning against any disposition to usurp God's prerogative of judging men's hearts by comparing them with ourselves or with one another in regard to the internal goodness of their will; encouragement against a too depressing view of ourselves or of the world at large. Deluged as the world is with every kind of moral disorder and irregularity of conduct, deplorable as such a state of things is to those who have God's Kingdom and glory at heart, yet it may well be that the worst evil of all, the internal evil of the will, is in no way coextensive with that outward material evil which is apparent.

Again, in estimating the effect of the sacraments

and means of grace upon ourselves and others, we
are often surprised to see so little fruit just because
we do not know what to look for. It is in the
maintenance and increase of good desires and
purposes that grace is directly perceptible, and not
always in the effectual and speedy correction of
outward conduct. If we find ourselves as resolved
as ever, and more so, to go on fighting and correcting
ourselves; if our faults displease us even more
vehemently, then, even though they resist our
efforts time after time, we are really progressing, or
at least we are not going back. Nay, even though
instead of making head against the current we are
carried down stream, it may be because the current
is stronger, and not because we are struggling less.
Had we not gone on struggling where should we be
now; how much worse should we be than we
actually are?

He, then, that shall persevere to the end shall be
saved, he whose face is ever set towards the goal,
who if the fixed eye of his intention blink an
instant through frailty or heaviness, recovers himself
promptly, without discouragement to begin again.

Perseverance does not imply one vehement act
of resolve followed by an unbroken record of steady
progress; it is not so that habits are formed; but
by alternations and oscillatory movements, as when
the tide creeps slowly in with rhythmic ebb and
flow till all the sand is covered; or as when a fire
is fed with fuel and blazes up and then burns low
and must be fed anew; or as when a little dog
follows his master, now lagging behind to be

whistled to heel, now running ahead to be recalled again, and at last reaches home having travelled the distance many times over. There is a like ebb and flow in the tide of our spiritual progress; there are times of renewal and fervour followed by times of chill and slackness; now we are lingering behind our Divine Master, now racing ahead; discouraged one moment, overconfident the next. Yet if we but persevere, we shall in the long run reach home, breathless and weary through our own folly, with graces innumerable wasted and squandered, but through the mercy of God—safe.

It is this humiliating but natural inconstancy of the human will that we have to recognize calmly and reckon with. "Were man but constant," could he but fix and perpetuate his nobler moods by a single act of will, "he were perfect." It is only by slowly inducing good habits that we can counteract this natural limitation, and cause a sort of artificial constancy, and this can only be effected through perseverance, of which discouragement is the great enemy. Discouragement is always surprised and resentful as the law of our moral growth makes itself felt in repeated failures and blunders. It makes new resolves only as long as it can do so with a belief that there is never to be another relapse; and when self-experience makes this belief no longer possible, it ceases to resolve. It does not know that perseverance means a dogged purpose of beginning again and again until a habit is formed. "Forgetting the things that are behind, and hastening to those which are before, I press forward to the mark," says St. Paul. A child's first effort to rise and walk is followed instantly by a fall, and this by a few brief tears; and then the fall is forgotten and the effort repeated. Were the child capable of memory and of a false prudence, it would never try again, but taught by Nature's wisdom it learns after many falls to stand, to walk, to run about; and so if after a brief act of sorrow we profit by our experience and rise at once to begin again, our falls will do us good instead of harm, and we shall learn, not only to walk, but to run in the way of God's commandments.

Nor does any wise, loving mother stand by and watch the efforts of her little one with such tenderness and carefulness as God watches us as we struggle and fall again and again—ever at hand to raise us up and console us and encourage us to begin afresh. What folly and mistaken kindness it would be were the mother never to allow her babe to risk the pain of a fall, but to carry it always in her bosom. God knows that there is no other way for us to learn but by experience, that pain and failure instruct and stimulate us. It is not when the pupil's hand is held and guided by the teacher and kept faithful to the headline that he learns and progresses, but when he is left at liberty to struggle alone. Doubtless there is an excess of liberty that tempts us beyond what we are able, and calls for more strength and skill than is yet even latent in us; but it is the part of the wise educator to graduate his lessons, to see that we get enough liberty to help us and not enough to harm us. So it is that God schools us by carefully adjusted trials and temptations and failures, that we may learn to become self-guiding, self-supporting, with that right independence which is the special dignity of free, intelligent creatures, masters of their own destiny—saving always the assistance of Divine grace, which is to us food, light, and air. In the order of grace as of nature, all evolution is the work of difficulty and opposition,—a truth verified by the common observation that the greatest saints have arisen in the corruptest ages. It is by temptation that God draws out all that is best in us, according to a law which may well be as necessary as the Divine Nature itself.

But in truth we have no business to look for so steady and even a progress as some of the foregoing illustrations might seem to imply. For there are disturbing conditions in ourselves and outside us which make it difficult to judge our advance save by the state of our interior will. It is only in the will-habit that we have a right to look for smooth, steady progress, and even there it is very difficult to gauge it. Were all the objective and subjective conditions precisely the same, we might reasonably expect to see a steady improvement in our outward conduct; but except in the very simplest matters this is never the case. It is not usually more difficult one day than another to say grace at meals or to perform some little exterior devotion; but it is not at all the same with regard to patience or keeping one's temper; for here much depends on the state of our nerves, on our weariness or freshness, our power of attention and self-control, and still more on the quite incalculable frequency of the occasions of victory or failure that may present themselves, so that often our seeming worst days are really our best, and *vice versa;* and when, as far as outward conduct goes, we are apparently relapsing, it is often then that the inward acts are most multiplied and the will-habit most strengthened and the advance most real. It is, in fact, almost as rash to judge ourselves by our outward conduct as it is to judge others. We may, indeed, judge ourselves by the attitude and set of our will, but of this we must not too readily take our conduct as an index. " Know thyself" is doubtless a precept of the highest wisdom; but as there is no folly like fancied self-knowledge, so perhaps he is the wisest of all who knows that he does not know himself, but has learnt to say with St. Peter: " Lord, Thou knowest all things."

Again, we must remember that habits are formed rapidly or slowly according as they favour or oppose our natural bent. It does not follow that because an evil habit is contracted in a month that it can be cured in a month; nor because a good habit has been formed after years that it cannot be uprooted in a week. Also, of good habits, some are more opposed to our inclination than others, and therefore take longer to form.

Once more, if we are really faithfully struggling after better things, it cannot but be that our standard of perfection and holiness will insensibly be raised higher and higher as we come to know

more of the spirit of Christ and His saints; while
at the same time a growing self-knowledge reveals
to us a thousand weaknesses which we were unconscious of when we first addressed ourselves to the
closer service of God.   Hence we necessarily will
seem to be much further from our ideals than when
we first set out to reach them; though, in truth, we
are far nearer in virtue of a truer conception, a
deeper and older love of the Divine will, a profounder
knowledge, a dislike of our own shortcomings.   The
beginner in every art, and the novice in the art of
Divine love, flushed with his first successes, is far
better pleased with himself than the skilled pro-
ficient; he is far nearer in imagination to the
attainment of his ambitions.   It should also be
remembered that a plant at first shoots up quickly
while all its energies are concentrated on the production of a single stalk, but more slowly when they
are dissipated among the many branches which it
afterwards puts forth, until a stage is reached when
growth is imperceptible; or again, that a stream
runs rapidly and forcibly while its waters are
confined to one narrow channel, but loiters as it
spreads out and shows a wider front.   At first our
efforts and attention are bestowed on the simpler
and more fundamental requirements of the spiritual
life, but later on we find new tasks branching out
before us on the right hand and the left.   We
cannot then expect to advance as rapidly in twenty
simultaneous undertakings as in one.

From all these considerations it seems to follow,
that the perseverance or constancy which we have

to aim at is a certain constancy of the will, a purpose of never giving up through discouragement, but of going on with a sort of spider-like persistency, patiently and promptly beginning again as often as the silken thread we have spun is snapped by one mishap or another. God will look less to the length we have accomplished than to the length we have designed to accomplish; nor will these painful, reiterated beginnings go unrewarded, unless faith and hope and courage and clinging love are without value in His eyes. " C'est qu'en aucune chose, peut être," says Guizot, "il n'est donné à l'homme d'arriver au but; sa gloire est d'y marcher." " He that shall persevere to the end," whom the hour of death shall find still struggling to gain the height, albeit beginning at the base for the thousandth time, he "shall be saved," and God in one purgatorial pang will perfect the unfinished task and will bring the storm-tossed, weary soul "to the haven of its desire."

THE MYSTICAL BODY.

"For as the body is one, and hath many members; and all the members of the body whereas they are many, yet are one body, so also is Christ. And the eye cannot say to the hand: I need not thy help; nor again the head to the feet: I have no need of you."—1 Cor. xii. 12, 21.

THE prominence given to the notion of the Church is notoriously characteristic of Catholic and historical Christianity, and distinguishes it from those many schools and Christian congregations which are called Churches in a widely different sense, and which professedly repudiate the Catholic's conception of the Church as they do his conception of priesthood and sacrifice, albeit retaining the terms with a modified signification.

It is not possible to define one idea truly, that is, to draw a line round it, without excluding false definitions; or to prove one position without disproving the contradictory. Still our present purpose is not to plead a cause, as it were, in the presence of inquirers or of opponents, but for our own pleasure and contemplation to set out in order our thoughts on so vast and complex a theme; to advance ourselves some little way towards a better apprehension of the "idea" of the Church, an idea which no one mind can hope to embrace in its entirety. We comprehend and exhaust nothing that is not simply the creature of our own brain—abstractions, forms, figures, generalizations; but when we come to concrete realities, to the works of God's hands, we know nothing, not the simple atomic creature, through and through, but at most, from this corner and from that; now under one aspect, now under another. If it is so of the dust of the earth, still more is it so of man made indeed from the dust, yet a world in himself were he but mere animal, a fathomless universe since he is also spiritual, and "little lower than the angels." Who then shall weigh and measure and sum up in vain words the "idea" of Him who is at once God and man, or the idea of that mystic Body, human and divine, earthly and heavenly, His Bride, the Catholic Church?

Were she but a society of man's making, a mere constitution and government imposed upon the Christian people that "all things might be done decently and in order," then indeed man's mind could quickly reach from end to end of its own creation; there would be nothing harder or more mysterious in the idea of the Church, than of any other polity ecclesiastical or civil; there would be no room for growth or progress in our knowledge of her nature. We might expect our forefathers who had framed that polity to have grasped the conception, not only as clearly, but more clearly than ourselves. But in the study of God's works natural and supernatural, we never near the end; our knowledge ever puts forth new branches, which in their turn branch out again, and these again, till we are lost and bewildered at the mazes which eternity alone will give us leisure to traverse. In these matters, in the study of realities, we can grow wiser than our elders, taught by the accumulated wisdom and experience of ages, transmitted from generation to generation.

Every Christian body or society, by the very fact that it is a body, admits the existence and the need of a Church in some sense of the word; nor is it ever disputed that Christ Himself approved, counselled, and commanded the association of His followers into some sort of external society; though the nature and meaning of that command is interpreted differently. The point in which the Catholic interpretation differs so markedly from all others, is the mediatorial character which it ascribes to the Church as an institution through which, and through which alone, the soul can be united to God. The good Catholic thinks and speaks of the Church as his spiritual Mother from whom his soul derives its supernatural life, by whom it is fed, nourished, healed, chastened, corrected, whom he is bound to love, reverence, and obey. Her name is ever on his lips and in his heart. We should think it strange to hear a Nonconformist speaking of " Holy Mother Church," for he has no thought which answers to the phrase, though he too believes in a Church otherwise conceived. It is precisely this exaltation of the Church to the side of Christ, her identification with Christ, that he quarrels with, the ascription to her of that

mediatorial office which is the prerogative of Him
alone, of whom it is said: "There is one God and
one Mediator between God and man, the man
Christ Jesus."

But what is mediatorship? For indeed it is
very doubtful if even those who vindicate it so
earnestly for our Blessed Lord as His exclusive
prerogative are altogether clear on the point.
Evidently it is some kind of "going between"
God and man, a drawing together of those who
were sundered and estranged. As God-Man, Christ
has the interests of God and of man at heart; and
in Him creation and the Creator are linked in one
personality. He is thus by nature fitted as none
other for the office of go-between or mediator, and
for the effecting of that union or atonement which
is its end.

But it is just here when we try to determine the nature of that union, and the mode
of its production, that two totally different conceptions of mediation present themselves; so that
while all Christians call Christ their mediator,
Catholics alone use the word in a sense which forbids
its application to any other than to Him; whereas
others, relying upon the text just quoted, refuse to
apply it to creatures in a sense in which it may
nevertheless be most rightly applied to them. For
indeed every creature that helps us in any way to
know or love or serve God better, is to be numbered
among the means of salvation, and so far mediates
between the soul and God. We do not see God
face to face yet, but must climb up to His throne

from His footstool, to Heaven from earth, by means
of the ladder of creation which bridges the otherwise impassable gulf. Still more, our fellow-men
here on earth, in so far as they help us, instruct us,
train us, pray for us, and are in a thousand ways
instrumental in our salvation, are truly mediators
between our souls and God, and not only occasion,
but to some extent effect, that union by a ministry
of reconciliation. It is not then wonderful that
Catholics who believe that "the effectual fervent
prayer of a just man availeth much," should ascribe
a still greater efficacy to the prayers of the saints in
Heaven, and speak of them as "mediators" and
"intercessors."

But such mediation as this is only a form of
ministry or service. The thing or person who
ministers or serves is thereby, or at least therein,
subordinated to the person served. "Who is
greater, he that sitteth at meat or he that serveth?"
Christ came into our midst as one that served, and
abased Himself at our feet in the abject humility
of love; and this manner of mediation he not only
allowed to all His disciples, but enjoined upon
them: "I have given **you** an example . . . If I,
your Lord and Master, wash your feet, much more
ought ye to wash one another's feet." So far as
Christ came to enlighten us by word and example,
to minister help to our souls and bodies, to promote
effectively our union with **God**, He was truly a
mediator, and the first of mediators, but not the
sole mediator, not the sole means of our salvation.

AA

But besides this ministerial mediation, there is another which for lack of a better term we might call "magisterial;" for in the exercise thereof the mediator is not abased, but exalted above him in whose behalf he mediates; he does not simply effect and produce direct union of the soul with God, and then stand aside having finished his service of mercy; but he is himself the link through which the soul is bound to God, standing as it were between the soul and God. He is not as a gardener who grafts the branch into the stock, and thereby gives it life, but He is Himself the stock into which the graft is set and through which it draws life from mother earth, one and the same life quickening both. "I am the vine," says Christ, "and you are the branches."

When Catholics say that Christ is the one and only mediator between God and man, that through Him alone we have access to the Father, that He alone is the door of the sheepfold, that no man cometh to the Father but by Him, they are speaking of this "magisterial" mediation, often so dimly understood outside the Church. They mean that no mere creature however holy or exalted can be directly and immediately united to God so as to be a sharer of the divine life and beatitude; but must first be united to Christ so as to make with Him one thing, one body, one moral personality, which "one thing," is united to God and receives His quickening grace. They mean to deny any separate or independent union with God, apart from Him who is the one channel of eternal life.

But where faith in the Divinity of Christ is clouded, and the purport of the Incarnation ill taught and ill apprehended, there is a danger of altogether ignoring this "magisterial" mediation of Christ, of regarding Him as merely the first of prophets, teachers, philanthropists, martyrs; by reason of His Divinity, infinite in dignity, infinite in power and wisdom, but still exercising only the same sort of ministerial mediation as they, though on a vastly extended scale. But salvation through Christ means salvation by incorporation with Christ, the sharing with Him of a gift of which we are incapable in our isolation; a gift which is indivisible, too great for our single soul to grasp or contain, except so far as, in union with Christ and with hands locked in His, it is strengthened to bear the burden.

No one will quarrel with us perhaps for conceiving the Church as a mediator in the ministerial sense of the term; for whether she be of human or Divine origin, she is evidently, under God, one of the principal means for the salvation of souls, in that she carries on the ministry of Christ, disseminates His teaching, applies the fruits of His Passion to the healing of the nations. When the Nonconformist repudiates sacerdotalism, it is not because it involves such mediation as this; for he himself is tolerant of such intervention on the part of his own ministers. Indeed he tolerates far more than any Catholic would endure; for he leaves it to the mood and caprice of his pastor, to determine on each occasion the substance of the public prayers, so that those present are willing to be represented before God as sad or joyful, as penitential or triumphant, as needing these graces rather than others, all according to the passing phases of the minister's own soul, and are ready to say Amen to whatever may come into his head. Also they are willing to listen patiently to his private interpretation of the word of God, and to accept it unless it manifestly disagrees with their own; they to a large extent trust him and allow their minds to be formed by him in doctrinal and religious questions. In a word, he is not merely their delegate before God, but their representative; his mediation is not passive, as his who repeats by rote the words entrusted to him by another; but rather active as of one to whom we commit our will and judgment.[1] The Catholic priest, on the other hand, is but the Church's delegate. Every word that he utters at the altar, nay, every little gesture and intonation is prescribed for him by the Christian republic not merely of to-day, but of the ages past; and even though the setting be his own, yet the doctrine that he sets forth in the pulpit is not his own but that

---

[1] Cf. the plea for "Common Prayer" quoted by Walton's "Piscator":

> But he that unto others leads the way
>   In public prayer,
>   Should do it so
>   As all that hear may know
>   They need not fear
> To tune their hearts unto his tongue and say,
>   Amen; not doubt they were betrayed
>   To blaspheme when they meant to have prayed.
>   (*Compleat Angler.*)

of the Church who has sent him, whose mouthpiece he is. Were he a reprobate or an unbeliever, he might be guilty of sacrilege in preaching and praying, but not of insincerity or hypocrisy, since he is understood to speak not in his own name but in the Church's. The very vestments in which she blots out his personality when he approaches the altar, are an indication of her desire that in his official work he should put off himself and should put on the Church. We do not for a moment deny that the individual will break through and assert himself in spite of all precautions; that he, and still more his followers and admirers, will often put the man before the priest. But wherever this tendency prevails, whether in the popular preacher or the popular confessor; in the ministry of the word or in that of the sacraments; whether by the intrusion of merely personal views and opinions into priestly teaching and direction, or by the substitution of personal tastes and fancies in place of the established liturgical observances of the Church, it is always felt to be uncatholic, an alien element hostile to that liberty from individual tyranny which the Church secures for her children.

It is not then the notion of instrumental or ministerial mediatorship which the Nonconformist objects to associating with his conception of the Church; but rather that of a mediatorship such as we have already declared to be the exclusive prerogative of Christ. "Exclusive," because for the Catholic, Christ and the Church are not two, but one, as head and body are one, as husband and

wife are one, two in one flesh. The vine is not all
stem, nor all branches, but stem and branches
together; and the Church is not all Head, nor all
members, but the two together are one Christ and
one Church, one mediator between God and man;
for she is the fulness, the complement, the extension
of Christ, as the branches are the extension of the
vine.

Thus all that we said of Christ's magisterial
mediation is to be understood of Christ in His
fulness, Christ and His Church; through the Church
alone we have access to the Father; no man comes
to the Father but through her. She is the immediate, the only adequate recipient of that grace
which flows into each single soul that is united to
her; she, too, is the recipient of that Eternal Life
hereafter, which single souls share only because
they are built into her fabric. We are not united to
God singly and independently as rays which converge
to a common centre and yet do not touch one
another on the road, but we are first knit together
into one living organic body under the Man Christ
as our Head, and then with Him and through Him
united to the very Godhead, whose life and beatitude flows down to the least and furthest member
of that living thing.

The happiness which the Christian looks forward
to hereafter is not that of his own personal triumph
over evil, of his own satisfaction in the realization
of his highest and best capacities; but it is that
of the triumph of God's cause for which he has
lived and laboured, recognizing himself as but an

instrument directed by reason and conscience to ends greater than personal, and but dimly conceived by himself; it is, by consequence, the happiness of the triumph of all those who with himself are sharers in the victory wrought by the right hand of God. The very terminology which speaks of the "Church militant" and the "Church triumphant" tells us of a collective and corporate joy. He is no true knight who fights but for his own skin, who triumphs only because he leaves the conflict scathless and rich with his own share of the booty; but rather he, whose solitary joy is all swallowed up and forgotten in the common joy of his prince and his country and his fellow-knights. For as the soul is not received and possessed by any one part or member of the organism but only by the whole; so that to which God gives Himself and unites Himself in glory, is no one soul, but all souls clustered round Christ into one living body. Nor is it a "common" beatitude, a "common" treasure, in the sense that all enjoy the same, albeit independently, as they do who gather round the same fire, each feeling its warmth neither more nor less for that many or few feel it together; but it is "common" because it is a rejoicing in the joy of others, and is therefore greater as there are more to participate in it.

For such a happiness and salvation as this, incorporation is plainly an absolute necessity; "outside the Church or outside Christ there is no salvation," becomes a truism as soon as we understand the nature of the salvation in question.

It must be admitted that this mediatorial conception of the Church, this notion of corporate
sanctification and salvation is not only subtle and
strange to modern minds of the prevalent type,
but also manifestly uncongenial to some of the
governing ideas which gave birth to Protestantism
in the sixteenth century,—ideas which had from
the very first been lurking here and there in the
pages of many a saintly mystic and illuminist more
happy in the enjoyment of Divine union than in
his analysis and exposition of that state and its
conditions. "I and my God," "My Beloved is mine
and I am His"—these, as the spontaneous self-
utterances of contemplative love, cannot be mis-
understood; but curious speculation may give them
an "excluding" sense savouring of a certain pride
and independence, of an indifference, nay, even a
sort of contempt for others, whom nevertheless God
has identified with Himself, and apart from whom
He cannot and will not be approached. To go to
God alone, to deal with Him immediately, to be
taught by Him privately and directly, to link ourselves with no other when we draw near to Him,
to stand or fall by ourselves, to account our fellow-
Christians in this matter as simply among those
creatures which are subordinated to us as helps and
ministers, but in no wise as making one body with
us; to view them as co-operators for a gain
"common" in a sense, but of which each takes
his share, nor gains in the gain of another, this is
the leading notion of what we might call a false
individualism in religion.

False as a fact, not because the idea is intrinsically absurd in any way. God most certainly
might have created each soul to be a separate little world, a church in itself, to be taught
and sanctified and saved independently, and not
merely as part of a body; and there is much *prima
facie* evidence to favour such a supposition. Even
the Catholic religion teaches that each soul is the
Church in epitome; that the first and absolutely
indispensable care of each man must be for his own
sanctification, which he may not sacrifice or injure,
however slightly, were it for the salvation of the
whole race. Nor is the Protestant conception
essentially selfish and egoistic, however inadequate
and defective. For it regards all souls as destined
to be united hereafter in God as rays are united in
their common centre, while here on earth they are
bound together by the ties of friendship and equality
as those engaged in the same profession or pursuit,
whose interest and pleasure it is to help one another;
or as fellow-travellers on the road making for the
same country, where, however, each has his own
home and private interest, which will not suffer
were all his companions to drop by the way. Yet
the Church, in contrast to the Catholic view, is
conceived simply as the aggregation of souls, as a
multitude of units in no way organized or inter-
dependent, nor is a love of the common good to
which each member ministers best by its own
perfection, the motive which makes self-care and self-
culture a supreme duty, but rather an implicit conviction that it is only the surplus and overflow of

our rational self-love that is due to our neighbour, since each man is regarded as a world and a church in himself, not in an analogical and defective sense, but in the fullest and most literal. It is the unit, and not, as with Catholics, the body, which is the archetype and exemplar.

When we say that our salvation not merely depends upon, but even consists formally in our incorporation into the Church, it is plain that we are speaking primarily of the invisible Church, and only in a conditional and qualified manner of the visible Church, which is but the sacrament and outward instrument of the former—a distinction which will occupy us later on. Speaking roughly, we might say that the Catholic idea of the Church is social in the good sense, while the Protestant is individualist in the bad sense. In the truest sense these notions are in no way antagonistic, for the ideal society is an organism whose every member works most fruitfully for the common good by securing its own fullest development; where there is no conflict between public and private interest; where mutual help and co-operation begets the only true liberty, which consists not in sterile isolation, but in the abundance of the means and opportunities for self-realization and the turning to account of every talent and energy; where the initiative and movement is from below, from the healthy vitality of the members themselves, needing but to be directed and guided by the head. It is no artificial product planned by theorists and imposed by force or fraud on a free people in the name of liberty, aiming at an impossible equality by reducing all to the condition of slavery, but the spontaneous growth of healthy social life freed from all morbid conditions.

Doubtless this ideal is at best a term of approximation never to be fully realized except in the Church triumphant; but it is ever preached, and to some degree realized, in the visible and militant Church, whose constitution is, as St. Paul teaches, that of a living body, not that of social contract. The very idea of the Church is a protest against the false individualism of the Reformation on the one hand, and against the false socialism of its reaction on the other. It is interesting to note how the following piece of otherwise very admirable criticism is vitiated by a failure to recognize the fact that if a certain individualism is un-catholic, a crude collectivism is no less so.

"Palestrina's music," writes H. E. Krehbiel, "must not be listened to with the notion in mind of dramatic expression such as we almost instinctively feel to-day. Palestrina does not seek to proclaim the varying sentiment which underlies his texts. That leads to individual interpretation, and is foreign to the habits of Churchmen in the old conception, when the individual was completely resolved in the organization. He aimed to exalt the mystery of the service, not to bring it down to popular comprehension and make it a personal utterance. For such a design in music we must wait till after the Reformation, when the ancient mysticism began to fall back before the demands of reason, when the idea of the sole and sufficient mediation of the

Church lost some of its power in the face of the growing conviction of the intimate personal relationship between man and his Creator. Now idealism had to yield some of its dominion to realism, and a more rugged art grew up in place of that which had been so wonderfully sublimated by mysticism.

" It is in Bach, who came in a century after Palestrina, that we find the most eloquent musical proclamation of the new *régime* . . .

" Palestrina's art is Roman; the spirit of restfulness, of celestial calm, of supernatural revelation and supernal beauty broods over it. Bach's is Gothic—rugged, massive, upward-striving, human. In Palestrina's music, the voice that speaks is the voice of angels; in Bach's, it is the voice of men.

" Bach is the publisher of the truest, tenderest, deepest, and most individual religious feeling. • His music is peculiarly a hymning of the religious sentiment of modern Germany, where salvation is to be wrought out with fear and trembling by each individual through faith and works, rather than the agency of even a divinely-constituted Church. . . . As the Church fell into the background, and the individual came to the fore, religious music took on the dramatic character which we find in the Passion music of Bach."

The critic is acute enough to feel that the idea of Catholicism and that of Protestantism are in some sense mutually exclusive; that the opposition can be roughly described to be such as exists between socialism and individualism; also, that this difference

and opposition permeates everywhere, not only
through doctrine, discipline, and ecclesiastical constitution, but even through liturgy, music, painting,
and literature. But he is wrong in assuming that
because the Reformation cast aside the social and
corporate element of the Catholic conception of
the Church, retaining only the individualist element
by which it was balanced, and which it balanced in
return, therefore the individual was, so to say, discovered by Protestantism, having been " in the old
conception " " completely resolved in the organization." The Church never for a moment in any
way accepted Plato's notion of the State (civil or
ecclesiastic, matters not) as of a distinct personality
or entity for whose sake the component members
existed collectively and individually. Nay, it was the
Catholic idea which gave slow and difficult birth to
belief in the absolute and ineffaceable value of the
individual, a belief fed and fostered by the application of the several sacraments to each several
soul, by the extinction of all artificial inequality,
and the recognition of perfect spiritual equality
among all those, from the Emperor to the lazer,
who feed at God's common board on the Bread of
Angels. It is a curious comment also on the
observation that Protestantism put man for the first
time into " intimate personal relationship with his
Creator," that while Protestants mostly speak of "*the*
Saviour," and " *the* Lord," Catholics invariably say,
" *our* Saviour," and " *our* Lord," and surely a glance
at the devotions and prayers of Catholics in any
age or country will show at once how absolutely

unfounded is the notion that the Church's mediation hinders immediate commerce between God and the individual.

Not such indeed is the mediation of the Church; she is not a barrier or a blind between the soul and her Maker. For though the quickening spirit can touch the parts and members only on condition of their incorporation with the body, separate from which they are dead; yet the body does not stand between them and the spirit, as though it absorbed without transmitting the vital flame. And so it is only through the Church, as making part of the Church, that the soul can come into direct contact with God our Father; it is only through the Mystic Vine that the sap of sanctifying grace can flow into our souls. Again, need we say, we speak of the invisible Church, the Communion of Saints, in which none is incorporated save by living faith; since no one can be so ignorant as to suppose that mere outward communion with the visible Church is sufficient for salvation, however necessary it may be in certain cases.

In fine, we may maintain fearlessly that Gothic architecture is every bit as Catholic as Roman, and Bach's style of music as Palestrina's. Both schools embody and set forth one aspect of the Catholic conception, each being complementary of the other. The exigencies and tastes of particular localities and times may call for an emphasis, now on this aspect, now on the other. Obviously the public and collective worship of the Church of its own nature demands the repression of individualism in liturgical observance, music, and other vehicles of expression. There is an impertinence which we instinctively resent in any attempt on the part of the individual to obtrude his private interpretations, sentiments, and emotions upon us by unauthorized vagaries and emphases of his own. He is but the mouthpiece of the Universal Church and of the traditions of centuries; let him deliver the message entrusted to him without comments or embellishments of his own. Originality is well in other spheres, but in the choir or the sanctuary it is the worst form of vulgarity.

To conclude the present matter, it is in this conception of the Church as mediating between God and the soul, as a mystical body in union with which alone salvation is possible, as the mother in whose womb we are conceived, on whose breasts we hang, that we find the reason of the prominence given to the Church in the mind and on the lips of Catholic Christians. Much even as we venerate Mary, the great Mother of God and man, yet even she is but a type and figure, but a part and member of this still greater Mother of us all—the Jerusalem from on high, our Holy Mother the Church.

II.

"The Church of the first-born who are written in the Heavens."—Hebrews xii. 23.

When we assert that salvation may be said in some sense to consist in being incorporated with the Church, we are not speaking of the visible, but of the invisible Church. With the former we are incorporated by mere profession of faith and obedience, although we be spiritually dead; with the latter we are incorporated only by divine charity. Let us now consider more closely this distinction between the invisible and the visible Church, and determine more accurately the relation of these two societies one to another.

We not uncommonly speak of them as the "Body" and the "Soul" of the Church, implying at least some kind of resemblance between their mutual relation and that of the components of our double nature. Of these components the soul is invisible, immortal, incorruptible, self-sustaining, principal; the body is visible, transitory, corruptible, dependent; it is the instrument and minister of the soul, its symbol and sacrament. For this reason we may apply the word "body" to the visible Church on earth, which shall end with time, which retains corrupt members in its communion, as tares amid the wheat; which is the outward symbol and sacrament of the invisible Church whose organ and instrument it is. And by contrast, this invisible Church of saints and angels may be called the "soul." But every metaphor is imperfect. Soul and body are at once distinct and in a sense co-extensive; whereas the invisible and visible Church are neither, some members being common to both, others belonging only to one. The saints in Heaven and legions of just men on earth do not belong to the visible Church or come under its external jurisdiction; while thousands of those that do have neither part nor lot with the saints in light. Again, speaking strictly, each of these societies has (like every society) a soul and body of its own. The saints in Heaven and all the just on earth, Catholic or non-Catholic, Christian or non-Christian, are invisibly bound together by the indwelling of the same Holy Spirit of Charity "which is the bond of peace," the cement which seals into one the stones of the Heavenly Salem—"one body and one spirit." And on earth the members of the visible Church are visibly united by the bond of obedience to that same Spirit viewed as the source of ecclesiastical authority and sacramental grace— "one body and one spirit."

However convenient, therefore, it may be to speak of the invisible and visible Churches as the soul and body of the Church, it is not without danger of confusion.

What, then, is the invisible Church?

It is that communion or society of saints and angels in Heaven and of just men on earth, of all nations and of all ages, of which St. Paul says: "But you have come nigh to Mount Sion and to the city of the living God, the Heavenly Jerusalem, and to the company of many thousands of angels, and to the Church of the first-born who are written in the heavens, and to God the Judge of all, and to the spirits of the just made perfect, and to Jesus the Mediator."

While, therefore, the members of the visible Church are upon earth, those of the invisible are both in Heaven and on earth—on earth, a handful;

BB

in Heaven, as the sands on the sea-shore. That portion .which is in Heaven is formed and perfected—has passed into its changeless condition; while the portion on earth is in process of formation, not yet accepted, shaped, or perfected. Here the stones of Solomon's temple are hewn and fashioned with many a rough blow and sharp incision; there they are noiselessly laid each in its peculiar and predestined place in the living structure.

> Scalpri salubris ictibus
> Et tunsione plurima,
> Fabri polita malleo,
> Hanc saxa molem construunt,
> Aptisque juncta nexibus
> Locantur in fastigio.[1]

We must not imagine that the visible Church is the same as the Church militant, and the invisible the same as the Church triumphant. For all upon earth who are engaged in God's cause belong to the militant Church, be they inside or outside the visible Church, while the triumphant Church comprehends only that portion of the invisible Church which is in Heaven.

In Heaven the invisible Church consists of the spirits of the just made perfect in love, purged seven-fold in the fire of suffering and great tribulation, developed into full correspondence with that

---

[1] By kindly chisel deftly formed,
    With showers of battering blows bestormed,
    Squared by the hand which Heaven hath skilled
    These polished blocks the fabric build
    And fastly jointed there unite
    To crown the rising summit's height.

Divine plan and pattern thought out and loved by
God from all eternity, and then by Him infused
slowly and laboriously into the often reluctant mind
and conscience, into the heart and affections of each
saint; a light that haunted the soul when it would
cower in the darkness; a fire that leaped up after
every futile quenching; a tormenting thought that
would not rest unlistened-to and unloved. And
though there dwells in the saints but one and the
same spirit, yet there is an infinite and most orderly
diversity of gifts and manifestations, even as the
same vital spark displays itself diversely in the
multitudinous members of our body—as sight in
the eye, as hearing in the ear, as motion in the
limbs, as thought in the mind, as love in the heart,
yet "one and the same spirit." In the gathering
together of the saints we have not merely an endless
chain of repetitions of the same idea or type—as it
were so many beads threaded on a string, or a
bundle of innumerable fagots each the exact counter-
part of its fellows; but rather a mighty and complex
organism, a vast mosaic of souls of every conceivable
pattern and complexion of sanctity, no two indeed
alike, albeit each indispensable for the perfection
of the entire design, each with its own place that
no other can fill, each with its own song of praise
that no other can sing, and yet which blends in a
chord of universal praise that would be thinned
and impoverished by its silence. As all creation
collectively makes one full utterance of the Divine
Goodness of which each several creature is but a
word or syllable, so in the communion of saints

the full idea of sanctity, the flower of human excellence wedded with Divine, is unfolded and expanded in all its parts to the glory and praise of God, and gives forth its fragrance *in odorem suavitatis.* There first shall we understand what God meant when He created man; not this man nor that, but man; there shall we see that governing idea which was forcing itself into reality and fact, through all the long, weary centuries of our miserable history; and seeing it we shall cry out: *Justus es, Domine, et rectum judicium tuum*—God was right after all.

There at last Christ shall be unfolded and made plain in that mystical body which is well called His *pleroma,* His fulness or extension. His Sacred Humanity while on earth, with its brief span of thirty years, could not within the narrow limits of a single experience reveal to us more than a fraction of the latent potentialities of His deified soul. He was but as the seed whose power and meaning lies hid till it has germinated, flowered, fructified, and multiplied from generation to generation. From Him all sanctity flows as from its source, whether we trace the stream from Calvary backward to the beginning or forward to the end of time. "I live," says the Christian, "yet not I, but Christ liveth in me," for sanctity is simply the prevalence in us of a "power that makes for righteousness," of a will that is not our own—in us, but not of us—ever pressing against the will of our egoism and self-centred love in the interests of a love which is God-centred and unselfish. It is the constant action upon us of God, who is, moreover, an Incarnate God; it is to our soul what gravitation is to our body, a force ever drawing us to our true centre and rest; so ever-abiding and persistent that we have come to confound it with the very constitution of our spiritual being. Yet were the earth suddenly annihilated from under our feet we should have no sense of weight; and were God to withdraw from us we should have no wish to do good, no love of the truth, no sense of right or wrong.

The tree is known by its fruits, and Christ is known by His deeds; not merely by the deeds of His earthly life, but by all that He has done and shall do in His saints from the beginning to the end. His spirit, in order to display its full content and significance, needs to be applied to every condition of human life, so that we may see Christ under every aspect; in every nationality and language, in every stage of development, social and individual, in Jew and Greek, in Barbarian and Scythian, in bond and free, in wealth and poverty, in prosperity and adversity, in health and sickness, in youth and age, in simplicity and culture, in weakness and strength; that we may see the leaven of the Kingdom of God in all its workings, in its actions and reactions under every possible variety of conditions, favourable and unfavourable, and may enter more fully into the mind and heart of Him whose life is thus manifested in His mystical body. "I saw a great multitude," says St. John, "which no man could number, of all nations and tribes and peoples and tongues, standing before the throne and in the sight of the Lamb;" for so it shall be in that day when the number of

the elect shall be filled up, and the last stone of the
mystical temple shall be laid in its predestined place,
and the last piece set to the perfect mosaic; when
the body of Christ shall have reached its fulness,
and the idea of Christian sanctity shall have attained
its complete expansion; and the potentialities of the
human soul shall have been revealed to the utmost;
when the long-sought chord of created and uncreated
praise shall have been struck at last, and time and
the things of time shall be needed no more.

III.

"In every nation he that feareth Him and worketh justice,
is acceptable to Him."—Acts x. 35.

We have now to ask ourselves: Who are the
members on earth of the Invisible Church? And
the first answer is simple enough, namely: All those
in whose hearts charity is diffused by the Holy
Ghost; all those who give God and God's cause the
first, if not always the only place in their affections;
all those who prefer right and truth and duty to
father, mother, spouse, children, brethren, kinsfolk,
home, and lands; all those who accept not only
with their mind, but with their heart and will, that
it profits a man nothing if he gain the whole world
to the hurt of his own soul. They may not yet have
learnt to love nothing else but in connection with
God and in sympathy with the Divine mind and
will; they have undoubtedly yet to be tried and
perfected through many tribulations, either here or
in Purgatory—for nothing defiled has ever entered

Heaven or reached the beatifying stage of love but at the cost of purifying pain. Still, as long as God weighs down all other treasures heaped together in the balance of their affections, so long do they keep their vital connection with the Mystical Body unsevered; but when singly or collectively creatures are preferred to Him in that same act they become as severed limbs; for nothing corrupt can enter into or remain in the Kingdom of Heaven.

But "without faith it is impossible to please God," it is impossible to possess charity, to cling to truth and goodness above all things and at every sacrifice. We cannot therefore suppose that the invisible Church on earth extends beyond the limits of the visible except so far as faith so extends. Faith is commonly and rightly explained to be a firm will or resolution to hold fast to truths taught us by God without discussing them or questioning them by any kind of practical doubt. We hold to them with that firmness which God's word merits; and we do so in obedience to God's command; not because we have necessarily sat in judgment either on the truths revealed or on God's claims as a witness; but simply because we recognize God's right to command the mind which He has made. Without such faith we cannot please God; for even where reason reaches the simple truths of religion and morality, its grasp is too feeble and its gaze too unsteady to prevent our mind being perverted in the hour of temptation and yielding to the fallacies of self-love, pride, and sensuality, or listening to the voice of worldly and carnal wisdom, or ceding to the influence of universal example. In that hour we have no strength alone; *Væ soli:* we must lean upon God and hear His voice and not our own; loyal obedience to Him will stand us in good stead when we are perhaps blinded by passion to our truest and highest self-interest. As hope lends us God's strength in the hour of weakness, so faith lends us God's light in the hour of darkness when our own lamp has gone out or flickers to extinction.

It is for this reason that theologians insist on some kind of divine speaking or revelation as a condition for faith, thus strictly interpreting, *Fides ex auditu—* "Faith comes by hearing." For faith is essentially trust in another whose wisdom and knowledge supplements what is defective. in our own. However clearly we may learn the same religious truths from reflection upon the phenomena of conscience or of physical nature, yet we are so far resting only upon ourselves, and our own reason and observation—a support that will prove insufficient in the time of trouble. We are trusting to the arm of flesh, and not to the arm of God; flesh and blood has revealed it to us, but not our Father who is in Heaven. Faith, hope, and love alike put God for self, and bind us to Him, and deliver us from the weakness of isolation.

There is nothing arbitrary in making faith a condition for salvation or at least of supernatural salvation. It is altogether natural and even necessary. Every wise moralist knows that we cannot lead a good life unless we resolve to stand firm in the hour of temptation and darkness, by those truths which we saw clearly in the hour of

calm and light, but which now we do not see
clearly and are disposed to question; in other
words, unless we are resolved not to rationalize
or doubt, but to hold on blindly to what we do not
now see, substituting a will-certainty for a mind-
certainty. This is faith, not in another, but in our
own better self; yet in principle it is the same. If
indeed we yield to the pressure of temptation and
reopen the question, we only offend against our own
better judgment—a fallible authority at best, though
surely more trustworthy than the judgment of passion.
In proportion as the spiritual truths by which we
must live are subtle and mysterious, we need still
greater support to supplement our wavering reason,
while for those that are strictly supernatural and out
of reason's ken, God's support is an absolute
necessity. Here, to doubt is to offend not against
fallible authority, but against the authority of God,
and the will-certainty must be measured to that
standard; it must be an unqualified adhesion of
the whole soul to God's word as such.

There can be no faith therefore where God is
not felt to have spoken and to have commanded
our obedient assent to the things that belong to
our peace, to the great fundamental truths that
there is a God, whose we are, and before whom
we continually stand; who is the Rewarder and the
Reward of them that seek Him, to whom we must
render an account and pay the last farthing of our
debt of reverence and service. There can be no
faith, no pleasing of God, where the idle speculative
questioning of these truths, implicitly admitted in

every act of conscience, is not recognized as immoral, as sinful, as a trespass not only against conscience itself, but against the revealed will of God; or where, with the full consciousness of being unduly excited or depressed, or otherwise biassed and unbalanced, one makes a resolve or chooses an opinion in accordance with such bias.

Yet if the soul is to listen not to itself but to God, if it is to cling to His word when its own word falters, it is needful that God should really speak to the soul, and should be apprehended distinctly as so speaking. For speech, in this stricter sense, it is not enough that the speaker betray his mind in words or signs, or even by direct "thought-transference" with the secret design that the perceiver shall take his meaning, as when one leaves a book open for another to read without bidding him read it, or showing any sign of a will that he should do so. To speak is not only to express one's mind, but also to express one's will that the hearer should listen. God utters His mind in creation and in our conscience, and designs these books for our instruction; but only so far as He also signifies that this message is expressly directed to us can He be said to speak to us; He rather soliloquizes in our presence; He speaks in us, or outside us, but not *to* us.

And what sort of sign is it that changes the voice of reason and of nature into a supernatural revelation; and by which God enters into personal relation with the soul and becomes her friend, her teacher, her support?

Were I in dire need of a very precise sum of money, and were I on the same day to find more or less the required amount, I should have no solid reason to think that it had been left in my way by design; but were I to find the exact sum to the very farthing, I could hardly resist the inference that it was intended for me by some one who knew my need, or if none knew it, by God who is over all. The exact correspondence of the sum to my need would change a "find" into a gift; it would equivalently address the money to me and mark it with my name.

It is peculiar to God, whose own the soul is, to call her by her most secret name known to Him alone. This was the reason of Christ's spell over Nathaniel, over the woman of Samaria, over all whom He has called. "Whence knowest thou Me?" they say, or, "Sir, I perceive Thou art a prophet." And so it is that God brings a truth home to a man, and changes it from a dead to a living word, when by its preternatural opportuneness, its altogether providential and otherwise unaccountable correspondence to his complex spiritual needs, it proves itself to be a message from One who knows him through and through, in all his individuality.

This waking up to the recognition of God's voice whether in conscience or in nature, or in the inspired word, this sense of its being directed to ourselves is well exemplified in what we so often read in saints' lives, where some text lighted on by chance, some naturally derived thought or suggestion presents

itself irresistibly as a Divine message and is listened
to as such.   Who does not remember St. Augustine's
Tolle et lege, the words of a child at play; or how
St. Anthony, as the Breviary says, took as said **to**
himself (*tamquam ea sibi dicta essent*), the words heard
on entering a church: " Go sell all and follow Me."
And besides innumerable instances in hagiography
there is perhaps no religious-minded person who
has not had some such experience real or fancied.
And if those who habitually seek such signs, forcing
God's hand, as it were, and not waiting for the time
of His free visitation, will be often deluded; and if
even those who do not seek them may often doubt
as to what is coincidence and what is design, yet
there are many instances where there is no room
for prudent or justifiable doubt.

However simple, frequent, and universal these
Divine utterances may be, in obedience to which
the soul which " hears from the Father," learns and
comes to Christ, yet they can be no more claimed
as a strict exigency of our nature, than any other
preternatural and personal intervention of Providence; they, and the faith they generate, are "the
gift of God."

It is not hard to believe that the fundamental
religious truths touching God the Rewarder which
are written in the secret of conscience and over
the face of Nature are brought home, not once in
a lifetime, but over and over again to every soul,
as a Divine message from without, claiming an
obedient voluntary assent, a will-certainty stronger
than death.   God speaks in divers manners; but to

all who are to be judged as to faith, speak He must in some form or other.

"No difficulty," says Aquinas, "follows from the position that one brought up in the woods among the wild beasts should be bound to certain explicit beliefs; for it is incumbent on Divine Providence to provide each soul with all necessary conditions for salvation, unless some hindrance is offered on the soul's part. For were one so brought up, to follow the lead of natural reason in the pursuit of good and the avoidance of evil, it is to be held for a perfect certainty (*certissimum tenendum est*), that God would either reveal all necessary beliefs to him by an internal inspiration, or He would send some one to preach the faith to him, as He sent Peter to Cornelius."[1]

In other words, where the fuller revelation is denied, where the light of the Gospel never penetrates, yet the internal revelation of the fundamental and germinal truths of all religion will surely never be wanting; one need not ascend into Heaven to bring it down, nor descend into Hell to bring it up, for the word is ever nigh to each human heart, ever whispering into the soul's ear, ever knocking at the gate of its love.

Wheresoever then and whensoever there is found a man who listens obediently and humbly to the voice of conscience; who bows to its sovereign authority as to a power above him and distinct from him, who admits its unqualified claims, not only in theory but in practice, there we may be sure that God, however

[1] *De Veritate*, xiv. a. ii. ad 1.

dimly recognized, has spoken and has been listened
to; since without faith it is impossible to please
God, impossible to live that life of sacrifice and
conflict which obedience to conscience entails.
This surely is the meaning of Peter's vision of all
manner of living creatures brought together in one
vessel knit at the four corners; a figure of all
nations, of all sorts and conditions of men, from the
four winds of heaven, and from the dawn of our
race till its consummation, all cleansed by God
through the Blood of Christ, all subjected to Peter
as the Vicar of Christ; even as was Cornelius whose
prayers and alms, ascending for a memorial in the
sight of God, were emblematic of the sacrifice of
justice offered daily by that large portion of the
invisible Church on earth, which stretches north,
south, east, and west, beyond the limits of the
visible. " In very deed," says Peter, interpreting
the vision, " I perceive that God is not a respecter
of persons; but in every nation, he that feareth
Him and worketh justice, is accepted of Him."

IV.

" The House of God, which is the Church of the living
God, the pillar and ground of the truth."—I Timothy iii. 15.

But if all this, which is matter rather of opinion
than of authoritative teaching, be admissible, it may
seem that we are letting in the heresy of moral and
dogmatic indifferentism, unless we also hold fast to
the truth that no one who professes indifferentism
is in good faith. A man who avowedly does not

care whether what he does *is* right or wrong so long as he *believes* it right, who professes not to care about breaking God's law so long as he does so unintentionally, is plainly an immoral man, and has no sympathy with justice for justice' sake, no wish to be like-minded with God. Similarly he who protests that it is indifferent what a man thinks or believes so long as he believes it sincerely, is an untruthful man, altogether insincere in his very profession of sincerity. It is preposterous to maintain that because conscious wrong-doing and error is a worse evil, therefore that which is unconscious is no evil. Good faith requires us to love truth and right not only where we recognize it, but everywhere and universally; and that we should give no sleep to our eyes till we have found out what is true and right. None, therefore, can be counted a member of the invisible Church who through any fault or negligence of his own remains outside the communion of the visible Church.

What, then, do we understand by the visible Church? It is the visible union of the faithful, under one visible head or government; understanding by the faithful those who with their lips and outward conduct subject themselves to the teaching and laws of the Church, in short, those who would be numbered in a census of Catholics. It is as definite an institution as the Roman or the British Empire, notorious in the history of the world for the last two thousand years. What need to define that which we have only to point to?

Here, too, we have an articulated organized

body, calling itself the mystical body of Christ, claiming in some measure His mediatorial office, making incorporation with itself a condition of salvation, and yet differing from the invisible Church in that it is wholly on earth, and nowise in Heaven; that its perpetuity is to the end of time but not to all eternity; that it numbers sinners as well as saints among its members, as a net containing good fish and worthless, or a field of wheat and tares; that it passes like a wave along the river of time, continually renewing its matter, while preserving its form, as succeeding generations creep up noiselessly and pass by.

Are these, then, two Churches, two mystical Bodies, two spouses of Christ, or are they one?

We have already seen to what extent they can be said to be related as soul and body, and where that metaphor falls short. For while neither soul nor body alone is a complete nature, each of these Churches is a complete society with a distinct constitution and bond of union. Yet this distinctness does not prevent one being wholly dependent upon and subordinate to the other, just as particular departments of a complex government are subjected to it, though distinctly organized; or as a religious order which exists only to serve the Church is, as a society, quite distinct from it. Though not precisely related as soul and body, yet we may say that the invisible and visible Church are two parts of one nature; that they are like the inner word of the mind and the outer word of the lips, distinct yet most intimately connected as symbol and reality, as sacrament and grace signified; that the visible Church is vicarious and the invisible is principal; that the one is the instrument of the other, as the hand is the instrument of the body, or even as the body is the instrument, the symbol, the sacrament, the expression of the soul.

The Church is the extension and body of Christ her Head, who is both God and Man, two natures in one person, the human being the organ and finite manifestation and sacrament of the Divine, effecting what it signifies, making us, by its touch, partakers of His Divinity, who vouchsafed to become a sharer of our humanity. And so the invisible Church is the extension of His Divinity, as the visible Church is of His sacred humanity, both being united in the personal unity of their head, and being related to one another as the two natures are in Him; the human being entirely organic and subordinate to the service and manifestation and communication of the divine.

The visible Church is pre-eminently a great sacrament and type, whose organization, whose indissoluble unity, whose perpetuity signifies dimly that of the Heavenly Church and archetype; even as the semblance of the Eucharistic bread signifies the Body of Christ. Moreover, incorporation and membership with the visible Church not only symbolizes but in due conditions effects that incorporation with the invisible, in which our salvation consists. Not, however, unconditionally or exclusively; for what is true of all particular sacraments holds here in like manner. God indeed has not tied

CC

His grace to the sacraments, and as there is a baptism and communion of desire for those who for one reason or another are inculpably cut off from the rites of the Church, so there is a membership of desire through which (though not without which) the graces of actual membership can be secured. Again, the sacraments may be not merely fruitless, but spiritually destructive to those who use them profanely; and similarly outward membership with the Church may be to many a cause of more grievous condemnation than that of Tyre and Sidon, or of Sodom and Gomorrah.

As of old, before Christ's advent, God worked in the souls of men unsacramentally, yet not without dependence on, and reference to, the coming Mediator and the sacraments, so now more freely does He lavish His saving grace broadcast wherever the Church is locally or intellectually inaccessiɓle, though not without reference to the Church from whose treasury and for whose sake, as it were, every grace is conferred. Not indeed that all rudimentary faith is destined or intended by God to reach on earth its last development in the full light of Catholic belief; but that it is a seed, of its own nature tending to that development when duly environed; it is the true religion in germ.

Since God has wedded into the human family and has become one of ourselves, the whole race, whether touched by the waters of baptism or left in the darkness of nature, has been raised to a supernatural dignity and favour quite independent of the internal dignity of sanctifying grace. As one of God's "poor relations" the most degraded savage, the "least of His brethren," has a distinction denied to the angels. If for ten just men God would have spared Sodom, what mercy will not the presence of the God-Man, of the Catholic Church and her sacraments, win for all humanity, for those even who trample them underfoot and revile them? For the Church is in the world as a tree that is rooted in the earth and whose secret fibres spread far and wide. God cannot draw the Church to Himself, but He must, in some sense, draw the whole world with her. She will not loose her grip: "If thou wilt not forgive them," she says, "then blot me out of the book of life."

But if those who do not know the visible Church can be saved without being actually incorporated with her and bound to her laws, it might seem that such knowledge profits nothing, except to make salvation more difficult for those to whom the obligation is revealed. This is an objection which might be urged against all the sacraments, against every additional means of light and grace. The instructed catechumen must seek water and a minister in order to be regenerated; whereas the pagan can be born again of the Holy Ghost in the fountain of his own tears. But plainly we must distinguish between the amply sufficient grace for salvation which God in His fidelity offers to all, and that superabundant grace which in His generosity He offers to millions, though not to all. Contrition in every case forgives our sins in the very moment we propose to seek absolution; but in the sacrament God overwhelms us with the grace of remission, He puts upon us the best robe, and a ring on our finger, and shoes on our feet, and banquets us, and rejoices over us with His angels. To every soul God supplies the daily bread of good thoughts and good desires, but in the Eucharist he satiates the hungry with the Bread of Angels, and causes the chalice of the thirsty to overflow and inebriate. To all in every religion He reveals Himself as God the rewarder of them that seek Him, but in the Catholic revelation these "broken lights" are gathered up and intensified into one steady ray of pure truth; and the corn that is meted in simple sufficiency to some is given to us in full measure, pressed down, shaken together, and running over.

Moreover, the sacraments are said to work their effect *ex opere operato, i.e.,* theirs is an effect produced in us by an external agency, not by ourselves; although as a condition they demand a certain receptivity, a certain disposition of the soil which multiplies the yield thirty, sixty, or a hundred-fold. That their effect is not directly, but only indirectly *ex opere operantis* and measured by our own industry, may seem to be but little advantage or gain; yet it is no small gain that instead of our waiting on God, as it were for the troubling of the waters, God should wait upon us, ready to serve us with His graces as often as we choose to approach the sacraments and dispose ourselves to receive them. Herein God has opened for us the fountains of salvation, that we may approach and draw living water when we will: "Whosoever will, let him come and drink freely."

Dare we then, even on these prudential grounds, and putting aside all question of the sovereign and universal authority of the Church over every soul upon earth, and of her commission to compel men to enter into her fold so far as Divine jurisdiction can compel them; dare we then refuse such a proffer of spiritual wealth, dare we hope even for the bare sufficiencies of salvation if we wilfully neglect this call to higher things?

Once more whether we regard ourselves as isolated units, or as members of the body, our union with the visible Church enables us both to get more and to give more than would be otherwise at all possible. For viewing the Church ministerially, as even Nonconformists view her, it is evident that by her ministration and government, and by the co-operation of our fellow-members, we are enlightened, guided, helped, prayed for, encouraged, and secure all the advantages which the individual gains in a society and loses in isolation, and are, therefore, able to serve and praise God with a fuller personal service. We profit by the accumulated experience of multitudes transmitted and added to from generation to generation; we are the inheritors of all that is meant by the Catholic tradition so far as we are capable of appropriating it. There is all the difference that exists between genius which has to teach itself everything from the beginning, and that which enters into the labours of others and starts where they have left off.

Still more as members of a living body do we participate in those special blessings and graces which God bestows on the Church collectively, seeing as He does the image of the Blessed Trinity, the Many in One, set forth in the society as it can never be set forth in the unit; " How good and pleasing it is for brethren to dwell together in unity . . . for there the Lord hath promised His blessing and life for evermore." And as happens analogously in the kingdoms of this world, there are benefits accruing to the faithful collectively in which even the wickedest and most unworthy members partake in such sort that their membership is to them a source of many graces otherwise denied them. Further there is a collective praise and service which we can give to God or participate in giving as parts and factors of a joint result, and which is wholly out of the power of those who praise and serve God singly and in isolation. The very same melody receives a new meaning and richness when sung in concert with others. And there is a collective prayer where many are gathered together as one, in His Name, a prayer which the Holy Ghost offers by the lips of the Universal Church in her liturgy, whose fruit is applied to our soul as often as we join in it or unite our intention with it.

All these considerations, and others that might be adduced, make it evident that membership with the visible Church is the condition and occasion of innumerable helps and graces otherwise inaccessible; and that to neglect wilfully such an offer of greater salvation would be an act, not only of rebellion against Divine authority, but also of presumption, meriting the forfeiture of all other but the most ordinary and barely sufficient means.

v.

"For by grace are you saved through faith, and that not of yourselves, for it is the gift of God."—Ephes. ii. 8.

We may now inquire for our own sakes rather than for theirs, how it comes to pass that so many of our fellow-Christians, who are to all appearances in perfect good faith, feel themselves in no way obliged to submit themselves to the Catholic Church: for we are bound in all justice—not to speak of charity—to find every excuse for them before we dare to condemn in our minds those whom perhaps God acquits as more faithful to their little light, than we to our abundance.

Why we ourselves believe is not a question whose discussion can interest us much more than a discussion of our own identity. We may dispute and deny the proofs usually alleged, but our belief is not shaken because our analysis of its origin is unsuccessful. A dogma is simply the skeleton of a living concrete reality which it but outlines and formulates; and the same might be said of the array of reasons we put forth for our recognition of the Church's claims. Our faith in her is the effect of an impression produced on our mind and heart by her whole concrete reality. We can never make another see what we see, or feel what we feel, by any verbal description however elaborate and detailed. To the Catholic born and bred, the claim of any other body to represent and continue the work of Christ is unthinkable; to the convert— if he has really grasped the point at issue—it is a dream sincerely accepted for truth, until set side by side with the facts of daylight when one wakens. For this very cause we are often indifferent, unsympathetic and harsh in our controversy; we are careless in our reasons, as the consciousness of certainty always makes men, we are inaccurate and slovenly in our answers, or else we are simply impatient of all discussion, feeling the hopeless inadequacy of language in the matter; we ourselves see, touch, and taste, but to convey that experience to others seems simply an interminable task.

First of all let us remember that in the expression of his reasons for not believing, the non-Catholic is as much embarrassed by this inadequacy of logic and languages as we are. His assigned reasons are at best the merest skeleton of that subjective impression about the Church by which he is really influenced in his heart. Very often they are not even so much; they have really no connection with it whatever, if they do not actually belie it. We may refute every reason he can put forth without touching the one true reason which he does not know how to disentangle or express.

It would betray a lamentable ignorance of the principles governing Divine election and favour, not to say of patent and notorious facts, to suppose that our seeing what so many are blind to is due in any degree to superior intellectual acumen or to more extensive information and erudition on our part; or even to our superior fidelity to grace and light. Though the Church has always had intellect and learning on her side in greater or less degree, she has never had a monopoly, and there is undoubtedly more arrayed against her than is with her. God has chosen the foolish and weak to confound the wise and strong; and it is so far as we are content to throw in our lot with that majority that we receive or retain the gift of faith. Nor are there many of us who have not been far more unfaithful to grace and light than some whom God has left outside the fold of Peter. Our faith is obviously matter for thanksgiving but not for boasting; it is not of works but of the gift of God.

But if the Church is conspicuous as a city set on a hill, how are they excusable who fail to see it?

Truly the Church is conspicuous and the features that distinguish her are broadly marked and recognizable by all. Were they subtle, microscopic, elusive, ambiguous; did they depend for their existence on niceties of history and exegesis and criticism; were it needful to be versed in the theology of valid orders, or to be competent to judge the precise requirements of unity, catholicity, sanctity, apostolicity—conceptions which theologians discuss and elaborate interminably—then indeed the trumpet might be said to give an uncertain sound. But we know it is not so, and that the evidence of the Church is like the evidence of the sun to those that have eyes. But eyes they must have, and here we come to the solution of our problem. For if

we search for some object, and are not clear as to
the nature and appearance of what we are searching
for, it may confront us time after time and be
passed over; not because its characteristics are
obscure, but because we do not know what to look
for. And so it is that the distinctive characteristics
of the Catholic Church are manifest to all, friends
and foes alike, but the latter find in them evidence
of her falsehood, while the former find in them
evidence of her truth.

For example, it is natural that every great
organization for universal and spiritual ends should
be brought to the birth by preaching; for it is the
embodiment and organ of an idea, and this idea
must be first preached to the ear, received in the
mind, and embraced by the affections of many,
before it can take shape in an institution or society.
So it was with the Christian Church. It is not,
therefore, wonderful that millions who have been
educated to believe that the Catholic Church
pretends to be the *unchanged* representative of the
Church as seen in the pages of the New Testament,
—a Church whose worship consisted of simple
eucharistic suppers, of informal, and even disorderly
prayings and prophesyings, of continual open-air
preaching and exhortation; a Church as yet soft
and formless, innocent of all definition in discipline or dogma or ritual, altogether in its general
exterior aspect far more like Methodism, or the
Salvation Army, than anything else;—it is not
wonderful that looking about for such a Church
as this they should fail to recognize it in the

Catholic Church, with her elaborate ecclesiastico-political organization, her complex and definite liturgy and canon law and dogma, her world-wide extension and authoritative government. They seek a tender sapling, and they find a gnarled, weather-beaten oak; they seek a babe in its crib, and they find a man on his cross.

We, on the other hand, seek a body that claims to carry on the work of Him who came to teach not the few but the millions, not the learned but the rude; to teach them, not the science of earth or the philosophy of man, but the wisdom of God and the mysteries of Heaven; and who, therefore, of necessity taught, not as the scribes by reasonings and discussion, but with authority as God, claiming the obedience of the mind, not its patronage; the assent of faith, not the critical approval of reason.

Looking for such a Church, our own eyes, and friend and foe alike lead us to Rome. Her exclusiveness and dogmatism is at once conspicuous and altogether distinctive. It is to us the mark or characteristic of Christ, to others of anti-Christ. But all alike allow that it is notorious and peculiar to Rome alone. Other bodies claim to have the true interpretation of Christianity; for such a claim is their *raison d'être*. But there is some modesty in their claim; they do not pretend to be infallibly right; they are open to conviction; they allow outsiders a right to their opinion. But Rome alone claims living infallibility, to be not only true, but certainly true, and alone true.

For this reason all antagonists join hands against her; whoever else is right she is infallibly wrong. She is the Ishmael of Christendom; a sign spoken against by all. And while this very concursus of opprobrium is for so many a conclusive proof of her imposture, it is for us the very impress of the stigmata of Christ.

But perhaps the commonest error is that which leads men to look for such a congregation of saints as we find in existence during the first days of the Church's infancy; before the tares had yet begun to make themselves noticeable to any great extent; to seek for the characteristics of the invisible Church in the visible. They forget, if they ever knew, that though the one Spirit which dwells in, quickens, and unites the members of the visible Church, as the source of its doctrinal light and of its sacramental grace, is unfailing and imperishable, yet it is as treasure stored in earthen and corruptible vessels; it is as leaven buried in an unleavened mass, slowly and with difficulty asserting its influence; and transforming into its own nature alien matter which cannot be leavened if separated from the mass. Christ surely was explicit enough on this point, to take away all surprise at the weakness or wickedness of the members of the visible Church of whatever degree or dignity. He came as the friend of publicans and sinners, to call, not the just, but sinners to repentance. We are not shocked to find the inmates of a hospital ailing and weakly; and the Church is little better than a hospital for sick and wounded souls, in whose midst

Christ sits down daily to meat. In this she emulates the patience as she shares the reproach of her Master. Those who come to her she will in no wise cast out; and if ever she excommunicates, it is only lest the disease spread from one to many, or else for the chastisement and ultimate healing of the sinner himself. While there is life there is hope. However dead and fruitless, yet until it is severed from the vine, the branch may yet be quickened; "although he hath sinned yet he hath not denied the Father, the Son, and the Holy Ghost."[1]

Much schism has originated in pharisaic scandal and a perverse application of the argument from fruits; and many still are kept outside the fold because they are offended that the following of the Church is so like the following which gathered round her Master when the righteous stood apart and drew close their garments from defiling contact.

Let us then be sure that if men of intelligence, learning, and good faith, hold aloof from us, it is simply because that of the countless aspects under which Christ and His Church can be viewed, they have not yet caught that one in which their resemblance or rather identity is so unmistakable. It is ever so with the seeing of likeness between face and face, what is missed by one is self-evident to another. Out of thousands there is some one angle to be taken, and the light breaks upon us irresistibly. We might call it chance were it not rather the free gift of God—*donum Dei est.*

[1] Commendation of the Dying.

Faith is the work of a massive impression produced by a concrete personality. We recognize, we believe, we trust, we love not in obedience to arguments and reasonings; but to a perception which wakes a response in every corner of our soul. We follow the Church for the same kind of reason that Peter of Galilee followed Christ. Had he been asked his reasons he would wisely have said: "Come and see;" and yet many who came, saw not, for their eyes were dim.

> Perceptions whole like that he sought
> To clothe, reject so pure a work of thought
> As language; thought may take perceptions place
> But hardly coexist in any case,
> Being its mere presentment,—of the whole
> By parts; the simultaneous and the sole,
> By the successive and the many.[1]

No man has ever yet uttered the whole, the real reason of his belief or of his unbelief. Therein he is alone with God, "to his own Maker he standeth or falleth." "Whatever be the happy arrangement of theses," writes a French Jesuit, *à propos* of Huysman's *En Route,* "according to which the theologian studies the preambles of faith, and plans a route for that abstract soul which he syllogizes about, the subject upon whom the touch of Divine grace is working makes little account of these scientific tactics. He is drawn by the cords of Love and by that bait which suits his particular appetite if he will but yield himself to follow; and the efficacity which the co-operation of his obedient will lends to grace, suffices to sanctify and justify

[1] R. Browning, *Sordello.*

him without inquiring for a moment whether or not he has numbered his steps in strict agreement with the theses or making sure that he has fallen into the Church's motherly arms according to all the pre-scribed rules."[1] And by way of illustration the critic quotes, without approving in every detail, the words in which the hero gives expression to some of the features of the Church by which he was most strongly drawn back to her bosom :

"Is it not then strange this invariable weakness on the part of defunct heresies? All of them from the very first have had the flesh enlisted in their service. Logically and naturally they should have triumphed for they pretended to allow men and women to follow their passions without condem-nation, and even, in the case of Gnostics, with profit to their sanctity, doing honour to God by the vilest excesses.

"And what has become of them? They have all gone to the bottom, while the Church, so rigid in this matter, is still to the fore, whole and entire. She commands the body to submit and the soul to suffer, and, contrary to all likelihood, human nature listens to her and sweeps aside as so much filth, the seductive pleasures which present themselves for acceptance."

And again :

"Is not this vitality which the Church preserves, in spite of the unfathomable stupidity of her children, something quite decisive? She has survived the alarming folly of her clergy (*Quoi qu'on*

---

[1] J. Pacheu, S.J., *De Dante à Verlaine.*

pense, says the critic, *de cette assertion incivile et outrée, elle a sa valeur*), she has not even been slain by the blunders and witlessness of her defenders! That is truly wonderful!"

Temper the irony, and this is only what St. Paul confesses and glories in when he says: "See your vocation, brethren, that there are not many wise according to the flesh, not many mighty, not many noble; but the foolish things of the world hath God chosen that He may confound the wise; and the weak things of the world hath God chosen that He may confound the strong; and the base things of the world and the things that are contemptible hath God chosen and the things that are not, that He might bring to nought things that are."[1]

[1] 1 Cor. i. 26—28.

APPENDIX.

IT may not be amiss to state a little more clearly the Christian doctrine of pain, which holds a position midway between two erroneous views. According to the hedonist and the stoic, pain is never in itself a means or cause of good, be that good pleasure or virtue. In this limited finite existence of ours, however, it is inseparably annexed to the means by which happiness is reached. In other words, bitterness, we are told, is never in itself medicinal, but being attached to other properties which are medicinal, it must be endured by those who desire health for themselves; it must be inflicted by those who desire health for others. Thus, if these thinkers profess any sort of Christianity, they regard Christ's mission of redemption as a mission primarily for the relief of suffering. If He calls on us to take up our cross and follow Him to Calvary and hang beside Him there, it is not because suffering is useful, but because it is inevitable if we would eventually minimize suffering for ourselves and for others. And therefore, though suffering is useless, sufferance is good, *i.e.*, being able to face suffering and fight it with a view to its extinction. Christ, in their view, is the exemplar philanthropist, who

DD

found joy in suffering, for the end that others might not suffer, who bore their burdens and griefs and sorrows, and imposed a like altruism on His disciples, as the Great Precept of the New Law. He bids the rich give to the poor, and those that have to those that have not. He promises life to those who devote themselves to the relief of pain and suffering, who feed the hungry, and clothe the naked, and minister to the needy. If this, then, be the true spirit of Christ, is it not evident that though it is good for us to be able and willing to suffer when necessary, yet the necessity of suffering is itself something to be deplored, something abnormal, irregular, the fruit of sin and disorder; that it is like the rust of a key which simply makes it difficult to turn it in the lock, and in no possible way helps to that effect; that suffering makes the food and medicine of life bitter, but is not itself nourishing or medicinal; that it is the great obstacle to holiness and goodness, and that were it not for the difficulty and pain to be encountered, the whole world would be virtuous and happy?

There is so much plausibility in this presentment of Christianity as to deceive at times even those whose spiritual instincts are truer than their reasoning, and who in attempting to formulate their religion do it scant justice.

Certain, indeed, it is that pain is never an ultimate end; that God never delights in suffering, even when He Himself inflicts it or wills it to be inflicted; that in some equivalent way, His love for the least of His creatures makes their pains His own, even as the father may suffer more than the child whom he chastises, yet shrinks not from doing what is for the child's greater good.

True it is also, that Christ went about relieving pain and sorrow, and that He requires like compassion from all His disciples; that He is the physician of the body no less than of the soul; that He cares for the temporal as well as for the eternal; for the State as well as for the Church; for the multitudes as well as for individuals., This aspect of Christianity is only too often ignored by those who would divorce grace and nature, Heaven and earth, Christianity and civilization, and set them at enmity one with another. No man need pretend to love God who has no pity for the hungry.

This is true, but it is not the whole truth. "Seek ye first God's Kingdom and its justice.'" This justice is the only supreme and unqualified good, by which all else is to be measured and estimated. Other things are to be sought or avoided according as they help or hinder the one thing needful. Nothing is absolute evil for man but what violates his humanity, the higher life of his reason. Were he mere animal, then pain would be an unqualified misfortune, and in no possible way a good or cause of good; though possibly it might be a condition of good. But belonging as he also does to the order of the Eternal and Absolute, and finding his highest perfection and happiness in the love of truth and right, of God and of God's cause—a love which is exerted, and thereby strengthened, in suffering and self-denial,—temporal and transitory crosses are evil only in a relative and conditional sense, *i.e.*, just so far as they hinder his higher and eternal life. But they may as often, perhaps more often, be not merely the condition but the very cause and direct means of his advance in the Kingdom of God and its justice; not merely something tolerated as inseparably annexed to the means, but themselves the means,—the very bitterness itself, and not merely the bitter thing, being medicinal. In a word, suffering is in itself good and useful, though not an ultimate and final good. The pain of the lance does the patient no good, and so perhaps we employ narcotics. But the pain of the lash does the criminal good, nor has philanthropy so far insisted on administering chloroform to him.

It seems, then, that "Humanitarianism" makes what is commonly understood as philanthropy the chief end of Christ's teaching and example; whereas Catholicity looks upon it as necessary indeed, but as secondary and subordinate. Where pain is an inseparable condition, still more where it is a direct cause and means of greater good, it must be embraced, not under protest, but with the love due to that which *in itself* is good and useful; which, though repugnant to feeling, is welcome to reason and faith.

No doubt there is a superstitious pain-worship connected with dualist religions, which, as they acknowledge an ultimate principle of evil, so also do they view pain as pleasing for its own sake to a cruel deity; or rather, because it tends to the destruction of the animal body, and of separate personal existence, which are regarded as of evil origin. Christian asceticism rests on no such foundation, but maintains that pain itself purifies the heart, as fire purifies gold.

For the heart is purified by detachment. Its purity is its perfect liberty from all that impedes its complete subjection to the Divine love, and reason, and will. Such subjection requires that it should be able to endure the pain of leaving what it likes, of embracing what it abhors—a power which may be possessed to an indefinite degree. Apart from supernatural intervention, the strength of Divine love in the soul, like every other habit, is increased by every act in advance of previous acts in point of intensity; by lesser acts it is sustained up to a corresponding point of capacity, but no further. It is not by the removal but by the graduated increase of obstacles that Divine love is exercised and strengthened; not by the extinction but by the mastery of rebellious feeling. Every new victory of Divine love over such rebellion is a new degree of liberty acquired, a further purification from hampering affections, another tie to earth and the lower life loosened.

As resistance draws out physical exertion and strengthens our muscles, so pain increases our moral strength, which is prized, not because to be able to endure pain is useful (that were a vicious circle), but because our perfection lies in loving God with our whole heart and strength, and drawing out every inch of our capacity in that respect. Normally, it is only by pain that this can be effected.[1] A life of pleasure unbroken by pain is in the moral order like a life of absolute bodily inactivity. It is the explicit teaching of Christianity that a man is sent into this world for no other end but to perfect himself in the love of God and of every form and aspect of Divine goodness; and if that love can be perfected and uttered only through labour and pain and suffering, it is hard to see why this life should be very much pleasanter than Purgatory, where the process which death finds imperfect is taken up and finished according to somewhat the same method. There is, indeed, true joy and peace mid the purgatorial pangs; and if there is any solid joy and peace on earth it is that which the saints have known in the midst of their many tribulations, and which the world could neither give nor take away. To say that life is but an

---

[1] Needless to say we speak of the natural order of things such as prevails now in consequence of the forfeiture of the preternatural through Adam's fall, and would have prevailed always had man not been created in Paradise. Even there man was not to be spiritually perfected, he could not make grace his own until it was, so to say, burnt into his soul by that mysterious temptation to which he, with all his advantages and helps, succumbed. We may be sure that the trial on which the destiny of the whole human race depended was one which could be borne only at the cost of great suffering,—since temptation implies suffering whether in the way of abstinence or of endurance. Thus the law of sanctification through suffering seems to be saved everywhere. As to the process by which the soul of the baptized infant is developed intellectually and morally and makes manifest the graces latent in it, we know too little to be certain that even here we have an exception.

inchoative purgatory may sound pessimistic to the thoughtless, but, in truth, it is very kindest optimism, the one answer that fits the riddle. Not, indeed, that there is **any** continuance of probation or increase of grace after death, but that the seeds of love here sown are there watered and matured, and spread their shoots and fibres to every corner of our spiritual being; it is a work, not of development as here on earth, but of simple evolution.

If once we accept the probation theory of life, it ought no longer to surprise us to find that the soul is so often on the rack, that every circumstance and condition of its existence is devised either to unite it more closely to God or else to separate it from God,—the latter purposes being seemingly contrary but really subordinate to the former, insomuch as the greater the force of the strain that would drag us away from God, *i.e.*, from faith, or hope, or charity, or justice, or purity, or truth, or any form of Divine goodness, the more firmly do we need to cling to Him and the stronger grows our grasp, if we are but faithful in clinging.

If the practice of Divine love were not painful, it would never take root or grow. No doubt it is the very idea of virtue that good actions should become easy; yet this is only because the habit of enduring pain has become deep-seated. "Easy" is not "painless." The pain is felt as much as ever, but the feeling is disregarded and promptly defied, owing to the strength of the counter-motive. Just as the strong man delights to exert his strength in order both to give expression to it, and to maintain and increase it, so the love of God, when it is strong, delights to give expression to itself, to exercise and perfect itself. The giant will not be satisfied to beat the air, but looks for something that will resist him, and if he finds no obstacle will make one; and the lover will not be satisfied with unresisting, easy tasks, but looks for something painful and hard; and if he finds it not to hand will devise it for himself. The Christian ascetic naturally, instinctively, reasonably (always supposing it be not to the hurt of greater good) takes to self-sought austerities simply and only to express, and incidentally therein to strengthen, his love of God, his sorrow for sin. In this he but co-operates in the dispensation whereby God Himself uses pain and suffering directly as a means for the spiritual formation of His saints.

In the mere fact of practising and inculcating fast and vigil, Christ our Saviour has allowed and taught asceticism; nor is there any difference in kind between His fast in the desert and the severest self-inflicted austerities of Catholic saints. It is quite immaterial whether we afflict ourselves by hunger, or thirst, or wakefulness, or scourge, or haircloth, if once we pass the boundary of mere temperance and uphold the lawfulness and the duty of fasting.

Christ's primary mission with respect to the sufferings and sorrows of life was, not to relieve them, but to teach men to bear them, to value them, to thank God for them. There are two ways of dealing with difficulties and trials—by

changing ourselves or by changing our surroundings; by running away from hardships or by
adapting ourselves to them and nerving ourselves
to bear them. There is no question as to which is
the wisest course. If we fly from one cross it is
only to fall into the arms of another. Go where
we will we carry ourselves with us, the source of
most of our trouble. Until we change ourselves, no
change of circumstances will avail. *Imaginatio locorum
et mutatio multos fefellit*, says à Kempis—many have
been deluded by the imaginary advantages of a
change. Men are constantly laying the blame of their
own faults on their surroundings; ever fancying that
they would be perfectly happy in some other place;
ever keen-eyed to their present grievances and
prospective advantages; ever blind to their present
advantages and prospective grievances; always loth
to face the inevitable truth, that life is a warfare
upon earth; that it is essentially a cross which must
be borne, whether willingly or unwillingly; that
"there is no other way to life and to true internal
peace but the way of the Holy Cross and of daily
mortification. Walk where you will, seek what you
will; yet you will find no higher way above, no safer
way below than the way of the Holy Cross. Arrange
and order everything after your own likings and
fancies, and yet you will always find something that
you have to suffer, whether willingly or unwillingly,
and thus you will always find the Cross. You will
have to put up either with bodily pain or with
spiritual troubles. At one time you will feel
abandoned by God; at another you will be tried by

your neighbour; and, what is worse, you will often be troublesome to yourself. Nor yet can you be released or relieved by any remedy or comfort, but needs must bear it as long as God wills. . . . Run where you will, you cannot escape, for wherever you go you carry yourself along with you, and so everywhere you will always find yourself. Turn where you will, above, or below, within or without, yet in every corner you will find the Cross; and everywhere you will need to exercise patience if you want to possess inward peace and deserve an everlasting crown. If you carry the Cross willingly, it will carry you; if you carry it unwillingly, you make a burden for yourself and weight yourself still more; and yet, bear it you must. If you cast off one cross you will surely find another, and perhaps a heavier one. Do you imagine you are going to escape what no man ever yet escaped? . . . You are sore mistaken* if you expect anything else but to suffer trials, for the whole of this earthly life is full of miseries and hedged round with crosses. Make up your mind that you will have to endure many adversities and all sorts of inconveniences in this wretched life, for so it will be with you wherever you are, and so you will surely find it wherever you lie hid. . . . When you shall have got so far that tribulation is sweet to you and savours of Christ, then indeed it will be well with you, and you will have discovered paradise upon earth. As long as suffering is an evil in your eyes, and you try to run away from it, so long will you be unhappy; and whithersoever you fly, the need of further flight will still follow you. But if you settle down to the inevitable, namely, to suffering and dying, things will quickly mend and you will find peace. . . . Had there been anything better or more useful for men's souls than suffering, surely Christ would have taught it by word and example! . . . And, therefore, let this be the final conclusion of all our study and investigation, that it is of necessity through many tribulations that we are to enter the Kingdom of God."[1]

In short, the Gospel has no belief in the perfectibility of human life here on earth. If suffering be the true, unmitigated evil, then Christianity is frankly pessimistic. Suffer we must on our cross, whether on the right hand of Christ or on the left; whether with faith, patience, and humility, or with unbelief, blasphemy, and proud indignation. Nor can there be any question as to who suffers more, he who makes the Cross not merely a basis of certain hope, but even an exercise and expression of present love, or he who finds in it not even the medicine, but the very poison of life.

We have already insisted that the good which positivism seeks to realize for humanity is not the ultimate good; nor is the evil it would mitigate a real, final evil. But we may go further with some plausibility, and urge that its aim is not only mistaken, but impossible; that it cheers us with hopes which can never be realized, that as every drop which the sun absorbs from the ocean comes back to it again sooner or later, so the efforts of

[1] *Imitation,* ii. 12.

philanthropy to drain the sea of man's sorrows are futile and unavailing.

It is vain for us to kick against the goad of suffering, for thereby we only feel it the more. We are comforted by promises of a golden age, or an age of gold, when poverty shall be no more. Yet He perchance knew the nature of human society better who said: "The poor you shall always have with you," and in so saying He may have enounced, not merely a fact of the future, but an iron law of life. If so, then as long as the world lasts the poor will always be in the majority and the destitute will be not a few. Indeed, it seems that the pursuit of social wealth is like the pursuit of truth—at every step a new and wider horizon opens out on our view. To solve ten problems is to suggest a hundred not dreamt of before; and so, to raise the standard of comfort and enjoyment is to multiply men's needs and make the conditions of their temporal happiness more difficult to realize. Let the wealth of the country increase as it will, yet the amount of discontent and suffering caused by poverty will be relatively much the same in one age as in another. The capacities for pleasure and for pain grow *pari passu*, and therefore the increase of social wealth does not lessen poverty, but only changes the standard. For poverty is something to a great extent relative. While society lasts there will always be inequality in possessions. As fast as we draw outsiders within the circle of economic comfort, others will be ready to take their place. For the more bread there is, the more mouths will there be to eat it; and if competitors multiply, the number of those weaklings is multiplied who are pushed to the wall in the struggle, and whose lot is poverty, if not destitution.

The stimulus to all progress is discontent with existing conditions, that is, misery of some kind or another; and therefore those who make material progress an end in itself, who fix no final point beyond which comfort may not go and where progress must cease, make discontent the normal lot of mankind.

Doubtless I shall be told that if we are to seek such "want-begotten rest," if we are to lower our standard of comfort to the minimum, in the first place we shall be relatively no happier, since with the contraction of our needs the means of satisfying them will proportionately dwindle down; and then, that we shall simply sacrifice the fulness of a life where all our capacities for enjoyment are developed to the utmost, for a lower and feebler vitality which suffers less, only because it lives less and enjoys less; that if our doctrine were carried to its extreme conclusion, we should (as Buddhism does) aim at the extinction of all desire and being.

This objection is valid if we accept the tenets of that hedonism which consciously or unconsciously pervades the thought of our day. For if indeed enjoyment be our highest good, then the only practical, though perhaps insoluble, question is as to whether pleasure or pain preponderates in this mortal life. If pleasure, then life should be sought in its greatest possible fulness; if pain, then life should be shunned, stifled, extinguished. The ancient East has learnt to take the bitter view; the sanguine West, with the buoyancy of comparative youth and inexperience, can still find hope in life apart from God.

If, therefore, pleasure were the last good, and pain the last ill, it might well be questioned whether the joys that culture and civilization bring to the majority are not more than cancelled by the attendant sorrows, and whether stagnation, numbness and sensibility were not the better wisdom, and *Nirvana* our best hope.

None perhaps ever entered more fully, more purely into the best that the highest culture can offer, than he who spoke not only in his own name, but in the name of that unique civilization he represented when he said: "For I believe that if one had to compare that night in which he slept so soundly as not to be troubled by any dream whatsoever, with all the other nights and days of his whole life, and had to confess how many days or nights he had passed more pleasantly and sweetly, I believe that neither the king on his throne, nor the beggar at his gate, could count many such."[1]

If, however, we deny that enjoyment is the chief good, or more than a subordinate condition of our highest and truest life, to be used or left as reason shall dictate; if we perceive that when sought for its own sake it becomes a tyrannical and insatiable greed, a source of chronic discontent and misery; that it tends to absorb all the interest and energy

[1] *Apol. Socratis.*

which would otherwise go to the quest of God, and of divine good, then it is no longer a concession to pessimism or Buddhism to advocate a simplifying of the conditions of life in the interests of a truer and nobler culture. Christianity has no quarrel with civilization or culture as such, but only with a false civilization which would usurp the place which belongs to the Kingdom of God and its justice. It not only allows but enjoins the futherance of all arts that minister to life, so long as due order be observed, and the lower be restrained by the higher, and nothing be sought without measure or restraint, save that which is highest of all. It defers to the claims of the body, of the passions and affections, of the æsthetic faculty and the imagination, yet always with the knowledge that restraint is the only antiseptic, and that when Nature breaks loose from the yoke of Grace, the liberty she seeks proves to be bondage, degradation, corruption.

But it is in justice, and in the inner Kingdom of God that we are to place our imperishable treasure of happiness, which no suffering in other respects can touch save superficially, leaving the soul's depths in imperturbable calm. This happiness, like the air and sunshine, is within the reach of all; and the supply being unlimited, there is no struggle of competition, no necessary poverty or destitution. In the spiritual soul, with its capacities for light and love, men possess an often unsuspected treasure of happiness, an instrument from which skilled fingers can at

pleasure draw sweetest music. Christ tells us that
our bliss depends more upon what we are, than upon
our circumstances; that these latter receive their
form and meaning from the soul; that the eye sees
what it brings with it, the power of seeing; that it
is more blessed to play an indifferent part nobly
than to play a noble part indifferently; that the
Kingdom is within us, and consists in that deep-
down, unbroken peace of the heart which the world
can neither give nor take away.

We are not then enemies to material progress
because we refuse to recognize it as an end in itself;
or because we forbid men to build all their hopes
upon it, and throw all their energies into it; or
because we refuse to believe that on the whole it
can ever seriously alter the relative proportions of
pain and pleasure in this world. On the contrary,
as nature in general is saved and perfected by its
subjection to grace and heavenly wisdom, so within
the many kingdoms of nature each lower realm is
best saved by subjection to that above it; nor can
any civilization escape corruption when the lower
life is sought luxuriously and extravagantly at the
expense of the higher; when the bulk of social
wealth goes, not to the necessities, but to the
superfluities of the body, while the soul is left
languishing.

And if the predictions of a future terrestrial
paradise consequent on the growth and distribution
of wealth are somewhat shortsighted, the same must
be said of those which point to the coming extermination of disease and the prolongation of life through

the progressive improvement of medical science. For if the art of healing finds new remedies and methods, it only means that many weaklings are born, and many survive whom Nature with rough kindness would have withheld or eliminated from the number of the living; and thus the proportion of those who can exist comfortably under improved medical science to those whose life is a burden to them, is about the same as before.

As for the far greater amount of human grief and sorrow which owes its birth to sin and selfishness, temptation and perverse free-will, it is hard to see how the most sanguine philanthropist can persuade himself that any diminution has been realized or is to be hoped for; and while death remains (as for such faithless thinkers it must remain) "the King of Terrors," the extinction of all they live for, and a sword of sorrow to loving survivors, it is vain to indulge in dreams of an earthly paradise from which all pain and sorrow is to be weeded out, and where comfort, if not luxury, shall be the unbroken lot of all. In flying from the Cross, humanity, with out-stretched arms, is flying from its own shadow.

Man is born for travail, as the sparks fly upwards. His life upon earth is a warfare; not a peaceful paradise. *Cur quæris quietem*, says à Kempis, *cum natus sis ad laborem*—"What business have you to expect rest, since you were born for labour and conflict?" Man that is born of woman hath but a short time to live, and is full of misery. This is "the iron law" of our nature, shirk it how we will,—*Furca expellas tamen usque recurret*. Against this

EE

tide of suffering, Christian, neo-Christian, and non-Christian philanthropy, each in obedience to the deepest and noblest instincts of the soul, casts up barriers of sand, to retard its advance here and there, or to break the force of its waves for a short hour or so. Nor herein is the Christian inconsistent, seeing as he does in these temporal needs and sorrows a true, though by no means unmitigated evil; one to be resisted, but not absolutely and unconditionally.

Yet it is not in the efforts and fruits of such philanthropy, not in the increased care for the poor and sick, that we are to look for the meaning of the Gospel proclamation, *Pauperes evangelizantur* —" Good news for the poor." Blessed are the poor, the mourners, the sick, the oppressed, the persecuted! Blessed indeed, because their Deliverer has come. But what manner of deliverance is Christ's ? Is it that the poor are to grow rich; the sick strong; the mourners gay and light-hearted; the oppressed victorious? In that case He should rather have said: Blessed are the rich, the prosperous, the gay. Yet though He bade His followers sell all and give to the poor, though He went about healing the sick, raising the dead, consoling the mourners,—as it were, robbing them of their blessing, yet He says, Blessed are you poor; and He chose their lot for Himself and for His Mother. Seeing that He had said it was easier for a camel to go through the eye of a needle than for a rich man to enter Heaven, He might well have given us an example of that more difficult sanctity, by coming among us as a rich man. But

His Heart was with the majority, to sweeten their lot. The rich, the great, and the learned live, so to say, on the crumbs that fall from the table God has spread for the poor and simple,—on the overflow of the Gospel graces. They get into Heaven by holding on to the skirts of the poor, and by making of them friends at court for themselves. Therefore our Saviour came rather to show the poor how to use their poverty, than to show the rich how to use their riches; to minister to the many, to sanctify their lot, to consecrate their ragged garments by wearing them Himself.

Who then is the true philanthropist? Is it he who, by the very manner in which he sympathizes with sorrow, and labours for its extinction, practically inculcates his own belief that it is an unmitigated evil; who dreams fondly and bids others dream of a future paradise on earth, who believes in the perfectibility, not only of the soul, but of the conditions of a comfortable and enjoyable existence? Or is it He who "knew what was in man," who knew that poverty, sorrow, suffering, and temptation would always and inevitably be the lot of the majority; who knew that there was wisdom and love veiled under God's seeming harsh dispensation, and who came not to change it, but to explain it; to touch the dark clouds with golden light; not to uproot the thorns which sin had sown, but to teach our bleeding fingers to weave them into a crown of glory for our own brow. A human comforter would stay us with false hopes of impossible amelioration; God shows us that poverty is wealth, and sorrow is joy, and death is life. He comes to us with His Cross on His shoulder and says: "Follow Me, I am the way;" He has taught us, if not to love, at least to adore the Cross; to carry it, if not joyfully, at least patiently.

There is no false kindness, but there is true and tender love in the hard, stern sayings of the Gospel. "Good news for the poor;" not that poverty is at an end, but that it can be turned into gold. And so of every sorrow and trial and temptation.

Pseudo-Christian philanthropy would take Christ down from the Cross. It forgets that He hung there by His own free-will; not in our stead, but that we might have courage to hang beside Him, for without the Cross there is no life. *In cruce vita*, says à Kempis, *in cruce salus—* "Only in the Cross is life and salvation to be found." *O Crux, Ave! Spes unica!* Can it be doubted but that this was the secret of the conquest of the world by Christianity? For what is strength but courage? and what is courage, when all is told, but the power of bearing pain, both moral and physical? And what force can resist a people whom love teaches, not merely to endure pain, but to seek it and to revel in it? The blood of the martyrs could not fail to be the seed of the Church; nor while the true doctrine of the Cross is preserved in the Church—as it must ever be preserved however at times neglected and forgotten,—need we fear for the eventual victory of Christianity over a feeble-minded world which grows daily more terrified at pain and suffering. Doubtless the children of the Church are at times largely infected with the world's sentiments in the matter, dainty members of a thorn-crowned Head—and so far the Church is feeble; but never while she clings to Christ crucified and His saints; never while she lifts the Cross for our adoration, and hails it: *Spes unica*—"our only hope," can the secret of her invincible strength be wholly forgotten: *In hoc signo vinces*—In this sign she must conquer.

———

NOVA ET VETERA:

INFORMAL MEDITATIONS

FOR TIMES OF SPIRITUAL DRYNESS.

BY

GEORGE TYRRELL, S.J.

OPINIONS OF THE PRESS.

———

" It is a book which can be opened at random with the certain result of finding a gem of thought, striking and original in its beauty. The reflections are all brief, but very much to the point, and of a depth which invites thought and ensures attention."—*Rosary Magazine.*

"As a book of meditations for those for whom it is intended it is in a certain degree perfection. Its great charm is its freshness."—*Catholic News.*

Reflections upon many topics of great interest to men and women who value their lives. There is nothing tiresome about the book to any moderately serious mind."—*American Ecclesiastical Review.*

"It is a book which one can open anywhere, with the certainty of finding something that will afford him consolation and instruction."—*American Catholic Quarterly.*

"This book excels most volumes of meditations in literary style and originality of thought-stimulus, and will be profitable both to clergymen, to religious, and to secular lay persons possessing a certain degree of education. It will be particularly valuable to preachers, who will be sure to find on every page many suggestions for fresh and powerful sermons."—*Church Progress.*

"A hearty reception will be given to the result of Father Tyrrell's labours. The subjects of the meditations are naturally various, and it only requires a glance through the index to be convinced that these subjects are introduced in a new and very striking manner ; and a closer acquaintance with the meditations proves to us most emphatically that the treatment of these subjects is likewise novel and striking. The meditations are in general short, but they are pregnant with ideas valuable to the soul at all times, and more particularly at seasons of spiritual dryness."—*Monitor.*

" We may turn to its pages and light at random upon some meditation that precisely suits our present state of mind ; and its suitability to our present condition is the very reason why it is spiritually useful to us."—*Book Notices.*

LONDON : LONGMANS, GREEN, AND CO.

Lightning Source UK Ltd.
Milton Keynes UK
UKHW02n0957120218
317657UK00003B/334/P